KF 9430 .C48 2009
Christol, Carl Quimby, 1913-
The American challenge

P9-CQL-302

WITHDRAWN
UNIVERSITY LIBRARY
THE UNIVERSITY OF TEXAS RIO GRANDE VALLEY

LIBRARY
THE UNIVERSITY OF TEXAS
AT BROWNSVILLE
Brownsville, Tx 78520-4991

The American Challenge

Terrorists, Detainees, Treaties, and Torture—Responses to the Rule of Law, 2001–2008

Carl Q. Christol

LIBRARY
THE UNIVERSITY OF TEXAS
AT BROWNSVILLE
Brownsville, Tx 78520-4991

UNIVERSITY PRESS OF AMERICA,® INC.
Lanham • Boulder • New York • Toronto • Plymouth, UK

Copyright © 2009 by
University Press of America,® Inc.
4501 Forbes Boulevard
Suite 200
Lanham, Maryland 20706
UPA Acquisitions Department (301) 459-3366

Estover Road
Plymouth PL6 7PY
United Kingdom

All rights reserved
Printed in the United States of America
British Library Cataloging in Publication Information Available

Library of Congress Control Number: 2009927163
ISBN: 978-0-7618-4344-3 (paperback : alk. paper)
eISBN: 978-0-7618-4345-0

♾™ The paper used in this publication meets the minimum
requirements of American National Standard for Information
Sciences—Permanence of Paper for Printed Library Materials,
ANSI Z39.48—1984

Contents

Preface

There is no cause for panic. Yet, things haven't been going so well. Problems have arisen faster than they have been resolved. Much work remains to be done.

Since 9/11 the acts and threats of terrorists and American responses have dominated the search for and the maintenance of national security. The means available to the American government to meet and to destroy such acts and threats are governed by the Constitution, by critically important statutes, and by international agreements designed to guarantee territorial integrity and national security. Federal courts have been called upon to clarify the lawful roles of those who bear these burdens. These interactions have provided a fascinating and fundamental test of the meaning to be given to the separation of powers principle of the Constitution. Informed and responsible citizens stand in awe of the integrity of the system as it selects and brings into play the responses to the challenges which must be met

During his tenure in office President George W. Bush was consistently and unwaveringly determined to treat terrorists, an especially hateful group of criminals, as unlawful enemy combatants, not as prisoners of war, and consequently not entitled to the privileges accorded to prisoners of war in the 1949 Geneva Prisoner of War (POW) Convention. The terrorists, when in the custody and control of the United States at the Guantanamo Bay Naval Station in Cuba, have been described as "detainees," and have been subject to two separate American legal regimes. The first, based on the Presidential Order of November 13, 2001 resulted in the establishment of Military Commissions and later in 2004 of Administrative Review Boards and Combatant Status Review Tribunals. At that stage the Military Commissions were to determine if detainees were enemy combatants and to prosecute detainees for terrorist acts.

The second regime resulted from the adoption of the Military Commissions Act (MCA) of October 17, 2006. The statute was enacted in response to the decision of the United States Supreme Court in the case of Hamdan v. Rumsfeld, 126 S. Ct. 2749 (June 29, 2006). It held that the Military Commission created by the Presidential Order of November 13, 2001 was unconstitutional.

President Bush has remained steadfast in his belief that an executive-proclaimed regime of military law rather than traditional civilian law based on legislative enactments should be applied to terrorists captured abroad and detained at the Guantanamo Naval Station in Cuba. He has strongly guarded his war time constitutional powers. This has been reflected in numerous "signing statements," attached to federal legislation. In them he announced the existence of his constitutional authority thereby serving notice that he was not bound by the indicated legislation if and when the statutory provisions conflicted with his constitutional powers. The adoption of the Detainee Treatment Act (DTA) of December 12, 2005 and the MCA on November 17, 2006 resulted in a revitalization of the system of Administrative Review Boards, Combat Status Review Tribunals, and Military Commissions to deal with offshore detainees held by the Department of Defense. Much of the military response following the Abu Ghraib debacle in 2004 has been to guarantee that the military detainees not be subject to torture or to other cruel, inhuman, or degrading treatment or punishment. There has been a concern that military practices and procedures would not conform to the standards of fair trials. Believing that military trials were best suited for unlawful enemy combatants, the DOD resisted efforts to have such cases transferred into Federal civilian trial courts. However, in instances where the alien detainee was a resident of and arrested in the United States, or where the detainee was an American citizen arrested abroad and removed to the United States these cases were tried in Federal District courts in the United States.

On July 20, 2007 President Bush signed a Directive mandating prohibitions to be followed by the CIA respecting detainees held by it and the interrogations engaged in by it. Though not identical with the regime established for the DOD, now governed by terms of Army Manual 2.22-3 of September 6, 2006, the CIA directive was patterned in many respects on the military regime. Critics have concluded that the Directive sets different standards than those required of the armed forces. In an actual case where a claim is made that a detainee's rights have been violated by an official of the CIA it will be necessary to obtain a judicial decision adjudicating the legality of the CIA Directive.

A number of serious problems remain to be resolved. On June 12, 2008 the United States Supreme Court in the case of Boumediene v. Bush (553 U. S.—) in a 5-4 decision held that the writ of habeas corpus could be claimed by Guantanamo Bay detainees. Section 7 of the Military Commissions Act was declared unconstitutional. Detainees, some held as long as 6 years without trial, were given the right to petition for the writ, or, optionally, to appeal from a decision of a Military Commission. This duality produced an invitation for additional litigation. Other matters in need of resolution are the extent and nature of additional rules governing the CIA's interrogation and detention of unlawful enemy combatants, the constitutionality of such rules and regulations, and, ultimately whether the United States can regain world confidence respecting the depth of its commitment to the world rule of law. American actions will have to demonstrate the seriousness of its commitment to this principle. The current world image is in need of repair. Suggestions have been made on how the American image can be improved.

The DOD has made some progress along such lines. The CIA is under intense public scrutiny. As the laws of armed conflict are reconsidered and revised it will be necessary to maintain the distinction between POWs and unlawful enemy combatants. Terrorists continue to constitute a major threat to world order.

Acknowledgments

I wish to express my appreciation to the University of Southern California Emeriti Faculty-Undergraduate Research Program which supported the research leading to the publication in 2004 of the first edition of INTERNATIONAL LAW AND U.S. FOREIGN POLICY, which included a Chapter on "Terrorism, Enemy Combatants, and Torture." The insights gained in that undertaking provided the momentum that has found expression in this book. I wish also to thank the University of Southern California Emeriti College and the Kenneth T. and Eileen L. Norris Foundation for providing financial support for the present undertaking. My understanding and awareness of the issues set forth in this book owe a great deal to the email postings of Charles B. Gittings, Jr., founder of the Project to Enforce the Geneva Conventions, to the many scholars who have contributed to Insights, asil.org, and to those professionals who have posted insightful "blogs" dealing with the subjects at hand. I have benefited from the highly professional help of Ms. Gerlanda Battles of the USC Political Science staff. I wish to express my deepest thanks to Susan, Jim, Dekker, and Kyle Deacon who steered me safely through the wilderness and wilds of computers and brought me safely home.

Carl Q. Christol
Santa Barbara, California
August 1, 2008

Chapter One

Problems and Challenges

1. A MORE PERFECT WORLD

In a more perfect world a book such as this, perhaps, might never have been written. Perhaps, with a greater sense of history and a higher level of acuity, reasons might have been found to prevent the development of the flaming hatred that came to possess the Al Qaeda terrorists. Perhaps humanitarian, cultural, and economic programs, or others of mutual interest, might have been negotiated. Major differences might have been identified and ameliorated. Perhaps, following 9/11, the American military responses in Afghanistan, and later in Iraq, might have been more discriminating and incisive, although no self-respecting country could have been expected to overlook the motives behind the devastation that occurred. Perhaps, while the search for weapons of mass destruction was under way in Iraq members of the Security Council could have found common interests to support the condition of collective security. Perhaps responsible elements of the Hussein regime could have been found and might have been entrusted to share, following Coalition successes, in the restoration of public order.

Perhaps American political and military leaders could have brought to the table a more knowledgeable understanding of the laws and customs of war, referred to as the law of war, and to the principles of Human Rights often referred to as humanitarian law. Perhaps they could have had a greater appreciation of the universality of the concept of the rule of law. Directly applicable were the Third Geneva Convention relating to the Treatment of Prisoners of War of August 12, 1949[1] the Fourth Geneva Convention relating to the Protection of Civilian Persons in Time of War of August 12, 1949,[2] and the Convention Against Torture and other Cruel, Inhuman or Degrading Treatment or

1

Punishment of December 10, 1984.[3] Also relevant was the Universal Declaration of Human Rights of December 10, 1948,[4] as well as all of the international and regional Covenants and Declarations on Human Rights which deal with torture and the cruel and inhuman treatment of individuals. Federal statutes enacted both before and after 9/11 were also relevant.

In the United States executive decisions were taken to create a new class of combatants identified as unlawful or illegal enemy combatants consisting of terrorists, as opposed to traditional military prisoners of war. The October 17, 2006 Military Commissions Act[5] provided for "alien unlawful enemy combatants" and "lawful enemy combatants." Military measures were taken to detain and interrogate them in order to obtain intelligence information and to prevent their returning to combat operations. It became necessary to identify the rights of such persons as well as their duties. They were considered by the Bush administration as separate and distinct from those appertaining to prisoners of war.

When it became known that detainees at the Abu Ghraib prison in Iraq had been tortured, American practices—viewed from the perspectives of CAT and federal statutes—reached headline proportions and moral sensibilities were traumatized. Assertions that detainees, who had been transferred from Afghanistan to the United States Naval Station at Guantanamo, Cuba, had been subjected to similar indignities, added fuel to the fire.

Dramatically posed were the preservation of national security coupled with military successes and the importance of winning two wars while maintaining and protecting the basic tenets of American democracy, including civil and political rights and liberties, and a firm commitment to the universal rule of law.

It became necessary to understand the respective roles of the President, of Congress, particularly the Senate in the area of international agreements, and Article III courts in assessing the legal condition of detainees. The President and the Secretary of Defense, as authorized by the President, have issued orders and created institutions to deal with detainees. Federal courts have decided cases relating to the rights and duties of such persons. The role of appellate courts has been particularly noteworthy. Congress, in turn, has enacted legislation designed to override the rulings of courts. Military Commissions in June, 2007, pointed to the limitations on their powers respecting Guantanamo Bay detainees regarding their classifications as enemy combatants and declined to exercise jurisdiction in two matters before them. Appellate procedures allowed for a correction of that decision.

Vital to an informed understanding of the issues and responses, if far from final answers, is the fact that each branch of the Federal government has zealously attempted to play its respective role. Each in turn has responded to the claims of designated constitutional authority when advanced by another branch, i.e., the concept of separation of powers. This has been a heartening outcome. This sequence has been repeated with the result that democratic processes have been engaged, and the search for acceptable solutions is in motion. This process has also produced a certain amount of friction, since absolute demarcation lines do not exist between the powers and duties of these three branches of government. Because of the importance and sensitivity of the situation the results of the process have received much public attention. Perhaps the debate has contributed to an understanding of the importance of the concept of a world rule of law. The bleakness of war and the uncertain conditions of mortality for those engaged in combat have emphasized the importance of the rule of law.

2. THE SEARCH FOR AND RELIANCE ON FACTS

To be of value a book with this title should be the product of a search for facts with the hope that they will give direction to public policy. Admittedly, old facts, that is old experiences, have been affected by and are laden with generally accepted values. Basic social science research should serve policy objectives. A linkage exists between good social science research and useful policy.

Basic social science research, dealing with specific facts and circumstances, which may be considered by some to be tedious, and perhaps inconsequential, in this case are fundamental. These facts and circumstances deal with the subject matter of this book. They cannot be inconsequential or trivial since they engage constitutional principles, as implemented by national legislation, executive orders, and high court decisions. They fix the boundaries for national behavior much as pure science and research can educate and enlighten the knowledge and practice of engineering or health care. Basic social science research should be called on by those who are privileged to engage in the choice between competing policies. Private persons, no less than governmental officials, must be guided by similar considerations.

3. A MULTITUDE OF QUESTIONS

Terrorism has become a dominant factor in national and world relations. With the collapse of time and space, fueled by an energetic and loosely knit global organization, renegade individuals, acting outside the traditional confines of nation-state authority, have engaged in shocking and inexcusable activities.

The responses, frequently calling for prohibitions and penalties have, in turn, often become the subject of very serious criticisms.

Attention has been drawn to the following: Can terrorists, acting without moral restraint, avoid culpability for violations of the laws and customs of war and the rights guaranteed to individuals under declarations and conventions dealing with Human Rights? What is the relevance of specifically oriented international agreements dealing with terrorist activity, such as the aerial hijacking convention or with the protection of diplomats? What is the significance of Article 3 (the Common Article) of the Third and Fourth 1949 Geneva Conventions dealing with torture and associated crimes? What is meant by the term "grave breaches" in the Geneva Conventions and the term "war crimes" used by Congress in 1977 when it enacted the Expanded War Crimes Act and substituted "war crimes" for "grave breaches"? What are the characteristics of a "competent tribunal" referred to in the POW Convention? How does a person captured during armed conflict qualify for the status of a POW?

How wide-ranging are the powers of the President as Commander–in–Chief? Have national leaders, who have waged a vigorous war on terrorist activity, been guided sufficiently by legal considerations, or has there been a practice on the part of some of "winking and nodding," thereby allowing for disregard of applicable international principles, standards, and rules?

What rights can be claimed under the 1984 CAT? What has been the impact of the Reservations, Understandings, and Declarations (RUDs) attached by the United States to the agreement? Is it possible to draw a satisfactory line between torture and other possibly similar but lesser forms of mistreatment and punishment? Is it ever legally or morally right to engage in acts of torture?

Do American legal documents, such as the Constitution and numerous Federal statutes meet the test of specificity, or are they challengeable on the ground of vagueness? Did the violations by Al Qaeda and the Taliban of the laws and customs of war provide justification for America's misreading or misunderstanding of the substantive and procedural contents of such laws? Can the lack of clarity in statements by the Department of Justice (DOJ) and the Department of Defense (DOD) regarding the requirements of international agreements offer to members of the armed forces in the field valid defenses on the ground that they had not been adequately trained and supervised in the conduct of detentions and interrogations?

Is the United States justified in applying one set of rules regarding torture to military personnel and another to civilian employees? Have sufficiently precise definitions and procedures regarding torture and similar practices been made by the DOD in the 2006 Field Manual 2-22.31 dealing with the detention and interrogation of alien enemy detainees? Do the procedures and rules applicable to administrative hearings before Administrative Review Boards and Combat Status Review Tribunals, and litigation in Military Commissions meet "civilized expectations"? What medical standards apply to the practice of governmental physicians whose patients consist of alien enemy unlawful combatants? Where the detainee is an American citizen? What are the implications of long-time and solitary confinements?

How does one respond when the legislative and executive departments of the government enact laws that purport to prevent the issuance by Federal District Courts of the writ of habeas corpus when sought by alien enemy unlawful combatants? More specifically, will the writ be available in Federal District Courts to detainees in custody at the Guantanamo Naval Station? On December 30, 2005, Congress enacted the Detainee Treatment Act which repealed Section 2241 of title 28 of the U. S. Code dealing with the issuance of writs of habeas corpus. The new statute provided that "No court . . . shall have jurisdiction to hear or consider . . . an application for a writ of habeas corpus filed by an alien enemy detained at Guanatnamo." On June 29, 2006 the Supreme Court in Hamdan v. Rumsfeld held that the legislative-stripping provision was unconstitutional.[6] This led to the enactment by the Congress on October 17, 2006 of the Military Commissions Act.[7] The statute, in effect, set aside the ruling made by the Supreme Court.

The statute, did, however, establish a limited habeas corpus process by allowing a claim by a detainee from an adverse decision of a Combatant Status Review Tribunal to be reviewed by the United States Court of Appeals for the District of Columbia. Members of Congress, including some who voted for the 2006 statute, have proposed new legislation, which, in turn, would open the door for an application for the writ. Public opinion articles have called for Congress to revise the existing legislation

The Supreme Court took into account the constitutional provision that Congress can suspend the issuance of the writ only in cases of rebellion or invasion when public safety may require it. Is the provision self-executing so that its benefit can be claimed by a person or is it necessary for Congress and the President to join in the adoption of legislation giving the constitutional provision legal force?

What is the significance of a "Presidential Signing Statement" attached by him to a statute in which he declares that the new law does not modify his constitutional powers? What is the significance of legislation designed to prohibit the Federal courts from considering or receiving guidance from international law or foreign laws? How does this affect the separation of powers principle? What is the force of a claim of "state secrets" made by the government in a case pending in a federal court?

These and other issue-based questions require suitable responses. In the following pages an assessment of these difficult issues will be attempted. Hopefully insights gained will open some doors to constructive outcomes.

4. THE RULE OF LAW

In a country proud of its history of freedom and democracy the concept of the universal rule of law is firmly rooted. It is a fundamental tenet to which Americans subscribe. But, when a country engages in armed conflict, for whatever reason, important challenges, to the applicability of laws, unfortunately, are bound to arise.

With the resort to armed force by the United States following 9/11, and with the attack on Iraq in March, 2003, the American people were presented with two important, but different, issues. The first "Was the American action lawful?" The second "Was it, taking into account moral considerations, the right thing to do?" Widely different outlooks on these questions quickly arose and remain alive at present. These outlooks have different weightings and are subject to different, but generally high, levels of intensity in public opinion.

In addition to the jus ad bellum concept, applicable to the initiation of armed conflict, there is the issue of the manner of its conduct, jus in bellum.[8] Regarding the latter, and in particular with respect to the persons captured in Afghanistan, the United States has issued a constantly modifying series of military orders creating a variety of procedures to deal with them. All have been based on the decision that combatants who had engaged in terrorist activities did not meet the Third Geneva POW qualifications, and that a new class of illegal enemy combatants was required. Trying to fit the latter into the category of POWs has been likened to trying to "put round pegs into square holes." But, while there were differences, leading to the conclusion that equal treatment of POWs and detainees was not an appropriate policy, it seemed to be in keeping with the broader concept of the rule of law that detainees should be accorded basic procedural rights when their terrorist roles came under review in military boards, tribunals, and commissions, and in the Federal courts.

The concept of the world rule of law separates the free from the unfree. Those who support the concept provide evidence of their support through their observable conduct. This means that behavior must be open and observable. Failure along such lines can bring down the wrath of national and international critics when they conclude that observable conduct has not measured up to reasonable expectations. Such opinion has played an important role in American responses, both public and private, to terrorist activities. Attention to such opinion is necessary if the United States wishes to be seen as a law-abiding citizen of the international community and enjoy the respect of its members. Self-interest, as usual, should be a motivating consideration. The foregoing scenario has been played out in the context of the need for the United States to protect public order and to insure security against foreign attack, and, equally importantly, to protect the civil and political rights and liberties of its citizens.

The Attorney General of the United Kingdom, Lord Goldsmith, in an address in the United States to members of the International and American Bar Associations on September 16, 2006, reflected on terrorism. He stated:

"I cannot agree with those civil libertarians who believe that 9/11 changed nothing and therefore no changes to our traditional ways of safeguarding fundamental values can be allowed. But, equally, I do not share the view of those who assert that 9/11 changed everything and therefore any changes are worth making if they might increase our security, whatever the impact on fundamental values and liberties on which our societies are based. What some would minimize as mere civil liberties are in fact the fundamental values on which our societies are based: liberty, justice, and equality before the law . . . These are the very freedoms and values that terrorists would destroy. We must not give them their victory by destroying them ourselves."[9]

This stirring assessment of the rule of law calls attention to the difference in rules governing trials in American Military Commissions and in the Federal District Courts. A subject in point is the use of torture-based confessions in the Commissions. This is governed by the DOD "Manual for Military Commissions" dated January 18, 2007, which does not entirely prohibit the use of such evidence. Another relates to the admission of hearsay evidence, and the weight to be given to it. A third deals with the burden of proof required to find an accused guilty of the charged act. In the Federal courts such guilt depends on a finding that it exists "beyond any reasonable doubt" as opposed in civil actions "by a preponderance of the evidence." The current approach for Military commissions suggests a finding of less than the former and more than the latter. Thus, section 949a. of the Military Commissions Act of October 17, 2006 (MCA) dealing with "Procedures and Rules of Evidence," provides that "A. Evidence shall be admissible if the military judge determines that the evidence would have probative value to a reasonable person."[10] This is the criteria or condition employed in Section 6(D.)(1) of the Presidential Order creating the earlier and now defunct version of Military Commissions. There was one change. In the 2001 Presidential Order creating the earlier a majority of the members of the Commission ruled on admissibility. In the 2006 version that decisions was vested in the Commission's military judge.

In the United States the ultimate authority regarding these matters is the Constitution, supplemented by valid statutes, such as the Uniform Code of Military Justice (UCMJ), as interpreted by holdings of the Supreme Court, unless and until overruled by subsequent legislation. These provide a more solid basis for national action than the vaguer and undefined content of the concept of the world rule of law, appealing as it is. By comparison, a more precise legal term is to be found in the Third Geneva Convention which states that duly constituted national courts are required to apply all of the "judicial guarantees which are recognized by civilized people." This, of course raises the question of the threshold of those "judicial guarantees" required in the United States.

By comparison countries, which employ civil law systems, and which enjoy high standards of civilization, but which do not adhere to the same substantive and procedural rights protected by the due process of law and the equal protection of the laws clauses in the U. S. Constitution, afford fewer protections. The standards for the administration of justice in these countries are high and certainly civilized. The substantive and procedural rights set forth in newly created national and international tribunals dealing with criminal and humanitarian matters do not reach the levels of protection contained in the criminal law jurisprudence of the United States. Yet, it is not likely, I think, that the particular procedures required in the International Criminal Tribunal for the former Yugoslavia, for matters now under consideration in the International Criminal Court, or the Special Tribunal for Crimes Against Humanity created for the prosecution of Saddam Hussein and other Iraqi defendants could be considered as not meeting the standards recognized and accepted by "civilized people."

In arriving at a working judgment in these matters, other factors must be considered. One is that of a world perspective summarized as "globalization" with its antecedents in multilateralism with its wide-ranging networks. This lively and practical concept is the product of scientific and technological progress including instant communications, rapid air travel, the common use of the English language, and the mobility of workers, despite the presence of national statutes calling for controls. It encompasses intensified and expanded contacts and involvements dealing with commercial, social, humanitarian, higher education, and political outlooks and engagements.[11] Not all of such influences have been hospitably received in foreign countries. In those areas where cultural traditions have been rapidly modified militant religious leaders and their followers have boldly pictured the United States as "the Great Satan."

This reflects the fact that dominant empires are feared, perhaps hated, and not trusted. America has been portrayed as a dominant hegemony. This has been coupled with the depiction of America's historic propensity to employ armed force in international relations. These situations have made many international leaders, and more than a few countries, suspicious of the U. S. claim to be supportive of the concept of the rule of law. This claim, frequently supported with vigor by American international lawyers, but relatively few others, is often doubted. Dominance, rather than high sounding proclamations and accompanying good behavior, frequently controls foreign and domestic appraisals. High degrees of subjectivity frequently influence such appraisals.

To overcome these mind sets the United States will have to provide convincing evidence that its commitment to freedom and democratic principles, including a cessation of its proclivity to engage in unilateral international military operations, will prevail. This can be demonstrated through compliance with constitutional principles, including the cooperative interactions of the three branches of government. It will have to pursue wholeheartedly and un remittingly generally perceived common international interests. It must demonstrate that it is giving meaningful attention to foreign perspectives. Policies of international accommodation, i.e., multilateralism, must replace failed policies having a unilateral focus. Peaceful change rather than the unilateral use of force in international relations will have to prevail. Where international diplomacy fails and the collective use of armed force is seen as the only remaining alternative, American participation must conform to the fundamental prescriptions of the United Nations Charter.

Not any easy task but worth the struggle.

NOTES

1. 77 UNTS 135, UST 3316, TIAS 3364. It entered into force for the United States on October 21, 1950. It was implemented in the Expanded War Crimes Act of 1997 with the substitution of "war crimes" for the term "grave breaches" appearing in the Convention. Pub. L. 104–192. For current developments see PROJECT to Enforce the Geneva Conventions (PEGC) containing a wealth of information on cases, articles, and books. www.pegc.US/. Authored by Charles B. Gittings, Jr.

2. 75 UNTS 287, 6 UST 3316, TIAS 3356. It entered into force for the United States on February 2, 1956. Both agreements had previously entered into force on October 21, 1950.

3. G. A. RES. 39/46 [annex, 39 GAOR Supp. (no. 51) at 197], U. N. Doc A/39/51 (1984)]. The Convention (CAT) entered into force on June 28, 1987. It was signed by the United States on April 18, 1988. It was deposited with the United Nations on October 21, 1994, with effect from November 20, 1994. 1830 UNTS A-2481.] It was subject to 2 Reservations, 5 Understandings (one of which consisted of 5 parts), 2 Declarations, and one proviso, which was not recorded with the United Nations.

Afghanistan is not a party to all of the foregoing treaties. Iraq was a signatory to both of the Geneva Conventions. It is not a party to the Torture Convention.

4. U. N. Doc. A/811.

5. Pub. L. 109-359.

6. 126 U.S. 2748 (June29, 2006).

7. Pub. L. 109-366, 124 Stat 2600.

8. L. MOIR, REAPPRAISING THE RESORT TO FORCE, JUS AD BELLUM AND THE WAR ON TERROR, (2008).

9. Rule of Law Symposium, International Bar and American Bar Association, Chicago, September 16, 2006. 36 International Law News, No. 1, p. 4 (Winter 2007).

10. Section 949a contains provisions addressed to the concept of a fair trial. Among them are: military commissions may receive evidence produced without a search warrant, an admissible statement by an accused is not to be excluded "on grounds of alleged coercion or compulsory self-incrimination so long as the evidence complies with the provisions of section 948r of this title." Where a self-incriminating statement was based on the torture of the detainee a distinction was made between statements obtained before the enactment if the DTA in 2005, where it is provided that if the degree of coercion is disputed such statement would be admissible only if the military judge finds that "(1) the totality of the circumstances renders the statement reliable and possessing sufficient probative value; and (2) the interests of justice would best be served by admission of the statement into evidence." However, for such statements obtained after the enactment of the DTA on December 30, 2005, their admissibility was to be conditioned by the foregoing provision on the totality of the circumstances and the interests of justice, and, in addition the military judge would have to determine "(3) that the interrogation methods used to obtain the statement do not amount to cruel, inhuman, or degrading treatment prohibited by Section 1003 . . ." of the 2005 DTA. Other conditions were established regarding "hearsay" evidence in Section 949a9(b)(E)(i). Such testimony was forthcoming, provided that (ii) "Hearsay evidence not otherwise admissible under the rules of evidence applicable to trials by general courts-martial shall not be admitted in a trial by military commission if the party opposing the admission of the evidence demonstrates that the evidence is unreliable or lacking in probative value." In general, evidence lacking in probative value, especially where it presented the "danger of unfair prejudice, confusion of the issues, or misleading the commission . . ." was to be excluded in military commission trials.

11. CARL Q. CHRISTOL, INTERNATIONAL LAW AND U.S.FOREIGN POLICY, Revised Second edition, (2006), JOHN V. MURPHY, THE UNITED STATES AND THE RULE OF LAW IN INTERNATIONAL AFFAIRS (2004). Other studies include THOMAS BUERGENTHAL and SEAN D. MURPHY, PUBLIC INTERNATIONAL LAW IN A NUTSHELL, Second edition (1990), G. VON GLAHN and JAMES L. TAULBEE, LAW AMONG NATIONS: AN INTRODUCTION TO PUBLIC INTERNATIONAL LAW, Eighth edition (2006) and MARK W. JANIS, AN INTRODUCTION TO INTERNATIONAL LAW, Revised Fourth edition (2003).

Chapter Two

The Convention against Torture and Other Cruel, Inhuman or Degrading Treatment or Punishment (CAT), December 10, 1984

1. INTRODUCTION

The 21st Century will probably be recorded as one of the bloodiest in history. Wars can produce extraordinarily heroic conduct. They can also provide occasions for the release of evil instincts with resulting torture and other cruel, inhuman, or degrading treatment or punishment.[1]

Will the 20th and the 21st be recorded as those in which the torture of humans reached a new high? Have the Reservations, Understandings, and Declarations (RUDs) attached by the United States to its ratification of the Convention weakened the basic provisions of the agreement? Who is responsible for conduct, seen as violations of the terms of the Convention, that has taken place during the wars in Afghanistan and Iraq, at the Guantanamo Naval Base in Cuba or in other countries where the United States has held detainees, considered to be terrorists, for interrogation?

Other questions have been raised: What caused American military personnel when engaged in the detention and interrogation of detainees to engage in acts of torture and the other accompanying offenses listed in the Convention? Who was ultimately responsible for departure from treaty norms? Had there been a failure in the training of those personnel who were assigned detention and interrogation functions? Had high level governmental authorities, both civilian and military, fully understood that in time of armed conflict that governing principles and rules of law were applicable? Had command authority been suitably understood? Was the chain of command properly implemented?

To preserve the dignity of humans the General Assembly of the United Nations on December 10, 1984 adopted a resolution bearing the above title.[2] Following the American signature on April 18, 1988, and intensive negotiations in which representatives of the Department of State, the Department of Defense, the Department of Justice and members of the Senate Committee on Foreign Relations participated, the Convention (CAT) was ratified by President Bush on October 20, 1994. It was deposited on the following day at the United Nations and entered into force for the United States on November 20, 1994. The non-acceptance by the United States of the Convention in its entirety was reflected in two reservations, five understandings, with one consisting of five parts, two declarations, and a proviso.[3] The RUDs accepted by the Bush administration were substantially different from those adopted by the Reagan Administration. Others that were considered by both administrations were also rejected following analysis. The negotiations between Senators, cognizant of their power under the advice and consent provision of the Constitution, and the White House were active with relevant exchanges of points of view.

The international law of war, which in recent years has been referred to as the law of armed conflict, has an extended history. During the 20th Century States placed emphasis on the humane treatment of military personnel during times of armed conflict. Through the development of international humanitarian law, advances were made for the protection of basic Human Rights for all individuals. Important and wide-ranging international agreements were agreed to having as their purpose the protection of both military personnel and civilians in time of armed conflict. While an earthly paradise was not contemplated there was real hope that the parties would comply with the international instruments, and that the broader needs of society would be served. In light of such expectations recent unlawful American military and civilian activities appear to be more than unusually reprehensible

Influencing the goals of CAT was the 1907 The Hague Convention on the Laws and Customs of War on Land. Dealing with prisoners of war (POW) and the inhabitants of occupied territories, it provided that prisoners "must be humanely treated."[4] Influencing CAT were the holdings of the Nuremberg Tribunal in 1945 with its reference to Crimes Against Humanity and War Crimes, including convictions and the imposition of sanctions. Also to be taken into account was the formation of the United Nations in 1945 with Article 55(c) calling for "universal respect for and observance of human rights and fundamental freedoms for all . . ." Equally important were the terms of Article 5 of the 1948 Universal Declaration of Human Rights reading "No one shall be subjected to torture or to cruel, inhuman or degrading treatment or punishment."[5]

On August 12, 1949, two long-negotiated and immensely important international agreements were signed in Geneva. They are the Convention Relating to Prisoners of War[6] and the Convention relating to the Protection of Civilian Persons in Time of War.[7]

The CAT had been preceded by substantial efforts. On December 9, 1975 the General Assembly had adopted a Declaration on the subject. Containing 12 articles it defined torture. It referred to measures seeking prevention and punishment.[8]

At the time of the negotiation and signature of the foregoing no one imagined they might become highly relevant as a result of the planning of terrorists which culminated with the attacks on 9/11. Those attacks and the wars in Afghanistan and Iraq resulted in conduct which made them relevant. Each of the Geneva Conventions contained a common article 3. It provided that "Persons taking no part in the hostilities . . . shall in all circumstances be treated humanely . . . To this end the following acts [referred to as "grave breaches" and later changed in the United States via legislation to "war crimes"] are and shall remain prohibited at any time and in any place whatsoever with respect to the above-mentioned persons:

(a) violence to life and person, in particular murder of all kinds, mutilation, cruel treatment and torture . . .

(c) outrages upon personal dignity, in particular, humiliating and degrading treatment . . .[9]

Additionally, Article 13 of the POW Convention requires that POWs must "at all times be humanely treated," that their "health must not be seriously endangered," and that they must be "protected against acts of violence and intimidation."

Article 17 of the Third Convention dealt with physical and mental torture. It stated: "No physical or mental torture, nor any other form of coercion, may be inflicted on prisoners of war to secure from them information of any kind whatever. Prisoners of war who refuse to answer may not be threatened, insulted, or exposed to any unpleasant or disadvantageous treatment of any kind."

Article 87 extends limitations on the conduct of captors. Thus, "Collective punishment for individual acts, corporal punishment, imprisonment in premises without daylight, and in general, any form of torture or cruelty, are forbidden."

The Fourth Convention created a somewhat different regime for civilian persons. Its Article 5 provided that "protected persons" shall "nevertheless be treated with humanity, and, in case of trial shall not be deprived of the rights of fair and regular trial prescribed in the present Convention." Its Articles 13 and 17 do not track the terms of the POW agreement. However Article 27 of the Civilian Convention repeats Article 13 of the POW Convention. Article

31 of the Civilian agreement employs different terms from those found in Article 17 of the POW treaty. Article 31 provides that "No physical or moral coercion [vice "physical and mental torture" in Article 17] shall be exercised against protected persons, in particular to obtain information from them or from third persons."

Article 32 of the Fourth Convention sets forth additional and highly specific rights for protected persons prohibiting Parties to the agreement from taking "any measures of such a character as to cause the physical suffering or extermination of protected persons in their hands. This prohibition applies not only to murder, torture, corporal punishments, mutilation and medical or scientific experiments not necessitated by the medical or scientific treatment of a protected person, but also to other measures of brutality whether applied by civilian or military agents." Article 33 of this Convention made specific reference to a subject not found in the POW agreement. It provided that "All measures of intimidation or of terrorism are prohibited."

In the years following 1949 these subjects have attracted substantial international attention. For example, in 1950 the International Law Commission announced principles which identified the mistreatment of POWs as "war crimes," and took into account "inhuman acts" affecting individuals. On December 16, 1966 agreement was reached on the terms of the International Covenant on Civil and Political Rights with Article 7 stating that "No one shall be subjected to torture, or to cruel, inhuman or degrading treatment or punishment."[10] Following acceptance by the United States of its terms the United States issued a reservation stating that it considered itself "bound by Article 7 to the extent that "cruel, inhuman or degrading treatment or punishment" means the "cruel and unusual treatment or punishment prohibited by the Fifth, Eighth, and/or Fourteenth Amendments to the Constitution of the United States." This was followed by regional agreements containing provisions relating to torture. Article 5 (2) of the American Convention on Human Rights of November 22, 1969 condemned such conduct. It was signed by the United States, but ratification did not follow. Nonetheless it entered into force on July 18, 1978.[11] Similar provisions are contained in Article 3 of the European Convention for the Protection of Human Rights and Fundamental Freedoms.[12] Article 5 of the June 27, 1981 African Charter on Human and Peoples' Rights promulgates the same principles.[13]

These widespread efforts over an extended period provide evidence of a constant commitment to the laws and customs of war and to the guarantees to individuals of basic Human Rights. The concerns reflecting American practices with respect to unlawful enemy combatants and their presumed terrorist activities have demonstrated how fundamental these principles have become. In light of the increase in the acts of terrorism during the past 10–15 years and the detention and interrogation of such persons, efforts have been made to identify the lawful extent of punitive governmental conduct and the remaining rights of those in custody.[14]

2. ESSENTIAL PROVISIONS OF CAT

The importance to the United States of the provisions of CAT can be judged by the attachment of RUDs to Articles 1, 3, 1–16, 21(1), and 30 (1) (2). Although the other articles were integral portions of the agreement, they were not signaled by the United States as so problematic as to require RUDs. To best understand the American debate and acceptance of CAT the provisions of the above articles need to be viewed.

Article 1 is the definitional article. It reads:

For the purposes of this Convention, the term "torture" means any act by which severe pain or suffering, whether physical or mental, is intentionally inflicted on a person for such purposes as obtaining from him or a third person information or a confession, punishing him for an act he or a third person has committed or is suspected of having committed, or intimidating or coercing him or a third person, or for any reason based on discrimination of any kind, when such pain or suffering is inflicted by or at the instigation of or with the consent or acquiescence of a public official or other person acting in an official capacity. It does not include pain or suffering arising only from, inherent in or incidental to lawful sanctions.

Article 2 provides:

1. Each State Party shall take effective legislative, administrative, judicial or other measures to prevent acts of torture in any territory under its jurisdiction.

2. No exceptional circumstances whatsoever, whether a state of war or a threat of war, internal political instability or any other public emergency, may be invoked as a justification of torture.

3. An order from a superior officer or a public authority may not be invoked as a justification of torture.

Article 3 deals with special aspects of implementation. It states:

1. No State shall expel, ("refouler") or extradite a person to another State where there are substantial grounds for believing that he would be in danger of being subjected to torture.

2. For the purposes of determining whether there are such grounds, the competent authorities shall take into account all relevant considerations including, where applicable, the existence in the State concerned or a consistent pattern of gross, flagrant or mass violations of human rights.

Article 4 requires national implementation by the parties. It reads:

1. Each Party shall ensure that all acts of torture are offenses under its criminal law. The same shall apply to an attempt to commit torture and to an act by any person which constitutes complicity or participation in torture.

2. Each State Party shall make these offenses punishable by appropriate penalties which take into account their grave nature.

Articles 5 through 13 dealt with the following:

5: the duty of a party to adopt measures dealing with special jurisdictional situations;

6: the duty to investigate and to insure the custody of a possible offender;

7: the duty to prosecute or to extradite an alleged offender;

8: conditions affecting extradition;

9: mutual assistance among the parties;

10: education on prohibition of torture for selected public officials;

11: systematic review of national detention and interrogation practices;

12: prompt and impartial investigations;

13: rights of alleged offenders to complain and have prompt inquiry by competent authorities.

Article 14 was of concern to the United States. Its terms are:

1. Each State Party shall ensure in its legal system that the victim of an act of torture obtains redress and has an enforceable right to fair and adequate compensation, including the means for as full rehabilitation as possible. In the event of the death of the victim as a result of an act of torture, his dependants shall be entitled to compensation.

2. Nothing in this article shall affect any right of the victim or other persons to compensation which may exist under national law.

Article 15 prohibited a statement made by a tortured person from being invoked as evidence in any proceedings, except as against the person accused of torture.

Article 16 identified crimes other than torture. It provided:

1. Each State party shall undertake to prevent in any territory under its jurisdiction other acts of cruel, inhuman or degrading treatment or punishment which do not amount to torture as defined in Article 1, when such acts are committed by or at the instigation of or with the consent or acquiescence of a public official or other person acting in an official capacity. In particular, the obligations contained in articles 10, 11, 12 and 13 shall apply with the substitution of references to torture of references to other forms of cruel, inhuman or degrading treatment or punishment.

2. The provisions of this Convention are without prejudice to the provisions of any other international instrument or national law which prohibits

cruel, inhuman or degrading treatment or punishment or which relates to extradition or expulsion.

Part II of the Convention, consisting of Articles 17–24, provided for the establishment and operation of a Committee against Torture. Article 17 identified the structure of governance. Article 18 referred to the election of officers and its relation to the United Nations. Article 19 called for reports by Parties on measures "taken to give effect to their undertakings under . . ." the Convention. Article 20 gave the Committee the power to invite Parties charged with violations of the agreement to "cooperate in the examination of the information and to this end to submit observations with regard to the information concerned."

Article 21 (1) enabled Parties to declare they recognized the competence of the Committee. The United States filed a declaration. The terms of Article 21(1) are:

1. A State Party to this Convention may at any time declare under this article that it recognizes the competence of the Committee to receive and consider communications to the effect that a State Party claims that another State Party is not fulfilling its obligations under this Convention. Such communications may be received and considered according to the procedures laid down in this article only if submitted by a State Party which has made a declaration recognizing in regard to itself the competence of the Committee. No communication shall be dealt with by the Committee under this article if it concerns a State Party which has not made such a declaration. Communications received under this article shall be dealt with in accordance with the following procedure;

(a) If a State Party considers that another State Party is not giving effect to the provisions of this Convention, it may, by written communication, bring the matter to the attention of that State Party. Within three months after the receipt of the communication the receiving State shall afford the State which sent the communication an explanation or any other statement in writing clarifying the matter, which should include, to the extent possible and pertinent, reference to domestic procedures and remedies taken, pending or available in the matter;

(b) If the matter is not adjusted to the satisfaction of both States Parties concerned within six months after the receipt by the receiving State of the initial communication, either State shall have the right to refer the matter to the Committee, by notice given to the Committee and to the other State;

(c) The Committee shall deal with a matter referred to it under this article only after it has ascertained that all domestic remedies have been invoked and exhausted in the matter, in conformity with the generally recognized principles

THE UNIVERSITY OF TEXAS
AT BROWNSVILLE
Brownsville, Tx 78520-4991

of international law. This shall not be the rule where the application of the remedies is unreasonably prolonged or is unlikely to bring effective relief to the person who is the victim of the violation of this Convention;

(d) The Committee shall hold closed meetings when examining communications under this article;

(e) Subject to the provisions of subparagraph (c), the Committee shall make available its good offices to the States Parties concerned with a view to a friendly solution of the matter on the basis of respect for the obligations provided for in this Convention. For this purpose, the Committee may, when appropriate, set up an ad hoc conciliation commission;

(f) In any matter referred to under this article, the Committee may call upon the States Parties concerned, referred to in subparagraph (b), to supply any relevant information;

(g) The States Parties concerned, referred to in subparagraph (b) shall have the right to be represented when the matter is being considered by the Committee and to make submissions orally and/or in writing;

(h) The Committee shall, within twelve months after the date of receipt of notice under subparagraph (b), submit a report:

(i) If a solution within the terms of subparagraph (e) is reached, the Committee shall confine its report to a brief statement of the facts and of the solution reached;

(ii) If a solution within the terms of subparagraph (e) is not reached, the Committee shall confine its report to a brief statement of the facts; the written submissions and record of the oral submissions made by the States Parties concerned shall be attached to the report;

In every matter, the report shall be communicated to the States Parties concerned.

Articles 22–29 dealt with the following:

Article 22: Competence of the Committee;

Article 23: Privileges and immunities of Committee members and of ad hoc conciliation commissions;

Article 24: Annual Report of Committee;

Article 25: Ratification of the Convention;

Article 26: Accession to the Convention;

Article 27: Entry into force of the Convention;

Article 28: Non-recognition of Committee, Withdrawal of Reservations,

Article 29: Proposal of Amendments.

Article 30 dealt with the resolution of disputes. It provides

1. Any dispute between two or more States Parties concerning the interpretation or application of this Convention which cannot be settled through negotiation shall, at the request of one of them, be submitted to arbitration. If

within six months from the date of the request for arbitration the Parties are unable to agree on the organization of the arbitration, any one of those Parties may refer the dispute to the International Court of Justice by request in conformity with the Statute of the Court.

2. Each State may, at the time of signature or ratification of this Convention or accession thereto, declare that it does not consider itself bound by paragraph 1 of this article. The other States Parties shall not be bound by paragraph 1 of this article with respect to any State Party having made such a reservation.

3. Any State Party having made a reservation in accordance with paragraph 2 of this article may at any time withdraw this reservation by notification to the Secretary-General of the United Nations.

Article 31 allows for a denunciation of the Convention. Article 32 requires the Secretary-General to notify parties of signatures, ratifications, accessions, and denunciations and the date of entry into force of the Convention. Article 33 prescribes the 5 languages having equal authenticity. Certified copies of the agreement are to be transmitted "to all States."[15]

3. THE AMERICAN RESERVATIONS, UNDERSTANDINGS AND DECLARATIONS (RUDS) TO CAT

After well-considered internal negotiation between the political branches of the Federal government, during which time numerous positions were advanced only to be rejected or replaced by other views, President Bush, after having received the advice and consent of the Senate,[16] ratified the Convention on October 21, 1994. A deposit of the ratification, together with the RUDs, was delivered to the Secretary-General on the same date, with a notice that it would become effective on November 20, 1994. The changes were affected by a substantial public interest in the subject, by the advent of a new administration, by the outlooks of powerful members of the U. S. Senate, and the persuasiveness of key members of the Departments of State, Justice, and Defense. In order to understand the shifting base for the final version of the RUDs it is worthwhile to refer to the earlier proposals. To allow for such analysis the terms of the final version need to be viewed. They follow:

I. The Senate's advice and consent is subject to the following reservations:

(1) That the United States considers itself bound by the obligation under Article 16 to prevent "cruel, inhuman or degrading treatment or punishment," only insofar as the term "cruel, inhuman or degrading treatment or punishment" means the cruel, unusual and inhumane treatment or punishment prohibited by the Fifth, Eighth, and/or Fourteenth Amendments to the Constitution of the United States.

(2) That pursuant to Article 30(2) the United States declares that it does not consider itself bound by Article 30(1), but reserves the right specifically to agree to follow this or any other procedure for arbitration in a particular case.

II. The Senate's advice and consent is subject to the following understandings, which shall apply to the obligations of the United States under this Convention:

(1)(a) That with reference to Article 1, the United States understands that, in order to constitute torture, an act must be specifically intended to inflict severe physical or mental pain or suffering and that mental pain or suffering refers to prolonged mental harm caused by or resulting from: (1) the intentional infliction or threatened infliction of severe physical pain or suffering; (2) the administration or application, or threatened administration or application, of mind altering substances or other procedures calculated to disrupt profoundly the senses or the personality; (3) the threat of imminent death; or (4) the threat that another person will imminently be subjected to death, severe physical pain or suffering, or the administration or application of mind altering substances or other procedures calculated to disrupt profoundly the senses or personality.

(b) That the United States understands that the definition of torture in Article 1 is intended to apply only to acts directed against persons in the offender's custody or physical control.

(c) That with reference to Article 1 of the Convention, the United States understands that "sanctions" includes judicially imposed sanctions and other enforcement actions authorized by United State law or judicial interpretation or such law. Nonetheless, the United States understands that a State Party could not through its domestic sanctions defeat the object and purpose of the Convention to prohibit torture.

(d) That with reference to Article 1 of the Convention, the United States understands that the term "acquiescence" requires that the public official, prior to the activity constituting torture, have awareness of such activity and thereafter breach his legal responsibility to intervene to prevent such activity.

(e) That with reference to Article 1 of the Convention, the United States understands that noncompliance with applicable legal procedural standards does not per se constitute torture.

(2) That the United States understands the phrase, "where there are substantial grounds for believing that he would be in danger of being subjected to torture," as used in Article 3 of the Convention, to mean "if it is more likely than not that he would be tortured."

(3) That it is the understanding of the United States that Article 14 requires a State Party to provide a private right of action for damages only for acts of torture committed in territory under the jurisdiction of that State Party.

(4) That the United States understands that international law does not prohibit the death penalty, and does not consider this Convention to restrict or prohibit the United States from applying the death penalty consistent with the Fifth, Eighth and/or Fourteenth Amendments to the Constitution of the United States, including any constitutional period of confinement prior to the imposition of the death penalty.

(5) That the United States understands that this Convention shall be implemented by the United States Government to the extent that it exercises legislative and judicial jurisdiction over the matters covered by the Convention and otherwise by the state and local governments. Accordingly, in implementing Articles 10–14 and 16, the United States Government shall take measures appropriate to the Federal system to the end that the competent authorities of the constituent units of the United States of America may take appropriate measures for the fulfillment of the Convention.

III. The Senate's advice and consent is subject to the following declarations:

(1) That the United States declares that the provisions of Articles 1 through 16 of the Convention are not self-executing.

(2) That the United States declares, pursuant to Article 21, paragraph 1, of the Convention, that it recognizes the competence of the Committee against Torture to receive and consider communications to the effect that a State Party claims that another State Party is not fulfilling its obligations under the Convention. It is the understanding of the United States that, pursuant to the above mentioned article, such communications shall be accepted and processed only if they come from a State Party which has made a similar declaration.

In addition the United States Senate adopted the following proviso which stated that the President was not to include it in the information deposited with the Secretary-General. The proviso stated: "The President of the United States shall not deposit the instrument of ratification until such time as he has notified all present and prospective ratifying parties to this Convention that nothing on this Convention requires or authorizes legislation, or other action, by the United States of America prohibited by the Constitution of the United States as interpreted by the United States."

Following the U. S. signature of CAT on April 18, 1988, President Reagan asked Secretary of State George Schultz for advice on ratification. He consulted with his own staff and with representatives of the Departments of Defense and Justice. In his May 1988 letter of transmittal to the President the Secretary of State pointed out that in view of the large number of countries concerned "it was not possible to negotiate a treaty that was acceptable to the United States in all respects."[17] He stated that RUDs had been drafted "to clarify the definition of 'torture,' to ensure that the provisions relating to extradition and deportation are consistent with U. S. treaty obligations and U. S. law and to reserve both to the compulsory jurisdiction of the International Court of Justice and to the competence of the Committee Against Torture to initiate investigations of the United States . . ."[18]

The Secretary of State also recommended that a declaration be made that the agreement was not to be self-executing. He also called attention to the need for recommended legislation to be submitted to Congress. His recommendation contained 4 resolutions, 9 understandings, and 4 declarations.[19]

On May 20, 1988 President Reagan submitted CAT to the Senate. He called attention to the proposed RUDs. He stated that with their inclusion he believed "there are no constitutional or other legal obstacles to United States ratification."[20] He later told the Senate that when he deposited the American ratification with the United Nations that he would add that the United States was not recognizing the competence of the Committee Against Torture "to make confidential investigations of charges that torture is being systematically practiced in the United States."[21] He also referred to the terms of Article 21.1 of the Convention, containing the requirement that a Party had to make a declaration granting the right to other countries to submit a communication alleging that another country was not fulfilling its obligations. President Reagan announced that the United States would not make such a declaration.[22]

Apparently overwhelmed by the nature of the challenge facing it the Senate Committee took no action until September, 1989, when its new chairman, Senator Pell, wrote to the new Secretary of State, James Baker, 1989–1992, inquiring as to the status of the Convention. He announced committee hearings on September 26, 1989. On December 10, 1989 Assistant Secretary of State Janet G. Mullins provided Senator Pell with a memorandum containing the proposals of the George H. W. Bush administration. In her letter she stated that the Bush administration had deleted a number of the RUDs that had been submitted to the Committee by the Reagan administration.

The first omitted reservation had provided: "The United States does not consider itself bound by Article 3 insofar as it conflicts with the obligations of the United States towards States not party to the Convention under bilateral extradition treaties with such States."[23] The reason for the withdrawal was that it was not necessary since it was subject to misconstruction, e. g., that the United States "was retaining, insofar as it relates to nonparties, the juridical right to send a person back to a country where that person would be tortured. Such was never the intent."[24]

The second omitted reservation had specified that the United States did not recognize the competence of the Committee against Torture under Article 20.

This was inconsistent with the declaration that was set forth in declaration III.(2) which accepted the competence of the Committee.

One understanding was omitted. It was considered that it was no longer necessary because it had been concluded that the terms of the Convention did not "preclude the availability of common law defenses, including but not limited to self-defense and the defense of others."[25]

Three of the Reagan declarations were omitted. The first related to the time when the instrument of ratification was to be deposited with the Secretary-General. Although it was the intent of both the Reagan and the Bush administration not to deposit the instrument of ratification until Congress had adopted implementing legislation, it was considered this consideration was not essential to the approval of the Senate.

The second referred to the phrase "competent authorities" as used in Article 3.2 of the Convention relating to the extradition or return of persons charged with torture. While such authority would be the Secretary of State in extradition matters and the Attorney General in deportation cases, it was considered this need not be included as a declaration.

The third related to the term "adequate alterative" in Article 7.1 of the Convention. This dealt with the extradition by the United States of an alien for alleged torture to the competent authorities of the requesting State for the purpose of prosecution "only if the extradition of the offender to the State where the offense was committed is not an adequate alternative."[26] This decision was based on the intent of the United States to conform to the above requirement, but it was deemed that this need not be included in a declaration dealing with a formal instrument of ratification.

On January 30, 1990 the Bush administration submitted a new set of conditions to the Senate including 3 reservations, 5 understandings, and one declaration.[27] On that date an extended hearing took place as reported below.

On October 27, 1990, during the administration of President Bush, the Senate gave its approval to the Convention. It attached its own set of RUDs which had been adopted by the Committee on Foreign Relations on July 19, 1990 and amended on October 27 by a Senate vote. During the period between the Reagan submission and the Senate approval, alternate proposals had been made. Numerous factors had contributed to new proposals and their analysis. There had been a substantial public interest, particularly on the part of the Human Rights community. Senators reflecting concerns for perceived American opinions, grounded in isolationist sentiment, voiced their views and added their own conditions. The need to protect national sovereignty was identified. Senators, holding to their traditional role in asserting oversight over executive foreign policy initiatives, exercised the prerogative of seeking to clarify the terms of the Convention and the underlying policies. Executive department responses had to be prepared and agreed to in the Departments of State, Defense, and Justice. These had to be reviewed by the Senate Committee. All of this took time, with much time elapsing between the Senate's first receipt of the presidential request on May 20, 1988 and the hearings conducted by the Committee on Foreign Relations on January 30, 1990.[28] It was not until July 19, 1990 that Senator Pell, Chairman of the Committee on Foreign Relations, deemed that the matter was ready for committee action. Even so, following floor action on August 3, 1990, the final debate occurred on October 27, 1990, at which time four proposals (S. Amdts. 3200–3203) were considered and agreed to.[29]

During this time it had become evident that the White House and the Senate were both engaged in "tightening up" an agreement containing general language as well as arriving at the required operational definitions. The Reagan and Bush administrations held different substantive views. The cooperative efforts of the White House and Congress meant that the alternative of an executive agreement in the form of a statutory enactment was not contemplated nor was the situation comparable to that facing Secretary of State Hay, when between 1899 and 1900 he was not able to find a common outlook with the Senate for the agreement which in 1901 became the Hay-Poncefote Treaty. In its final form there were also many Senate-based reservations.

Parallels exist between the CAT RUDs and the RUDs attached to the 1948 International Convention on the Prevention and Punishment of the Crime of Genocide.[30] During the course of the Committee's hearings on the CAT the issue arose whether a reservation were necessary to ensure that ratification of the Convention did not bind the United States to take actions prohibited by the Constitution. It was considered that such a constitutional reservation would not add anything in the way of constitutional protection. It was noted that such a reservation could create numerous problems at the international level and would, under international law, automatically become available to all other Parties. The United States had invoked the constitutional proviso in the Genocide Convention. One outcome was the filing of written objections by 12 Western European countries to the reservation. It was considered that such an American reservation to the CAT would lead to the adoption of the same reservation by other countries with the adverse consequences of such reservations being magnified.

The American understandings to the CAT demonstrated a concern over such definitional terms as "intent to destroy," "specific intent to destroy," and "mental harm." One American understanding dealt with the American right not to participate in an international penal tribunal, such as the new International Criminal Court, while one reservation reserved the right of the United States to prevent litigation in the International Court of Justice. In both agreements a considerable amount of time elapsed between the signing of the agreement and its ratification and entry into force.

A second issue was whether the United States should accept the competence of the Committee Against Torture. Although favored initially by the Reagan administration it changed its outlook and created a reservation in its submission to the Senate stating that the competence of such a committee would not be recognized by the United States.

A third issue dealt with the meaning to be accorded to the term "lawful sanctions" in the definition of "torture" in Article 1 of the Convention. The American concern was grounded on the possibility that other Parties might justify actions which were torture by declaring such sanctions to be lawful under domestic law.

It was not until October 20, 1994 that CAT was signed by President Bush. It entered into force for the United States one month later. The uncertainty of the United States regarding the appropriateness of the conditions finally attached to its ratification characterized the period from the date of signature (April 18, 1988) through the ratification by President Bush.

Although the terms of the Convention and the RUDs received bipartisan support during the business meetings of the Committee, a favorable report to the President was given only by the Democrat members of the Committee. Republican members of the Committee were not present when the vote was called by Senator Pell. They responded that this had been a "failure of comity which implied a diminished appreciation of our international obligations."[31] The early vote had prevented Republican members of the Committee from accepting some of the proposed RUDs. They asked for another business meeting in which they would have an opportunity to propose amendments. This occurred on October 27, 1990 with the acceptance of joint proposals by Senator Pell and Senator Helms.

The Department of State provided the members of the Committee with a report identifying the administrations views on May 23, 1988.[32] This was followed by a second assessment of the proposed RUDs on December 10, 1989.[33] The latter consisted of a report submitted by Janet G. Mullins, Assistant Secretary of State, Legislative Affairs, to Senator Pell. It identified changes from the 1988 proposed RUDs. The 1989 version included some of the terms that were finally accepted by the Committee and by the administration, were approved by the Senate and deposited with the United Nations.

The Mullins memorandum called attention to the acceptance in 1989 of provisions that had been retained from 1988 without modification, reassignment of identifications, and identification of revisions. Thus, the federal government's responsibility for the acts of constituent units, while retained from 1988, was changed from a reservation to understandings, and included in

II.(5). The understanding relating to Article 16 became a reservation without a changed in its formulation. The reservation relating to Article 30 (2) was retained without modification. This reservation with its reference to the use of arbitration resulted from Senator Pressler's statement at the hearings conducted in September, 1989. He told the Committee he would not accept the compulsory jurisdiction of the World Court in disputes involving CAT. Consultations within the administration disclosed that this view was shared. This led to the reservation set forth in Section I.(2) of the RUDs.

The 1988 Understandings were also identified. Article 1 (a) dealing with the definition of torture was revised to clarify the definition of mental harm. It became a final Understanding. It influenced profoundly subsequent legislation and Department of Justice memoranda and produced unanticipated outcomes. Article 1 (b) was adopted without modification. Article 1 (c) dealing with the meaning of lawful sanctions was revised "to require that, for purposes of the definition of lawful sanctions, any U. S. sanctions or sanctions permitted under U. S. law be not clearly prohibited under international law." Article 1 (d) in the 1988 understanding stated that the U. S. "understands that the term 'acquiescence' requires that the public official, prior to the activity constituting torture, have awareness of such activity and thereafter breach his legal responsibility to intervene to prevent such activity." The 1989 change from "knowledge" to "awareness" was intended to "make it clearer that both actual knowledge and willful blindness fall within the meaning of acquiescence." Article 1(e) was retained without modification.

Hearings on the RUDs took place before the Committee on January 30, 1990.[34] Testifying were Abraham D. Sofaer, State Department Legal Adviser, and Mark Richard, a Deputy Attorney General. In his testimony Mr. Sofaer in referring to the section II.1(a) understanding on torture stated it was a "codified proposal which does not raise the high threshold of pain already required under international law, but clarifies the definition of mental pain and suffering, and maintains the position that specific intent is required for torture."[35]

Mr. Sofaer also referred to the 1998 package of American RUDs and, in particular the reference to the term "sanctions," as including "not only judicially imposed sanctions but also other enforcement actions authorized by United States law or judicial interpretations of such law." When the U. S. government realized that the use of this formula by a foreign government would allow it to attempt to legitimize "officially-sanctioned torture simply by authorizing it specifically as a matter of domestic law,"[36] the United States included in its understanding II.(1)(c) that "nonetheless, the United States understands that a State Party could not through its domestic sanctions defeat the object and purpose of the Convention to prohibit torture."

Mr. Richard, from the perspective of officials engaged in the administration of justice, expressed the need for having a clear understanding of the meanings assigned to treaty terms and to the RUDs. He envisioned the engrafting of treaty provisions onto the criminal law of the United States. Failure to obtain clarity would lead to unwarranted litigation. He noted the treaty provision allowing for international jurisdiction over American defendants and expressed concern that a lack of clarity respecting treaty provisions could lead to fundamental unfairness. He was concerned that the absence of clear definitions might encourage unscrupulous foreign nations to take hostile actions against American defendants in those countries.

Mr. Richard assessed the II.(1) (a) understanding relating to torture. He pointed out that the definition of torture in CAT was relatively general and that torture was a more severe form of human misconduct than inhuman or degrading behavior. He also observed that the Parties to the agreement had not defined cruel, inhuman, or degrading conduct, although Article 16 called upon signatories to undertake to prevent such conduct and to punish such actions within the territories under their jurisdiction. In arriving at his presentation he reviewed international efforts to deal with torture in the laws of war and earlier efforts to arrive at a legal meaning for "torture." With regard to torture it was his view that the drafters of the Convention did not have a "significant body of international legal precedent on which to draw."[37] As a result the CAT contained a fairly general definition.

He reported that a careful distinction should be made between physical and mental pain. As to the former, because "severe" required a high level of pain caused in a deliberate or calculated manner, this could be translated into the requirement in American law for a "specific intent to inflict a high level of pain."[38] He noted that mental pain could be subjective, since the "action that causes one person severe mental suffering may seem inconsequential to another person. Moreover, mental suffering is often transitory, causing no lasting harm."[39] He concluded that in 1990 there was no consensus or well-defined body of law concerning the degree of mental suffering that would have to be experienced in order to constitute torture.

He observed that severe pain or suffering could be produced by intentional acts and that they would constitute torture when such acts damaged or destroyed the human personality. In furtherance of the distinction between torture and inhuman or degrading treatment he made a further distinction. This was the condition of "legal compulsion" which he described as being "properly a part of the criminal justice system, interrogation, incarceration, prosecution, compelled testimony against a friend, etc.-not withstanding the fact that they may have the incidental effect for producing mental strain."[40]

Mr. Richard then reviewed (1)(b) of Section II. He stated that the U. S. understanding was intended to apply only to acts directed against persons in the offender's custody or physical control. Thus, "the rules relating to proportionality in the use of force in effecting an arrest and in self-defense are essentially unaffected by this Convention, as these rules normally relate to actions occurring prior to a public official's having effected custody of the subject."[41]

Turning to (1)(c) and the meaning of "sanctions," he noted that this would allow for law enforcement actions "undertaken consistent with statute or case law, as opposed to judicial order,[when or where] not interfered with by the Convention unless such conduct clearly violates international law. This makes it clear, that, for example, the use of reasonable force to maintain order in a penal institution is not prohibited by the Convention."[42]

Paragraph (1)(d) dealt with the meaning of "acquiescence" as used in Article 1 of CAT. It contemplated a situation where a public official had a prior awareness of torture and had breached his legal responsibility by not intervening. According to Mr. Richard the understanding was designed to ensure that Article 1 was consistent with the due process requirements of the U. S. Constitution. Further, the criminal sanctions in CAT relating to torture were to be focused on "knowing misconduct as opposed to negligent inaction."[43] Thus, guilt would result from a superior's active direction of or participation in the prohibited activity. It would also lead to prosecutions for willful blindness.

With regard to (1)(e) Mr. Richard noted that it dealt with "noncompliance with applicable legal procedural standards" and that failure to meet such standards "does not per se constitute torture. He viewed this understanding as required to demonstrate, for example, "that court orders suppressing evidence based on inaction by enforcement agents do not, in and of themselves, establish the existence of torture."[44]

Moving on to additional understandings Section II.(2) referred to the provision contained in Article 3 of the treaty relating to a person's being subjected to torture. The concern reflected in Article 3 was that if an individual were expelled, returned, or extradited to another State that the individual might, on the basis of substantial grounds, be "in danger of being subjected to torture." The final U. S. position focused on "whether" it was "more likely than not that he would be tortured." This contrasted with the reservation proposed by the United States in 1988 reading "The United States does not consider itself bound by Article 3 insofar as it conflicts with the obligations of the United States toward States not party to the Convention under bilateral extradition treaties with the United States." At the 1990 hearings Mr. Sofaer testified that the United States "never intended to suggest by the proposed reservation that we wished to retain the right to send a person back to a country where that person could be tortured."[45] The proposed reservation was withdrawn by the United States in 1989 because it had been construed, as it related to non-parties to the Convention, as not preventing the sending of an individual back to a country where that person would be tortured.[46]

A further American understanding, Section II.(3), dealt with the creation by Parties of a private right of action for damages provided for in Article 14 of the Convention. The United States interpreted this as applying only to territory under national jurisdiction. The understanding was identical with proposed declarations put forward in 1988 and 1989.

In Section II.(4) the United States referred to its view of the death penalty in international law. This understanding, advanced for the first time at the Committee hearing on January 30, 1990, asserted that the United States did not consider that the CAT "restrict[ed] or prohibit[ed] the United States from applying the death penalty consistent with the Fifth, Eighth and/or Fourteenth Amendments to the Constitution of the United States, including any constitutional period of confinement prior to the imposition of the death penalty." This later became Reservation I.(1) to Article 16 of the Convention, but only to the extent that it stated that there was an obligation "to prevent 'cruel, inhuman or degrading treatment or punishment' only insofar as the term 'cruel, inhuman or degrading treatment or punishment' means the cruel, unusual and inhumane treatment or punishment prohibited by the Fifth, Eighth, and/or Fourteenth Amendments to the Constitution of the United States."

In Section II.(5) the United States engaged itself to implement the constituent units provisions of Articles 10–14 and 16 of the Convention. The national government promised to take measures to ensure compliance by constituent units with the terms of the agreement. This understanding replaced and added to the general reservation announced in 1988.

The United States in Section III of its RUDs set forth two declarations. The 1990 version retained without modification that of 1988. It provided that Articles 1–16 of the Convention were not self-executing.

Section III.(2) dealt with the functions of the Committee against Torture created in Article 17 of the Convention. Article 21.1. allowed a Party to accept the competence of the Committee to inquire into claims that another signatory was not fulfilling its treaty obligations. In the original package of RUDs put forward by the Reagan administration on May 23, 1988, the United States declared that it would not recognize the competence of the Committee. This extreme position found little support, and was modified in the 1989 package with the understanding, which became a part of the final U. S. commitment to the treaty reading "It is the understanding of the United States that, pursuant to the above mentioned article, such communications shall be accepted and processed only if they come from a State Party which has made a similar declaration."[47] This allowed the United States to accept the competence of the Committee. In January, 1990, Mr. Sofaer told the Foreign Relations Committee that "We believe that by participating in the work of the committee the United States will have a positive influence on its work and enhance our ability to focus the attention of the committee on the practices of other States which we may conclude engage in torture."[48]

Article 22 of CAT offered the parties an opportunity to declare that the Committee possessed the competence to "receive and consider communications from or on behalf of individuals subject to its jurisdiction who claim to be victims of a violation by a State Party of the provisions of the Convention. No communication shall be received by the Committee if it concerns a State Party which has not made such a declaration." The United States elected not to subscribe to this option.

Mr. Sofaer advised the Foreign Relations Committee that individual complaints were likely to be frivolous and aimed at embarrassing a country rather than "rectifying the form of injustice with which the Convention was intended to deal. Any legitimate complaints of torture by officials of the United States would be remedied in our Federal and State courts. Defending such claims in an international tribunal would waste limited resources and entail unwarranted risks."[49]

During the January 30, 1990 hearings Senator Jesse Helms urged that the "sovereignty clause," which had been intensely debated in the Senate when it was considering the Genocide Convention and the Mutual Legal Assistance Treaties dealing with foreign bank secrecy laws and American efforts to stem the international commerce in narcotics, should an additional reservation. The clause was designed to ensure that ratification of the Convention would not bind the United States to adopt any action prohibited by the Constitution. The pedigree of the Helms proposal can be traced back to the wide-ranging debates concerning the Bricker Resolution relating to the American acceptance of the compulsory jurisdiction of the World Court. It was designed to allow the United States to make that determination through the expression "as determined by the United States." The introduction of this proposition into the American RUDs proved to be the most contentious of the proposals (following the adjustment of the varying positions taken by the Reagan and Bush administrations) facing the President and the Senate.

In 1990 the Committee pointed out that "the administration opposes the so-called 'constitutional reservation' on the grounds that it is 'unnecessary' at the domestic level and 'damaging' at the international level. A majority of the committee shares this view."[50] The majority relied on the holding of the United States Supreme Court in Reid. v. Covert (354 U. S. 1, 17 (1957) which held unambiguously that treaty provisions were subordinate to the Constitution. Since the CAT did not and could not require the United States to enact legislation or to take any action prohibited by the Constitution the proposed condition was considered redundant. Moreover, while the "sovereignty clause" could not extend constitutional protections, it was likely to create international problems. It raised questions "as to the exact nature of the treaty obligations undertaken by the United States. Moreover, under international treaty law, it automatically becomes available to all other States."[51] Concern was also expressed that the presence of this American condition might inhibit or limit compliance with the Convention if other Parties were to limit or modify their own constitutional provisions dealing with the prosecution or extradition of alleged torturers so that the absolute provision against torture would be "severely undermined."[52]

Despite these considerations following the lead of the members of the Foreign Relations Committee the Senate adopted Executive Amendment No. 3203 on October 27, 1990. It was at the end of and not a part of the resolution of ratification. It stated:

IV. The Senate's advice and consent is subject to the following proviso, which shall not be included in the instrument of ratification to be deposited by the President:

The President of the United States shall not deposit the instrument of ratification until such time as he has notified all present and prospective ratifying parties to this Convention that nothing in this Convention requires or authorizes legislation, or other action, by the United States of America prohibited by the Constitution of the United States as interpreted by the United States.

On June 3, 1994 the United States asked the Secretary-General of the United Nations to give notice of the above to present and prospective ratifying parties. Thus, on this issue the Senate prevailed over the President but only because the above was labeled a "proviso" rather than a RUD. It was considered that such a characterization would avoid its being employed by other countries on a reciprocal basis.

Statutes, including those adopted prior to the entry into force of CAT, and other governmental actions, are relevant to the American approach to torture.

4. THE 1969 VIENNA CONVENTION ON THE LAW OF TREATIES: RESERVATIONS AND OBJECTIONS TO THE AMERICAN RESERVATIONS AND UNDERSTANDINGS

The Convention was signed on May 23, 1969 and entered into force on January 27, 1980.[53] The United States is not a party. However, the agreement is generally regarded as the authoritative source of international treaty law. The

United States has not opposed the terms of the agreement. American officials and scholars have affirmed the status of the Convention. American practice has followed the terms of the agreement. A leading authority has written that "there are no conflicts between treaty law and practice as set out in the Convention and present U. S. law and practice."[54]

Article 1(d) defined "reservation" as a "unilateral statement, however phrased or named, made by a State when . . . signing [or] ratifying . . . a treaty, whereby it purports to exclude or to modify the legal effect of certain provisions of the treaty in their application to that State." The Convention makes no mention of declarations, understandings, or provisos. Such unilateral statements are permissible pursuant to Article 1 (d).

However, such statements under the terms of Article 19(2) may not negate the treaty through the introduction of conditions that would be incompatible with the object and purpose of the agreement. Under Article 20 parties are allowed to determine if a condition is or is not acceptable and to object to it. However, pursuant to paragraph 4(b) this does not "preclude the entry into force of the treaty between the objecting and the reserving States unless a contrary intention is definitely expressed by an objecting State."

The CAT made brief reference to the use of reservations. Article 28.2 allowed a Party that had declared that it did not recognize the competence of the Committee Against Torture to withdraw that reservation. Article 30.3. Allowed a Party to withdraw a reservation relating to the settlement of disputes by way of arbitration or by reference to the World Court. The CAT did not refer to national understandings or declarations. Only a handful of States filed reservations, including France, Israel, New Zealand, and the United States. The American reservation I.(1), relating to the meaning of allowable punishments, did not fit into the terms of Article 28.2 or Article 30.3 of the Convention. Understandings or declarations were voiced by the following: Australia, Austria, France, Greece, Italy, the Netherlands, Spain, the United Kingdom, and the United States. Countries which made neither reservations or declarations included Germany, Japan, South Africa, the Russian Federation, South Africa, and Sweden.

America's approach to the treaty process was identified by the Department of State Legal Adviser to foreign international lawyers on June 6, 2007. Identified as a "rigorous approach," he observed that "during negotiations, we try to eliminate ambiguities and pin down important issues of policy. This makes it harder to paper over disagreements, and sometimes harder to reach consensus. But we don't do this to be obstructionist. Rather, we want the treaty obligations to be as clear as possible. This is in part a matter of good draftsmanship, and an attempt to head off disputes and promote compliance. But it is also a reflection of the reality in which we operate: We need to explain to our Senate exactly what obligations we are taking on and what the implications of joining a particular treaty are. Important too, is what happens after we join the treaty. More than almost any other state, we are subject to broad and vigorous oversight through private litigation and scrutiny by the press, civil society, and the international community as a whole. If we do not get the words in the treaty exactly right, we will have to answer the consequences."[55] He added: "[t]his accountability, coupled with the seriousness with which we implement our obligations, also explains why we are so careful from the very start to determine whether we need to subject our ratifications of treaties to any reservations or understanding and why we make sure to line up any implementing legislation in advance. Unlike certain countries, we do not join treaties lightly as a good will gesture, or as a substitute for taking meaningful steps to comply."[56]

In February 1996 Finland, Germany, the Netherlands, and Sweden filed objections to the American reservations and understandings with the Secretary-General. These countries did not state that the CAT was inapplicable to their relationship with the United States. However, important positions were voiced.[57]

In its objection of February 27, 1996 Finland stated that the American reservation I.(1) "making reference to a national law without specifying its content fails to inform other Parties of a reserving State's commitment to the treaty."[58] To this was added: the reservation is subject to "general principles of treaty interpretation whereby a State may not invoke the provisions of its internal law as justification for failure to perform a treaty."[59] Further objection was voiced respecting the American declaration regarding Articles 7 and 16 of the Convention.

The German communication of February 26, 1996 made reference to the American reservation contained in its item I.(1) and its understandings set out in items II.(2) and (3). Germany stated that they "do not touch upon the obligations of the United States of America as State Party to the Convention."[60]

The Netherlands'communication of February 26, 1996, contained sweeping statements. First, it challenged the views of the United States relating to Article 16 of the Convention stating that they were "incompatible with the object and purpose of the Convention"[61] with Article 16 being characterized as an "essential" aspect of the agreement. The objection noted that it was not clear "how the provisions of the Constitution of the United States of America related to the obligations under the Convention." Further, "The Netherlands considered that the understandings of the United States had "no impact on the obligations of the United States." In its view the terms of the American II.1(a) understanding restricted the scope of the definition contained in Article 1 of the Convention while II.1(d) diminished "the continued responsibility of public officials for

behavior of their subordinates." The Netherlands also reserved its position relating to the American understandings contained in II.(1) (b) and 1(c) as well
as (2) on the ground that the contents were not "sufficiently clear."

The Swedish objection of February 27, 1996 to the American reservation
to Article 16. 1. of the treaty referred to its position taken regarding the
American reservations to Article 7 of the International Covenant on Civil
and Political Rights dealing with torture or cruel, inhuman or degrading
treatment or punishment The United States in that document conditioned its
acceptance by interpreting the term "cruel, inhuman or degrading treatment
or punishment" as set forth in Article 16. 1. of CAT to mean "the cruel, unusual and inhumane treatment or punishment prohibited by the Fifth, Eighth,
and/or Fourteenth Amendments to the Constitution of the United States."
Additionally Sweden objected to the American understandings to CAT. Such
understandings, it was claimed do not "relieve the United States of America
or a Party to the Convention from the responsibility to fulfill the obligations
undertaken therein."[62]

No other countries have objected to the American reservations or understandings. Thus, the provision of Article 20.5 of the Vienna Convention
would apply, namely "a reservation is considered to have been accepted by a
State if it shall have raised no objection to the reservation by the end of a period of twelve months after it was notified of the reservation or by the date on
which it is expressed its consent to be bound by the treaty, whichever is later."

Article 21 deals with the legal effects of reservations and of objections to
reservations. It reads:

1. A reservation established with regard to another party in accordance with
articles 19, 20 and 23: (a) modifies for the reserving State in its relations with
that other party the provisions of the treaty to which the reservation relates to
the extent of the reservation; and (b) modifies those provisions to the same
extent for that other party in its relations with the reserving State;

2. The reservation does not modify the provisions of the treaty for the other
parties to the treaty inter se.

3. When a State objecting to a reservation has not opposed the entry into
force of the treaty between itself and the reserving State, the provision to
which the reservation relates do not apply as between the two States to the extent of the reservation.

In a study published in 2001 specific meanings, based on U. S. practice,
were assigned to "reservations," "understandings," and "declarations." Reservations are "proposed revisions in the obligations undertaken by the United
States pursuant to the treaty. [They are] specific qualifications of stipulations
that modify language."[63] Understandings "are interpretive statements that
clarify or elaborate, rather then change, the provisions of the agreement and

that are deemed to be consistent with the obligations imposed by the agreement."[64] They are designed to clarify and provide reassurances rather than to revise the agreement. Declarations were described as statements of "purpose, policy, or position related to matters raised by a treaty in question but not altering or limiting any of its provisions."[65] It also has been noted that "proviso," which was employed by the Senate in CAT could be viewed as a "declaration." Since international agreements are the product of many national proposals, and since the efforts of accommodation of varying outlooks may result in broadly stated obligations, sometimes seen to be vague, or, on the other hand so restrictive that a country cannot accept proposed terminology, a practicable outcome is to allow for RUDs.[66]

NOTES

1. It should be noted that engaging in conduct resulting from the exercise of "evil instincts" or authoritative positions is not confined to armed conflicts. The Stanford Prison Experiment demonstrated how quite normal individuals could engage in serious abuses and mistreatments involving civilians. The structured use of electrical shock treatments was described by S. MILGRAM in OBEDIENCE TO AUTHORITY: AN EXPERIMENTAL VIEW (1974). A recent book by PHILIP ZIMBARGO, THE LUCIFER EFFECT: UNDERSTANDING HOW GOOD PEOPLE TURN EVIL (2007) serves as a reminder. However, the laws and customs of war, acknowledging that evil misconduct may be more likely to occur on a mass level during a time of armed conflict, constitute a special legal regime. By uniquely addressing the problem, as reflected in the following citations, a special condition was created seeking to avert and to punish against transgressions. For a commentary, see M. NOVAK, THE UNITED NATIONS CONVENTION AGAINST TORTURE (2008).

2. G. A. Res. 39/46 [annex, 39 U.N. GAOR Supp. (no. 51) at 197, U. N. Doc. A/30/51 (1984)]. It entered into force on June 26, 1987. 1465 UNTS 85, United States Treaty Doc. 100-20. At the beginning of 2008 there were more than 140 parties, many of which had filed reservations or understandings with the United Nations.

3. 1830 UNTS A-24841. Subsequently, on June 3, 1994, the Secretary-General received a communication from the United States government "requesting, in compliance with a condition set forth by the Senate of the United States, in giving advice and consent to the ratification of the Convention by the United States of America, that a notification should be made to all present and prospective ratifying Parties of the Convention to the effect that . . . nothing in this Convention requires or authorizes legislation, or other action, by the United States of America prohibited by the Constitution of the United States as interpreted by the United States." Report of the Office of the High Commission for Human Rights, April, 2004.

4. Annex, Regulations, Article 4.

5. G. A. Res. 217A (III), U.N. Doc. A/810 (1948).

6. TIAS 3364, 6 UST 3316, 75 UNTS 135. It entered into force for the United States on February 2, 1956.

7. TIAS 3365, 6 UST 6516, 75 USTS 287. It entered into force for the United States on February 2, 1956. It had previously entered into force on October 21, 1950.

8. GA (RES) 3452 (XXX).

9. Supra, notes 6 and 7. `Subparagraph (b) prohibits "the taking of hostages," and specifies that there must not be the "passing of sentences and the carrying out of executions without a previous judgment pronounced by a regularly constituted court which offers all of the juridical guarantees which are recognized as indispensable by civilized peoples." The importance of this provision has been accorded major attention in the United States with the President, Congress, and the Courts having critical roles to play. Among the subjects dealt with have been the presumption of innocence of an accused, burden of proof, right to effective counsel, the role of "hearsay" evidence, availability of the writ of habeas corpus, due process of law, equal protection, bills of attainder, and the substantive differences between military and civilian courts and commissions. These subjects will be dealt with in detail below.

10. 999 UNTS 171, 6 ILM 368.

11. OAS Treaty Series No. 36.

12. 213 UNTS 221.

13. 20 ILM, No. 1, 58 (January 1981). It entered into force on October 21, 1986.

14. W. P. Nagan and L. Atkins, The International Law of Torture: From Universal Prescription to Effective Application and Enforcement, 14 Harvard Human Rights Journal 87 (Spring 2001). Important studies on torture are N. S. RODLEY, THE TREATMENT OF PRISONERS UNDER INTERNATIONAL LAW (1987) and H. BURGESS and H. DANIELUS, THE UNITED NATIONS CONVENTION AGAINST TORTURE (1988). For important short essays, see S. LEVINSON, ed., TORTUE; A COLLECTION, revised ed. (2007). For an extensive source of official United States views relating to the Iraq war see K. S. GREENBERG and J. C. PATEL, eds., THE TORTURE PAPERS: THE ROAD TO ABU GHRAIB (2005).

15. An Optional Protocol was adopted on December 18, 2002 at the 57th session of the General Assembly by Resolution A/RES/57/199 42 ILM 26 (2003). It entered into force on June 22, 2006. It called for the establishment of a system of regular visits by independent international and national bodies to places where people were being deprived of their liberty, to prevent torture, and to forestall lesser forms of individual harms. The United States is not a party. For a brief account see CARL Q. CHRISTOL, INTERNATIONAL LAW AND U. S. FOREIGN POLICY, Second Revised Edition, 366–367. (2006).

16. Article II, Section 2 of the Constitution provides that the Senate's advice and consent depends on a vote in which "two thirds of the Senators present concur." This may raise the issue of whether a quorum is present. This determination has been described "The Senate operates on the presumption that a quorum is present at all times, under all circumstances, unless the question to the contrary is raised, or the absence of a quorum is officially shown, or until a point of no quorum is made even though a voice vote is taken and announced in the meantime." S. Bach, Voting and Quorum Procedures in the Senate, CRS-2 (no date). Support for this was found in Riddick's

Senate Procedure, 1041–1042 (no date). The presiding official would be controlled by Article I, Section 5 of the Constitution which states that a "Majority of each [house] shall constitute a Quorum." It seems unlikely that any international agreement receiving public attention would ever come to a vote in the Senate where two-thirds of a quorum of 51 would provide the required advice and consent.

17. Message of the President of the United States Transmitting Torture Convention, Senate Treaty Document 100-20, 100th Cong. 2nd Sess., May 10, 1988, p. vi (1988).

18. Ibid.

19. Ibid.

20. Ibid.

21. Senate Exe. Rept. 101-30, August 30, 1990, p. 37.

22. Ibid.

23. Ibid.

24. Ibid.

25. Id. at p. 35.

26. Ibid.

27. Ibid.

28. Hearings, S. hrg 101-718, Convention Against Torture, Government Printing Office (1990) p. 7.

29. Ibid.

30. U.S. reservations, declarations, and understandings. Cong. Rec. S1355-01 (daily ed., Feb. 19, 1986).

31. Supra, note 22, p. 33.

32. Supra, note 22.

33. Ibid., p. 10.

34. Ibid.

35. Sofaer, Id. at 16.

36. Id. at 17.

37. Richard, Ibid.

38 Richard, Id.

39. Ibid. Reference was made to PAUL SIEGART, THE INTERNATIONAL LAW OF HUMAN RIGHTS, who had suggested that mental pain or suffering might be produced by solitary confinement, insulting language, or being required to be naked. Citing other observers, Mr. Richard speculated that such instances might constitute overstatements. Nonetheless, they have served to demonstrate that there was no consensus or well-defined body of international law identifying the degrees of mental suffering that must be experienced in order to constitute torture.

40. Ibid.

41. Ibid.

42. Ibid.

43. Sofaer, supra, note 22, at 9.

44. Richard, supra, note 22, at 17.

45. Sofaer, Ibid. at 37.

46. Ibid.

47. Ibid.

48. Id. at 1–3.

49. Id., at 4–5.

50. Id., at 4.

51. Id., at 6.

52. Id.

53. 1155 UNTS 331.

54. John B. Bellinger, III, The United States and International Law, http://www
.state.gov/s1/rs/86123.htm. p. 2.

55. Ibid.

56. Ibid.

57. Office of the High Commissioner for Human Rights, Declarations and Reservations (April 2004), p. 60.

58. Ibid.

59. Id.

60. Id.

61. Id.

62. Id.

63. R. F. Grimmett, Treaties and Other International Agreements, The Role of the United States Senate, Committee Print, 106th Cong., 2d Sess. S. Prt., 106-71 (2001).

64. Ibid.

65. Ibid. It was noted by Grimmett that a more comprehensive term encompassing all of the above is "conditions." Further, no matter what name was encompassed in the "condition," if the President considered that it "alters an international obligation under a treaty, he is expected to transmit it to the other party or parties." Id.

66. A. Rovine, Defense of Declarations, Reservations, and Understandings, in R. B. LILLICH, ed., UNITED STATES RATIFICTIONS OF HUMAN RIGHTS TREATIES: WITH OR WITHOUT RESERVATIONS (1981). To achieve standard uses of terms in international agreements the Department of State issued Circular 175 in 1955. Its procedures have been codified in Foreign Affairs Manual, Volume 1, May 26, 2006. Reservations and understandings are identified in section 11 FAM 748.1. It provides that "it is necessary to inform other governments concerned, and perhaps obtain their consent, with respect to an understanding, interpretation, or reservation included by the Senate on advice and consent, this Government communicates with the depositary, which then, carries on the necessary correspondence with the other government concerned."

Chapter Three

Statutes Dealing with or Related to Torture and Other Cruel, Inhuman, or Degrading Treatment or Punishment

1. THE TORTURE VICTIM PROTECTION ACT OF 1991

During the lengthy proceedings involving the identification of the RUDs and the conditions under which the United States could accept the terms of CAT it became evident that there was no federal legislation identifying the conditions to be met by American citizens who might have monetary claims in civil actions for torture or extrajudicial killings. This resulted in the Torture Victim Protection Act of 1991.[1]

Section 1350 of the statute allows for claims for damages against "An individual who, under actual or apparent authority, or color of law, of any foreign nation . . ." engages either in torture of an "individual" or in an "extrajudicial killing." In the event of torture the claim is that of the tortured individual. If it were an extrajudicial killing the suit would be instituted by the legal representative or by any person "who may be a claimant in an action for wrongful death." The statute requires the exhaustion of the "adequate and available remedies in the place in which the conduct giving rise to the claim occurred." The provision for a statute of limitations requires that the action be commenced within 10 years after the cause of action arose.

The statute contained definitions of "extrajudicial killing" and "torture." The former "means a deliberated killing not authorized by a previous judgment pronounced by a regularly constituted court according all the judicial guarantees which are recognized as indispensable by civilized peoples. Such term, however, does not include any killing that, under international law, is lawfully carried out under the authority of a foreign nation."

The definition of torture varies slightly from that adopted by the United States in Section II.(1)(a) in its understanding of CAT. The 1991 statute employs the term "torture" as meaning "any act, directed against an individual in the offender's custody or physical control, by which severe pain or suffering (other than pain or suffering arising only from or inherent in, or incidental to, lawful sanctions), whether physical or mental, is intentionally inflicted on that individual for such purposes as obtaining from that individual, or a third person information or a confession, punishing that individual for an act that individual or a third person has committed or is suspected of having committed, intimidating or coercing that individual or a third person, or for any reason based on discrimination of any kind . . ." Among the major differences are that Section II.(1)(a) uses "specifically intended" rather than "intentionally inflicted," that II.(1)(a) combines "severe physical or mental pain or suffering," while section 1350 separately references "mental pain or suffering." Both identify mental pain or suffering with "prolonged mental harm." Both consider the "threat of imminent death" as constituting torture. Section 1350 uses the term "under color of law" while the understanding does not. Section 1350 generally employs the term "individual," while the understanding uses "person" or "persons." The similarities outweigh the differences and demonstrate that the 1991 statute influenced materially the terms of the 1994 RUDs.

2. THE CRIMINAL TORTURE ACT OF 1994

The statute was adopted on April 30, 1994, pursuant to the requirement of Article 3 of CAT. It became effective on November 20, 1994. The enactment was included in the Foreign Relations Authorization Act Fiscal Years 1994 and 1995.[2] The federal statute, Section 2340, codified as Title 18 of the United States Code, dealing with crimes and criminal procedure, was based on Understanding II.1.(a) of the American RUDs. The new statute tied the effective date to the date the Convention entered into force for the United States.

Section 2340 was composed of three parts. The first, tailored to meet United States criminal law requirements, defined torture as meaning "an act committed by a person acting under the color of law specifically intended to inflict severe physical or mental pain or suffering (other than the pain or suffering incidental to lawful sanctions) upon another person within his custody or physical control." The phrase in the statute "acting under the color of law" does not appear in CAT or in the American RUDs. The phrase "specifically intended to inflict severe physical or mental pain or suffering" was taken from the U. S. understanding II.(1)(a) . The phrase in the statute "(other than pain or suffering incidental to lawful sanctions)" does not appear in the American RUDs. However, the expression in the statute "upon another person within his custody or physical control" was taken from the American understanding II.(1)(b).

The second section of the new law defined "severe mental pain or suffering" as the "prolonged mental harm caused by or resulting from" the conditions enumerated in understanding II.(1)(a). These are: "(A) the intentional infliction or threatened infliction of severe physical pain or suffering; (B) the administration or application, or threatened administration or application, of mind-altering substances or other procedures calculated to disrupt profoundly the senses or the personality; (C) the threat of imminent death; (D) the threat that another person will imminently be subjected to death, severe physical pain or suffering, or the administration or application of mind-altering substances or other procedures calculated to disrupt profoundly the senses or personality . . ." The third section described the United States as meaning "the several States of the United States, the District of Columbia, and the commonwealth, territories, and possessions of the United States." This allowed for the further definition of the United States to include all areas under the jurisdiction of the United States as identified in various statutes. Included were "all areas under the jurisdiction of the United States including any of the places described in sections 5 and 7 of this title and section 46501(2) of title 49."

Section 3 defined the United States in a territorial sense. Pursuant to the provisions of the above title 49 included were "all places and waters, continental or insular, subject to the jurisdiction of the United States except the Canal Zone." Section 7 spells out the "Special maritime and territorial jurisdiction of the United States. Included in this category are ocean areas, vessels registered in the United States, guano islands, government and citizen owned aircraft operating in specified offshore areas, spacecraft registered in the United States, places outside the jurisdiction of any nation, foreign naval vessels scheduled to depart from or arrive in the United States when the offense is committed against a U. S. national, and U. S. diplomatic, consular, and military missions or entities." The Section also stipulates that jurisdiction extends to "Any lands reserved or acquired for the use of the United States, and under the exclusive or concurrent jurisdiction thereof . . ." Section 46501(2) refers to aircraft. Section 46502 governs aerial piracy.

Section 2340A of the statute imposes penalties. It refers to jurisdiction and to conspiracy. An offense is committed by "Whoever outside the United States commits or attempts to commit torture." Fines or imprisonments are imposed, with a 20 year maximum imprisonment except where death occurs. In that event the penalty may be death or imprisonment for any term of years or for life. There is jurisdiction over the activity if "the alleged offender is a national of the United States; or the alleged offender is present in the United

States, irrespective of the nationality of the victim or alleged offender." The statute in dealing with conspiracy states "A person who conspires to commit an offense under this section shall be subject to the same penalties (other than the penalty of death) as the penalties prescribed for the offense, the commission of which was the object of the conspiracy." The statute did not make specific reference to the definitional terms of Article 1 of CAT although both have the object and purpose of bringing torture into the fold of international criminal law.

Section 2340B refers to exclusive remedies. It provides that "Nothing in this chapter shall be construed as precluding the application of State or local laws on the same subject, nor shall anything in this chapter be construed as creating any substantive or procedural right enforceable by law by any party in any civil proceeding."

Section 2340A(a) extended the criminal law jurisdiction of the United States to "whoever," which includes an American national, engages in acts or attempts to commit torture outside of the United States. It provide for prosecutions within the United States of an alleged offender without regard for nationality.

The efforts by Department of Justice lawyers to provide a "fine-tuning" of the definitional terms relating to "torture" created much of the turmoil recounted in this book.

A. The 2004 Supreme Court Decision on "Lands Under the Exclusive or Concurrent Jurisdiction of the United States"

The Supreme Court in Rasul et.al. v. Bush, President of the United States,[3] in a case dealing with a habeas corpus petition, expressed views concerning the meaning of Section 7, Title 18, Part 1, Chapter 1 dealing with "lands under the exclusive or concurrent jurisdiction of the United States.[4] In deciding that the petitioners, non-U. S. nationals held in detention at the U. S. Naval War Station, Guantanamo, Cuba, were entitled to have access to the use of writs of habeas corpus, the Court reviewed the February 23, 1903 Lease Agreement between the United States and Cuba providing that "the United States recognizes the continuance of the ultimate sovereignty of the Republic of Cuba over the [leased areas]" while "the Republic of Cuba consents that during the period of occupation by the United States . . . the United States shall exercise complete jurisdiction and control over and within such areas."

In a concurring opinion Justice Kennedy observed that the Naval Base "is in every practical respect a United States territory, and is one far removed from hostilities." If this position is accepted the 1994 Torture Statute would apply to U. S. military personnel stationed at the Naval Base who are charged with violating the rights of victims irrespective of their nationality. The statute (2340A(a)) in any event makes U. S. nationals subject to prosecution in Federal courts for torture occurring outside the United States. In dissenting opinions Justices Scalia and Thomas urged that the right to a writ of habeas corpus was only available to persons within the territorial boundaries of the United States, and that the Naval Base was not a part of U. S. territory. In their view the issuance of the writ depended on legislation and that 28 U.S.C. 2241 would have to be amended to allow its availability to aliens in a foreign country.

3. THE WAR CRIMES ACT OF 1996 AND THE 1997 AMENDMENT

This statute carried out the obligation of the United States incurred when it ratified the 1949 Geneva Conventions to provide criminal penalties for grave breaches of the conventions. Section 2441 of Chapter 118 of title 18 of the U. S. Code entitled "War Crimes Act of 1996" provided that "whoever, whether inside or outside the United States, commits a grave breach of the Geneva Conventions in two specified circumstances shall be fined under title 18 or imprisoned for life or any term of years, or both, and if death results to the victim, shall also be subject to the death penalty."[5]

The two circumstances were where "(1) the person committing the breach is a member of the armed forces of the United States or a national of the United States, and (2) the victim of the breach is a member of the armed forces of the United States or a national of the United States. 'Grave breach of the Geneva Conventions' means conduct defined as a grave breach in any of the four Geneva Conventions, or any protocol to the conventions to which the United States is a party."[6]

Grave breaches were defined as a series of particularly serious violations including "torture or inhumane treatment" and "willfully causing great suffering or serious injury to body or health." The statute also referred to crimes committed in violation of common Article Three of the 1949 Conventions, applicable to persons detained in noninternational armed conflicts. This article prohibited, among other things, "violence to life and person," "cruel treatment and torture," and "outrages upon personal dignity, in particular, humiliating and degrading treatment." The 1996 statute was amended in the Expanded War Crimes Act of 1997 in which the term "grave breaches" was replaced by "war crimes."[7]

The reference to Article Three of the Convention in the 1996 statute became an issue in Hamdan v. Rumsfeld (126 S. Ct. 2749, 2006) where the Court rejected the administrations's argument that the statute was inapplicable to the conflict with Al Qaeda. The majority ruled that Article Three was applicable to all conflicts within the territory of a party to the Convention, other than conflicts between States. The holding constituted a major reason why the administration sought the enactment of the Military Commissions Act of 2006 so that restrictions would be placed upon the "degree to which criminal sanctions under the War Crimes Act applied to violations of common Article 3."[8] Abusive interrogation practices deserve to be sanctioned. By its terms it would apply to CIA personnel when nationals of the United States.

According to M.J. Matheson, a Department of State official who participated in the drafting of the War Crimes Act, the changes made by the MCA divided Article 3 of the Convention into three parts creating different remedies. "First is a series of particularly serious violations that are referred to as 'grave breache[s] of common Article 3' — including torture, 'cruel or inhuman treatment,' and intentionally causing 'serious bodily injury'; these remain subject to criminal penalties. [18 U.S.C. #2441 note]. Second is 'degrading treatment or punishment,' which is prohibited but not subject to criminal penalties. [42 U.S.C. #2999dd-0]. Third are any other violations of common Article 3, as to which the amended Act states that the president has the authority to prescribe administrative regulations on enforcement. [18 U.S.C. 2441 note]."[9]

Another aspect of the 1996 statute has been criticized. Section six states that "[n]o foreign or international source of law shall supply a basis for a rule of decision in the courts of the United States in interpreting the prohibitions enumerated" in the amended War Crimes Act. Since the identified crimes resulted from the negotiation of rules of international law in international forums and were "created and defined by international sources of law — namely the Geneva Conventions," this portion of the statute as been described as "bizarre and unfortunate.[10]

4. THE FOREIGN AFFAIRS REFORM AND
RESTRUCTURING ACT OF 1998

Section 2242(b) of this statute fixed responsibilities for "the heads of appropriate agencies" regarding the provisions of Article 3 of CAT. It provided that a Party could not expel, return, or extradite a person to another State where there were substantial grounds for believing that such person would be "in danger of being subjected to torture."[11] The new provision required the appropriate authorities to "prescribe regulations" to implement Article 3, subject to the RUDs and provisos contained in the Senate resolution of ratification of CAT.[12]

5. THE TORTURE VICTIM RELIEF ACT OF 1998

The American government has recognized that a third dimension, going beyond statutes calling for criminal prosecutions and providing for civil actions for damages for torture and extrajudicial killings, exists. The Torture Victim Relief Act of 1998 addresses the identification of victims, their rehabilitation, and world-wide prevention.[13] The statute provided support for the Committee Against Torture established in CAT, for the UN Voluntary Fund for the Victims of Torture, and for foreign and domestic treatment centers. American support was designated for the investigation of Human Rights violations where it was suspected that a "systematic practice of torture" was present. So that American foreign service officers may become alert to and conversant with the problem the Secretary of State was required to provide training with a wide-ranging curriculum so they will be sensitized to the situation.

This statute defined torture by reference to Section 2340(1) of Title 18 of the U. S. Code.[14] To this was added "the use of rape and other forms of sexual violence by a person acting under the color of law upon another person under his custody or control." This provision adopted the recently promulgated view that rape constitutes a major violation of Human Rights as indicated in Article 5 entitled "Crimes Against Humanity" of the 1993 Statute of the International Criminal Tribunal for the Former Yugoslavia where both torture and rape are listed.[15] Rape is also included in Article 8.2.(e)(vi) of the 1998 Statute of the International Criminal Court as a violation of the laws and customs of war applicable in armed conflicts not of an international character.[16]

Congressional findings used to support the 1998 statute identified torture as a means to "destroy individual personality and to destroy society." It declared that torture is used by "repressive governments . . . .as a weapon against democracy." A major goal is to "help to heal the effects of torture and prevent its use around the world."

The statute also made provision for "assistance for victims of torture." Rehabilitation is to be furthered through subventions to treatment centers and programs in foreign countries which are "carrying out projects or activities specifically designed to treat victims of torture for the physical and psychological effects of torture." Federal funds will not be paid to the harmed person. They will receive "direct services" at treatment centers. Providers of health care may also obtain funding for research and training purposes. Private organizations and individuals have also supported the physical and psychological repair of tortured individuals.

6. THE JOHN WARNER NATIONAL DEFENSE AUTHORIZATION ACT FOR FISCAL YEAR 2007

When the proposed statute was considered by the Congressional Conference Committee it contained provisions dealing with numerous forms of torture and cruel, inhuman or degrading treatment or punishment with the requirement that the President report to Congress if and when such actions had taken place. The proposed Section 1061 of the bill did not make it through Congress. Instead the statute called for the President to give notice to Congress of each investigation or prosecution on account of any violation of international law or obligations regarding the treatment of detainees. It also provided that the Secretary of Defense was to report regularly to Congress of each investigation or prosecution. The President attached a "signing statement" reading "the executive branch will construe . . . in a manner consistent with the President's constitutional authority to withhold information the disclosure of which could impair foreign relations, the national security, the deliberative processes of the Executive, or the performance of the Executive's constitutional duties."

The statute, signed by President Bush on October 17, 2006, contained a provision introduced by Senator Lindsey Graham amending article 2(a) of Section 802(a) of Chapter 47, Title 10 of the United States Code. The amendment was to the Uniform Code of Military Justice, which until its amendment gave such courts jurisdiction over "persons accompanying an armed force in the field . . . in time of war." The amendment called for the striking of the term "war" and inserting "declared war or a contingency operation."[17] This gave court-martial jurisdiction "in time of declared war or contingency operations [over] persons serving with or accompanying an armed force in the field."[18] This will result in civilians being subject to the same rules as military personnel in such conflicts. In a June 26, 2006 Press Release issued by Senator Graham it noted that the amendment would "give military commanders a new, fair, and efficient means of discipline on the battlefield. The provision clarifies the Uniform Code of Military Justice to place civilian contractors accompanying the Armed Forces in the field under court-martial jurisdiction during contingency operations as well as in time of declared war." The term "contingency operations" was not defined. If such civilians were

U. S. nationals and engaged in acts of torture, prosecutions would be subject to well established procedural and substantive law. There is very sparse legislative history on the Graham amendment, and it might be supposed that its principal application will be to the vast numbers of persons employed by American contractors who provide goods and services to the American forces in Iraq and Afghanistan. Its terms indicate that it would not have application to prisoners of war or to detainees.

7. TORTURE AND THE FEDERAL ALIEN TORT CLAIMS ACT OF 1789

The importance of the crime of torture, and the lesser associated crimes, has been emphasized by the entry into force of the international agreements prohibiting such conduct and by treaties establishing the mechanisms and the rules of procedure for the prosecutions of violations. There is presently no doubt respecting the gravity of the crime of torture and the need for national and international tribunals equipped to deal with the subject. A consensus exists that civil actions for damages must also be available.

One of the most pressing and sustained questions confronting American international lawyers and the federal courts is the meaning to be accorded to the 1789 statute which by its terms allows alien claimants to sue in U. S. federal courts "for a tort only, committed in violation of the law of nations or treaty of the United States."[19] Much of the debate has focused on the term "law of nations," and in particular whether this applies only to the status of international law in 1789, or whether it can include the expansion of international law since that time via customary processes and procedures. With the incorporation into international law of many Human Rights principles and concepts, and with the right of individuals to initiate independently, and without governmental intercession or representation, civil claims for the violation of such rights, assertions have been made that such claims now deserve to be included in the present-day concept of "the law of nations." Civil actions as well as criminal proceedings, it is being claimed, with increasing intensity, should be included in "the law of nations."

The issue was addressed by the United States Supreme Court in Sosa v. Alvarez-Machain involving a claim for damage resulting from an extraterritorial kidnapping.[20] The Court declined to extend the statute to cover this conduct since Congress had not adopted a statute or endorsed a procedure allowing for damages for such conduct. It was considered that the relatively short detention of the plaintiff did not equate to the type of offense that would have been actionable at the time the statute was enacted. The holding has been construed by some government lawyers as allowing for a valid cause of action if the conduct had been clearly identified by Congress.

Opposing this outlook there is considerable support for the view that the 18th century violations of customary international law, such as slave trading or piracy, do meet the tests set forth in the opinion. These proponents also have included genocide, the practice of apartheid, torture, and crimes against humanity, and other serious violations of Human Rights as falling within the scope of the opinion. However, Justice Souter opined that the practical implications of the 1789 statute would allow only for a "modest" number of actions where the violations of international law were most evident. He stated that "other considerations persuade us that the judicial power should be exercised on the understanding that the door is still ajar subject to vigilant doorkeeping, and thus open to a narrow class of international norms today." He also stated that in the narrow area of international relations "federal common law continues to exist." By this statement he intended to convey that Federal district courts could identify new causes of action under the statute. This was addressed to the criticism of Justice Scalia that courts were not well-equipped to perform judicial functions in such areas. Only after trial courts had passed judgment on such claims could there be a determination by the Supreme Court.

The "door ajar" approach received further support from Justice Souter when he stated: "It would take some explaining to say now that federal courts must avert their gaze entirely from any international norm intended to protect individuals." In short, he urged that the Supreme Court should not "shut the door to the law of nations entirely." And, more specifically: "For purposes of civil liability . . . torture has become like the pirate and slave trader before him-*hostes humani generis*, an enemy of all mankind."

In the torture cases coming before the former Yugoslavia and Rwanda courts there has been no practical difficulty in offering evidence. There is no reason to believe that it would present a major problem to the Federal district courts. However, means would have to be devised for the introduction of classified intelligence evidence by governmental witnesses whose anonymity had to be protected.

In determining if a plaintiff is to rely on the Torture Victim Protection Act of 1991 or the 1789 statute certain differences would have to be considered. The former allows individuals (without regard for nationality) to sue if the misconduct were the act of an individual acting "under actual or apparent authority, or color of law, of any foreign nation . . ." The 1991 statute clearly encompasses claims for torture. The latter may be used only by aliens against defendants who may or may not have been acting in private capacities. It remains to be seen if American courts will consider torture to be within the coverage of the statute.

Unrelated to claims related to torture or to the lesser associated crimes have been the claims presented to U. S. military authorities in Afghanistan and Iraq by civilians who have been caught up in the guerilla-type warfare being waged there. It has become necessary to distinguish between lawful "combat activity" and conditions where the harms to civilians, though innocent, may have been deemed to have been unnecessary. Claim forms have been prepared, reviewed, and payments made. Payments have covered loss of life, personal injuries, and property damage. The payments have been treated by the United States as condolence or ex gratae payments, that is, gratuitous without admission of liability for the harms incurred.

Congress, as illustrated by the foregoing statutes, has demonstrated a capacity to address particular issues. Following 9/11 it quickly enacted on September 18 the Authorization for the Use of Military Force. On October 6 agreement was reached on the Patriot Act. As the war on terrorism continued in 2005 the Detainee Treatment statute was enacted, and in 2006 the Military Commission Act was adopted. In taking a longer view of the relationships between the President and Congress during the "war" an important fact has emerged. The Chief Executive, through the issuance of orders and decrees, based on assertions of his war powers, supplemented by those emanating from the DOD, has overshadowed the role of Congress. Some observers have suggested that Congress has ceded a considerable amount of authority to the White House thereby modifying the always uneasy balance of power between the two branches.

While there remains an active role for Congress during this "war", its principal functions have been considerably aided by members of the public through the initiation of lawsuits, seeking the aid of the federal courts in order to achieve the proper balance. These litigants have been faced with the determined policy of the executive branch to secure the dominance of military law claiming that in these troubled times national interests are better left to it rather than to the traditional approaches favored in times of a civilian ascendancy. The Supreme Court cases dealt with below and those yet to be resolved will offer some guidance on the subject.

NOTES

1. 28 U.S.C. Section 1350, Pub. L. 102–256, 106 Stat 73.
2. 18 U.S.C. Section 2340, Pub. L. 103–236, 108 Stat.463, title V, Sec. 506)a), April 30, 1994.

3. 124 S. Ct. 2686 (June 28, 2004) 42 ILM 1207 (September, 2004) The case will be analyzed in detail below.

4. Ibid.

5. Pub. L. 104–192, #2a, 110 Stat. 2104, H.R. 104–698 (1996). (1996).

6. Pub. L. 104–192, August 21, 1996. House of Representatives Report 105–204, 105th Cong. 1st Sess.

7. The Expanded War Crimes Act of 1997, House of Representatives Report 105–204, HR 105–204.

8. M. J. Matheson, The Amendment of the War Crimes Act. As Principal Department of State Legal Advisor he urged that "war crimes" other than "grave breaches" should be criminalized. Additionally he noted that "it would be odd and undesirable for U. S. military personnel who might be prosecuted under the Act to be denied recourse to international standards and sources of law that might aid in their defense, or for U. S. prosecutors who are seeking convictions for crimes against U. S. personnel to be denied the use of such materials to establish their cases. " 101 AJIL 50 (No. 1, January 2007).

9. Id., at 51.

10. Id., at 55.

11. Pub. L. 105–277. It has been noted that in 1980 the Office of Legal Counsel in the Department of Justice stated that "irregular renditions are a violation of customary international law because it would be an invasion of sovereignty of one country to carry out law enforcement activities in another country without that country's consent." M. J. Garcia, The United Nations Convention Against Torture: Overview of United States Implementation Polciy Concerning Aliens, Congressional Reference Service-1e8, note 1099, March 11, 2004. This view was repudiated by the Department of Justice in 1989. Ibid. Nonetheless, Garcia concluded the "The express language of Section 2340A of the Criminal Code "does not appear to prevent the United States from rendering a person to another country so that he could be treated harshly, so long as such treatment does not reach the level of torture." CRS-19. In general, pp. 15–22.

12. For Department of Homeland Security and Justice Regulations, see C.F.R. ##208.16; 208.17; 208.18; 208.30; 208.31; 235.8. For Department of State Regulations see C.F.R. Part 95.

13. 22 U.S.C. Section 2152, Pub. L. 105–320, 112 Stat. 3016, 113 Stat. 1302.

14. 18 U.S.C. Section 3261, Pub. L. 106-523, 114 Stat. 2488.

15. U. N. Doc. S/RES/827, May 14, 1993.

16. U. N. Doc. A/CONF.183/94, July 17, 1998.

17. H. R. 5122, H.R. 109-504.

18. Ibid.

19. 28 U.S.C. 1350 (2000). The statute reads: "The district courts shall have original jurisdiction of any civil action by an alien for a tort only, committed in violation of the law of nations or a treaty of the United States."

20. 124 S. Ct. 2633 (June 28, 2004); 43 ILM 1207 (September 2004). For a short review of the case see 98 AJIL 798 (No. 4 , October 2004).

Chapter Four

American Responses to the Third Geneva Convention Relating to the Treatment of Prisoners of War, August 12, 1949 and to the CAT

With the advent of the "war against terrorism" and the wars against Afghanistan and Iraq United States military forces, aided by CIA employees, captured or obtained custody and control over thousands of persons. Two decisive issues, other than the basic need to preserve a freedom-based distinction between national security needs and civil and political rights and liberties, quickly arose. Rejecting the view that the captured persons should be treated as POWs, as defined in the Third Geneva Convention, 1949, they were described by the Bush administration as "illegal enemy combatants." Important disagreements were voiced in the Departments of State and Defense. Secondly, of equal importance were the efforts to finalize the meaning of torture as defined in CAT and interpreted by the U. S. in the reservations, understandings, and declarations contained in its notice of ratification deposited with the United Nations.

The "war" produced a new era of American military and civilian law. The executive department relying on presidential war powers endeavored to vest in the armed forces extensive authority to deal with captured persons. The new era included the interpretation and application of international law and U. S. constitutional law, particularly in the context of CAT. American responses to its use of torture, involved the issuance of executive orders, military regulations, administrative procedures, federal legislation, and federal court opinions, including those of the U. S. Supreme Court. These efforts will occupy more than a footnote in the history of American jurisprudence.

Terrorists and terrorism have been around for a long time. While it has been difficult for the average American to understand their motivations and the depth of their grievances it is entirely evident that the measures they are willing to employ are extreme. For Americans the shocking and dramatic events of September 11, 2001, involving the World Trade Center in New York, the

Pentagon, and the fiery airline crash in Pennsylvania, created an abrupt awareness of their presence, their organizational capabilities, the extent of their malice, and their ongoing capacity to produce enormous, and unrivaled harm. Leaders, near and far, cannot be complacent in an era in which terrorists contemplate the acquisition of bacterial, chemical, electronic, and nuclear weapons and the means for activating them. Out of these circumstances has emerged the expression "the war on terrorism." Drawn from such expressions as the wars against drugs, homelessness, and hunger, questions have been asked how imminent are the threats of terrorism. Responses have varied: very, fairly proximate, moderately near, and distant. One's grasp on timeliness will serve as a guide to making decisions and taking responsive action. One's access to relevant intelligence will serve those who have the responsibility for such decisions and actions. Owing to the potential dangers national leaders are confronted with monumental responsibilities

Major legal themes have emerged regarding the treatment and disposition of terrorists. The first has been to effect an appropriate characterization, namely, are they to be accorded, pursuant to the laws and customs of war the status of POWs? In particular, are such individuals to have the rights and duties set forth in the 1949 Geneva POW Convention and its applicable protocols? Second, what are the norms relating to the detention and interrogation of such individuals? Third, what, if any, legal benefits are to be applied depending on U. S. nationality or being an alien or whether they were captured abroad, or apprehended in the United States? Fourth, what are the political and legal dynamics of the U. S. understanding and application of the separation of powers principle? Fifth, are democratic principles giving way to the need for military successes? Sixth, more generally, when viewed from abroad, how has U. S. behavior affected perceptions of its support for the world rule of law?

1. THE PRESIDENTIAL EXECUTIVE ORDER OF SEPTEMBER 25, 2001

On September 23, 2001, the President issued Executive Order 13224 dealing with "Blocking and prohibiting transactions with persons who commit, threaten to commit, or support terrorism." For the purposes of the Order, which linked intent and conduct, terrorism was described as an activity that "(i) involves a violent act or an act dangerous to human life, property, or infrastructure; and (ii) appears to be intended (A) to intimidate or coerce a civilian population; (B) to influence the policy of a government by intimidation or coercion; or (C) to affect the conduct of government by mass destruction, assassination, kidnapping, or hostage taking." Its focus was on activities and not on a condition. The implementation of the Order, although difficult owing to the need to obtain the support of domestic and foreign financial institutions, via Department of Treasury regulations, has resulted in "flattening the pocketbooks" of the supporters of terrorism. The Order was supplemented in 2002 by the "Suppression of the Financing of Terrorism Implementation Act."

By January, 2002, the U. S. government had identified 168 organizations and individuals as financers of terrorism and blocked $34.2 million. On January 9, 2002, the Secretary of the Treasury reported that the Coalition "partners had blocked another $33.9 million. 196 nations have expressed support for disrupting terrorist financing and 144 have blocking orders in force."[1] On April 20, 2003, Secretary of State Powell announced that since 9/11 more than $134 million of terrorist assets in the United States had been frozen.

On October 26, 2001 the International Money Laundering Abatement Act of 2001 was signed into law.[2] Important provisions dealt with due diligence measures, bank secrecy, and money laundering. The statute gave the government many new weapons to combat international terrorism. Sanctions were increased. With regard to money laundering, long-arm jurisdiction was established over foreign money launderers including financial institutions, which were defined to include foreign banks. The civil and criminal penalties for laundering were increased from $100,000 to $1,000,000.[3]

The members of the United Nations have taken an active interest in the subject. On January 10, 2002 it opened for signature the International Convention for the Financing of Terrorism, which was signed by the United States on January 20, 2002. On September 28, 2001 the Security Council adopted Resolution 1373. It called for strong measures by all States to prevent and to criminalize money laundering intended to further terrorist activities. This was followed by Security Council Resolution 1390 of January 16, 2002. It required "all States" to:

"Freeze without delay the funds and other financial assets or economic resources of these individuals, groups, undertakings and entities, including funds derived from property owned or controlled, directly or indirectly by them or by persons acting on their behalf or at their direction, and ensure that neither these nor any other funds, financial assets or economic resources are made available, directly or indirectly, for such persons' benefit, by their nationals or by any persons within their territory."[4]

The 2002 Resolution also called for the interdiction of travel by identified terrorists through a member's territory. It required the withholding of military supplies and prohibited the delivery of such materials to identified terrorists.

Relying on existing statutes, including the 2001 Patriot Act, the government began its special war against accountants, auditors, and bankers who served as conduits between U. S. residents and terrorist organizations. One such body was the Chicago-based Global Relief Organization. It had been under governmental surveillance since 2001. This body had links to Osama bin Laden and Al Qaeda networks. When it was prosecuted in a Federal District Court a demand was made on the government to produce its evidence and the sources of its information. It declined to do so because of secret sources. Officers of the organization, were, nonetheless, convicted. On appeal to the Court of Appeals in Illinois the conviction was upheld despite the secrecy contention

Providing military training to terrorist organizations also is unlawful. Earnest James Usama, an American citizen living in Seattle, received training at an Al Qaeda camp in Afghanistan, where he installed computer software programs for Taliban officials. Following his arrest in the United States he was refused bail and was charged with terrorist activities including providing money, goods, services, and technical assistance to the enemy. He received a two year prison sentence which resulted from his willingness to assist the government in investigating other terrorists. The outcome met with the approval of the Attorney General who stated that a part of the war against terrorism consisted in gaining the "cooperation of insiders who have direct knowledge of activities" of terrorists.

In a separate case a naturalized American citizen, living in Chicago, created the Benevolence International Foundation devoted to humanitarian purposes. He was charged with unlawfully bankrolling Muslim fighters in Chechnya and Bosnia-Herzegovina. He denied assisting Al Qaeda. Following a guilty plea to a single count of racketeering he was convicted. His engagement in plea bargaining led to the requirement that he cooperate with the government in identifying terrorists. The Department of Justice has brought several criminal prosecutions against persons who collected funds for foreign terrorists. In proceedings of this kind the court hearings will receive public airing. Americans can be provided with a deeper understanding of the activities of terrorists.The proceedings were instructive. U. S. citizens and aliens living in the United States charged with such crimes were accorded trials in Federal District Courts rather than by Military Commissions

2. THE PRESIDENTIAL ORDER OF NOVEMBER 13, 2001: MILITARY COMMISSIONS

A variety of legal measures have been addressed to terrorism and torture, accompanied by Presidential and Department of Defense Orders, Decrees, and Regulations, and litigation has marked efforts to ensure the prosecution and sentencing of illegal alien combatants and Americans charged with having engaged in making war against the United States and in acts of torture. It became necessary to identify those persons who, as "detainees," could be held in U. S. custody. However, executive action, unaccompanied by confirming legislation, produced uncertainty and legal turmoil. This was reflected in the Presidential Order of November 13, 2001 which authorized the Secretary of Defense to detain in the United States or abroad "terrorists" as defined in that order.[5] The Order was based on the President's general powers, including the constitutional office of Commander in Chief, and the laws of the United States including the "Authorization for the Use of Military Force Joint Resolution " of September 18, 2001.[6]

The Bush Order, based on the efforts of lawyers in the Departments of State, Defense, and Justice, endeavored to make provision for military commissions that were consistent with historic practices, including the Order issued by President Roosevelt that had been upheld in Ex Parte Quirin.[7] The Order called for the prosecution of unlawful enemy combatants. It was the position of the Bush administration that Al Qaeda was, in effect, a "band of brigands," and not entitled to the protection of the laws and customs of war and relevant treaties, and that the Taliban in 2001 was under the domination of Al Qaeda, and, therefore, not entitled to such protections. The underlying assumption was that the executive department should have considerable latitude in the course of implementing practical means of control.

Section One of the Presidential Order recited findings of terrorist attacks at home and abroad, the existence of a state of armed conflict requiring the use of America's armed forces, and referred to the Declaration of Emergency of December 14, 2001. The finding proclaimed that the prospects for massive destruction were so grave that a risk existed regarding the "continuity of the operations of the United States government." Protective measures were required to bring the attacks to an end.

To obtain stability the Order called for the detention of terrorists and when prosecuted to be "tried for violations of the laws of war and applicable laws by military tribunals." In Section 1(f) the President stated "to the extent provided by and under this Order I find consistent with sections 836 of Title 18, United States Code, that it is not practicable to apply in military commissions under this Order the principles and rules of evidence generally recognized in the trial of cases in the United States district courts." This was based on the finding that an extraordinary emergency existed for national defense purposes.

Section 2 was entitled "Definition and Policy." Subject to the various provisions of the Order were "individuals" who were not United States citizens, who were identified from time to time in writing, who was or had been a member of Al Qaeda, who "has engage in, aided or abetted, or conspired to commit, acts of international terrorism, or acts in preparation thereof, who have caused, threatened to cause, or have as their aim to cause, injury to or adverse effects on the United States, its citizens, national security, foreign policy, or economy; or has knowingly harbored one or more individuals described . . ." therein.

Section 3 referred to the detention policy of the Secretary of Defense. Detentions might be within or outside the United States. Detainees were entitled to humane treatment "without adverse distinctions based on race, color, religion, gender, birth, wealth, or any similar criteria." While in detention a detainee was to be afforded adequate food, drinking water, and the amenities usually accorded to prisoners of war.

Section 4 referred to penalties and to conditions designed to insure fair trials with the military commission sitting as a trier of both fact and law. The admission of evidence was to be determined by the officer presiding at the hearing, but was subject to the determination of the entire commission. Evidence was to have "probative value to a reasonable person." Penalties were subject to applicable law and could be incarcerations up to death, and the death penalty.

Section 4 was also designed to protect against "unauthorized disclosure" or "as otherwise protected by law" the "handling of, admission into evidence or, and access to materials and information" and "the conduct, closure of, and access to proceedings . . ." Section 4 also dealt with the conduct of counsel appointed to prosecute cases and the conduct of the defense of the individuals who were subject to the order. A two-thirds vote of members of the commission was required for conviction and sentencing. The record of the trial was to be submitted to the President or to the Secretary of Defense, as so prescribed, for review and final decision

Section 5 required governmental agencies to assist the Department of Defense to assist in the implementation of the order. Section 6 delegated to the Secretary of Defense the authority to issue orders and regulations to implement the order, subject to the exception that there could be no delegation respecting review and final decision.

Section 7 was entitled "Relationship to Other Law and Forums." It provided that unauthorized persons were not to possess "state secrets." The President was given exclusive authority to grant reprieves and pardons, The Order was not to be construed as prohibiting the Secretary of Defense, military commanders, or any other officer or agent of the United States from detaining or trying any "person who is not an individual subject to this or any other order." Persons subject to the order were subject to the exclusive jurisdiction of a commission. Section 7 also provided that a detained individual "shall not be privileged to seek any remedy or maintain any proceeding, directly or indirectly, or to have any such remedy or proceeding sought on the individual's behalf, in (i) any court of the United States, or any State thereof, (ii) any court of any foreign nation, or (iii) any international tribunal . . ." The Order in sweeping terms announced that it was "not intended to and does not create any right, benefit, or privilege, substantial or procedural enforceable at law or equity by any party against the United States, its departments, or other entities, its officers or employees or any other person." The word "State" was defined to include any State, district, territory, or possession of the United States.

Section 7(e) authorized the President to transfer a detainee from one governmental authority to another. No limitations were promulgated on the prosecution of a transferred individual. The order made no mention of the Uniform Code of Military Justice.

In the case of Hamdan v. Rumsfeld decided by the Supreme Court on June 29, 2006, it was ruled that the President did not possess the power to issue the 2001 Military Commission Order. Prior to the invalidation of the 2001 Order elaborate efforts had been made in the Department of Defense to provide a legal infrastructure, including procedural matters, designed to made the Commission a meaningful institution. Following the adoption of the Military Commissions Act at the end of 2006 a new Military Commission was created. Much of the earlier infrastructure, plus new ideas, were added to its characteristics so that jurisdiction would still be vested in a Military Commission. It is worth noting that the first Commission did not resolve a single matter, and that the new Commission has gotten off to a slow start.

3. THE DEPARTMENT OF DEFENSE MILITARY COMMISSION ORDER NO. 1, MARCH 21, 2002

It was not until March 21, 2002, that the Secretary of Defense, following extensive consultations with leading members of the private bar, as well as with government officials, implemented the Bush Order of November 13, 2001.[8] The Secretary's Order, consisting of 26 pages, and entitled "Procedures for Trials by Military Commissions of Certain Non-United States Citizens in the War Against Terrorism,"[9] paralleled the Bush Order, made some changes, and was not subject to all of the negative criticism that had been evoked by the former.[10] The Secretary's Order made it clear that jurisdiction over members of Al Qaeda, other persons engaged in acts of international terrorism against the United States, and those persons who knowingly harbored such terrorists would be prosecuted in military commissions. The Secretary's Order did not repeat those provisions of the Bush Order denying access by detainees to other U. S. courts, foreign courts, and international tribunals. Under the Bush Order triable offenses were those falling under "the laws of war and other applicable laws." The Rumsfeld Order changed this to read "violations of the laws of war and all other offenses triable by military commissions." Charges could be made only against an individual or individuals.

The Rumsfeld Order provided for the presumption of innocence for an accused. The test of evidence was that which "would have probative value to a reasonable person." Provision was also made for the protection of witnesses against recrimination, open proceedings, unless secrecy required a closing to the public, the availability of counsel, which was to be supplied either at government costs or through private employment, the right of an accused to testify, and the availability of cross examination. As before the members of the commission were to determine the facts and the applicable law. Provision was made for post-trial procedures, including appellate review conducted by three judges. Both civilian lawyers and government lawyers can serve on such agencies. One of the foregoing must have had judicial experience. There was to be an automatic review by the Secretary of Defense. The power to grant pardons or reprieves was reserved to the President.

Order No. 1 consisted of the following parts: 1. Purpose, 2. Establishment of Military Commissions, 3. Jurisdiction, 4. Commission Personnel, 5. Procedures Accorded to the Accused, 6. Conduct of the Trial, 7. Regulations, 8. Authority, 9. Protection of State Secrets, 10.Other, 11 Amendment, 12. Deletions, and 13. Effective Date. Under the heading "Purpose" the Order called for its implementation and construction in a manner ensuring that the persons who were prosecuted would "receive a full and fair trial . . ."

Section 2 identified the Secretary of Defense as the "appointing authority" for the establishment of the commissions. Section 3 dealt with jurisdiction over persons and offenses constituting "violations of the laws of war and all other offenses triable by military commissions." Section 4 made provision for commission members, prosecuting and defense counsel and supporting personnel. The powers of the Presiding Officer, who had to be a qualified judge advocate serving in the Armed Forces, were identified. Procedures for the conduct of a trial were identified. He was empowered to admit or reject the introduction of evidence. Under specified conditions he was allowed to close the proceedings. If the commission were presented with an interlocutory question, the disposition of which would require termination of the trial, he was instructed to certify the question to the Appointing Authority for disposition. This section called for the appointment of military judge advocates to defend accused individuals. They were instructed to defend their clients zealously within the bounds of the law without regard to personal opinion as to innocence or guilt. An accused was authorized to select another military judge advocate in the event of incompatibility and to employ outside civilian counsel. The latter were obliged to meet designated security clearances.

Section 5 dealt with the important procedures accorded an accused. Based on those available in trials in Federal District Courts a detainee was to receive the charge written in English prior to trial with sufficient time for the preparation of a defense, to have the presumption of innocence with proof to be beyond "a reasonable doubt, based on the evidence admitted at trial . . ." The detainee was given the right to be present at every stage of the trial, the right to counsel including continuity of representation. Further rights included the right to call witnesses, that of cross-examination of adverse witnesses, the right to remain silent, the right to an open trial, subject to identified limitations, and, in keeping with the right to a full and fair trial to have access prior to trial of materials obtained by the government in its investigations. An accused was entitled to an interpreter if his understanding of the English language was limited. He was to have advanced notice of evidence to be presented by the prosecution at the time of sentencing. Section 9 of the Order contained a "states secrets" provision prohibiting an accused from having access to such materials.

Section 6(B)(3) called for public trials in order to demonstrate that they were full and fair. Limitations, however, were based on the need to protect classified information where there were prohibitions against unauthorized disclosure, as well as the need to protect "the physical safety of participants . . . including prospective witnesses, intelligence and law enforcement sources, methods, or activities," and "other national security interests." He was entitled to access to evidence intended to be introduced at time of trial, including that which tended to "exculpate" the prisoner. Much of the foregoing was borrowed from the Uniform Code of Military Justice

Military Commission Order No. 2 was issued on August 1, 2003. Nos. 3 and 4 were issued on February 6, 2004, and No. 5 on March 17, 2004. They were designed to clarify the terms of the prior orders. The roles of a presiding officer, trial advocates, and defense counsel were identified with greater specificity. Changes were made in the composition of the commission.

The military authorities following the issuance of the Presidential Order of November 13, 2001, based on their assumption that it was constitutional, put together the foregoing procedures. Pending their announcement, and subject to changes promulgated periodically until May 2003, efforts were made to establish the case histories of each detainee . As a result some were released. Others, deemed to be prospective cases for classification as unlawful enemy combatants were slowly investigated. These activities did not result in a final decision of the original commission. In the meantime, the military was establishing Review Boards and Combatant Status Review Tribunals. It was considered that they would make the investigations allowing for an appeal to the Commission, subject to an ongoing review of the terms of final authority following the 2006 enactment of the Military Commissions statute. During the time that efforts were being made for the institution of legal procedures for the detainees, the record of abuses of detainees at Guantanamo was becoming increasingly evident. Under these circumstances detainees sought writs of habeas corpus so that the might prove their innocence and escape the harsh measures being applied during their detention.

4. THE DEPARTMENT OF DEFENSE MILITARY COMMISSION INSTRUCTION, NO. 2, APRIL 30, 2003

The Instruction bearing the title "Crimes and Elements for Trials by Military Commissions" also offered guidance" relating to the crimes prosecutable in military commissions and the elements of those crimes." Like Order Number 1 it had been circulated widely prior to issuance in order to obtain commentary and points of view. The crimes and the elements identified in the Instruction were derived from the existing principles of the law of armed conflict. Convictions may be based only on intentional and wrongful conduct. The Instruction was applicable to detainees held at the Guantanamo Naval Base unless previously released following interrogation.

The jurisdiction of the commissions, pursuant to this Instruction, extended to 25 enumerated crimes. The list was not to be regarded as definitive. Among the identified crimes are the willful killing of protected persons (diplomats), rape, hijacking or hazarding a vessel or aircraft, terrorism, which was defined as the killing or inflicting of bodily harm, or engaging in inherently dangerous conduct when such harm or destruction was "intended to intimidate or coerce a civilian population, or to influence the policy of a government by intimidation or coercion," "aiding the enemy," and "engaging in a conspiracy" to commit a substantive offense identified in the Instruction.

To insure fairness in a prosecution an accused was entitled to all of the defenses "available under the law of armed conflict." The burden of presenting "evidence of lawful justification or excuse or any applicable defense" rests with the accused. Once this had been demonstrated "the burden is on the prosecution to establish beyond a reasonable doubt that the conduct was wrongful or that the defense did not apply."

The defense may raise the issue of severe mental disease or defect. This must be proven by an accused by clear and convincing evidence; not beyond a reasonable doubt. Violations of the laws of war are not subject to a statute of limitations.[11]

The Instruction maintained the distinction between "lawful" and "unlawful" combatant immunity and "belligerent privilege." The term "enemy" was described broadly. Included was an "entity" with which the United States or allied forces may be engaged in armed conflict, or which is "preparing to attack the United States." "Enemy" specifically included any organization composed of "terrorists with international reach." In using "any" it would appear to include a "domestic" entity having meaningful contacts with an organized body of foreign terrorists. If so, it, as well as individuals, would be subject to the jurisdiction of a military commission.

The Instruction bearing the title "Crimes and Elements for Trials by Military Commissions" also offered guidance relating to "the crimes prosecutable in military commissions and the elements of those crimes." Like Order Number 1 it had been circulated widely prior to its issuance in order to obtain commentary and points of view. The crimes and elements identified in the Instruction were derived from the existing principles of the law of armed conflict. The Instruction was applied to detainees held at the Guantanamo Naval Base unless previously released following interrogation.

5. ADDITIONAL MILITARY COMMISSION INSTRUCTIONS, MAY 2, 2003

On May 2, 2003 the Department of Defense issued eight further instructions. They were intended to guide "full and fair" Commission trials in the event they were presented with charges against detainees. One set of instructions bore the title "Crimes and Elements for Trials by Military Commission." The others focused on the procedures of the Commissions. They were: Guidance on Military Commission Instructions Themselves, Responsibilities of the Chief Prosecutor, Prosecutors, and Assistant Prosecutors, Responsibilities of the Chief Defense Counsel, Detailed Defense Counsel, and Civilian Counsel, Qualifications of Civilian Defense Counsel, Reporting Relationships for Military Commission Personnel, Sentencing, and Administrative Procedures. They were intended to regularize the proceedings of the first set of commissions, if and when they were activated.

A. Assessment of the Presidential Commissions

The creation of Executive Department Military Commissions in 2001 brought with it from the beginning basic and difficult questions relating to the powers of the president and whether the detailed and extensive procedural and substantive rules and regulations met constitutional and statutory standards. The formation of the commissions was based on the assumption that the conduct of terrorists required a response in which the Department of Defense would be engaged in both the criminal prosecution of terrorists with suitable punishments and in its management of traditional war-making activities. This has resulted in "the confluence of what might previously have been viewed as disparate legal regimes—law enforcement and war—and the lacunae that reveal themselves in our attempts to merge the boundaries of these separate disciplines."[12] At issue was the concurrent presence of military law, duly enacted by Congress, and the instrumentality of commissions, operating from November 2001 by Executive Department orders until they were declared unconstitutional in Hamdan v. Rumsfeld in November, 2004, and civilian law, creating separate categories of defendants. The jurisdiction of military commissions, comparable to military authority vested in domestic courts-martials, would relate to "alien unlawful enemy combatants" pursuant to the "Manual for Military Commissions" announced by the Secretary of Defense on January 18, 2007.[13] However, before that date, and before November, 2004, and that classification the Executive Department had endeavored to implement a two-level (or bimodal) jurisdictional distinction. The administration's perseverance in maintaining the distinction is best reflected in its submission of the January, 2007, Manual to Congress in accordance with the Military Commissions Act of 2006. In drafting the new Manual the Department of Defense benefited from its experience with the 2001 Bush Commissions. The legal authority, however, for the new Manual was the Military Commissions Act of 2006.

The Department of Defense, with much sensitivity to the role of the federal courts, with their traditional safeguards in the prosecution of persons charged with crime, sought to alleviate such concerns for the new military commissions created in 2006. Thus, the Manual designated as 2-22.3 according to its proponents would "ensure that alien unlawful enemy combatants who are suspected of war crimes and certain other offenses are prosecuted before regularly constituted courts affording all the judicial guarantees which area recognized as indispensable by civilized people."[14] To meet this standard Manual 2-22.3 set forth procedural rules, evidentiary rules, and a detailed recitation of the crimes punishable by Commissions, and the elements of those crimes. This conscientious and consolidating approach to such prosecutions, should not, however, detract from the fact that detailed rules and regulations, designed to secure the protections of due process of law, had been promulgated before January 18, 2007 respecting hearings before Administrative Review Boards, Combatant Status Review Tribunals, and for the 2001 Commissions.

The Department of Defense moved slowly in setting up the 2001 Commissions. Upon activation in 2004 Guantanamo detainees challenged their legal status. Detainees who had been held under the invalidated Presidential Order remained in custody after the enactment of the Military Commissions Act. This meant that some of the first of the captives may have been in custody up to six years in December 2007, although the government has noted that many had not been captured more than three or four years prior to December 2007. That extended period was referred to by justices of the U. S. Supreme Court when the cases of Boumediene v. Bush and Al Odah v. United States were argued before the court on December 5, 2007.[15]

NOTES

1. U. S. Department of Treasury, Treasury News, Office of Public Affairs, Fact Sheet, 2 January 2002.

2. U. S. Patriot Act, Pub. L. 107-56, 115 Stat.296-3342, October 24, 2001.

3. E. J. Krauland and S. Lagonico, The Counter-Money Laundering and Anti-Terrorist Financing Law, 31 International Law News, No. 1, 16 (Winter, 2002).

4. S/RES/1390 (2002), 2, January 28, 2002. Reprinted in 41 ILM 511, No. 2 (March 2002). An assessment of earlier Security Council Resolutions appears in M. Kantor, Effective Enforcement of International Obligations to Suppress the Financing of Terror, The American Society of International Law Task Force on Terrorism, 5–8 (September 2002).

5. Detention, Treatment, and Trial of Certain Non-Citizens in the War Against Terrorism, 66 F.R. 57833 (Nov. 16, 2001), Pub. L. 107-40, 115 Stat 224 (2001).

6. Pub. L. 107-40, 115 Stat. 224 (2001). The joint resolution stated: "That the President is authorized to use all necessary and appropriate force against those nations, organizations, or persons he determines planned, authorized, committed, or aided the terrorist attacks that occurred on September 11, 2001, or harbored such organizations or persons, in order to prevent any future acts of international terrorism against the United States by such nations, organizations or persons." It affirmed that the resolution met with and was not inconsistent with the provisions of the War Powers Resolution of 1973. Frequently referred to as the War Powers Act. R. F. Grimmett, Authorization For Use Of Military Force in Response to the 9/11 Attacks (P.L. 107): Legislative History, CRS Report for Congress, January 4, 2006.

7. 317 U. S. 1 (1942).

8. http://www.defenselink.mil/news/commissions.html. Los Angeles Times, A22, January 18, 2002.

9. Ibid.

10. The military commissions created by the executive department have been assessed by J.Elsea, Congressional Reference Service, in The Department of Defense Rules for Military Commissions: Analysis of Procedural Rules and Comparison with

Proposed Legislation and the Uniform Code of Military Justice (November 2004). On March 3, 2002, William H. Taft, IV, Department of State Legal Advisor issued a memorandum U. S. Military Commissions: Fair Trials and Justice. http://usinfro.state.gov. See also N. K. Katyal and L. H. Tribe, Waging War, Deciding Guilt: Trying the Military Tribunals, 111 Yale L. J. 1259, No. , 4 (April 2002); Jordan J. Paust in 23 Mich. J. Intl Law, Nos. 1 and 4 (2001–2002); D. M. Aman, Guantanamo, 42 Colum. J. Transnat'l Law 262, No. 2 (2004).

11. The Instructions were amended from time to time. For example, on December 30, 2003 Instruction No. 9 was issued. As noted in DOD Press Release No. 384-04 of April 20, 2004, the changes were designed to ensure that defense counsel possessed sufficient independence from command prejudice.

12. W. K. Lietzau, Military Commsission: Old Law for New Wars, in INTERNATIONAL LAW CHALLENGES; HOMLEAND SECURITY AND COMBATTING TERRORISM, 81 INTERNATIONAL LAW STUDIES, U. S. NAVAL WAR COLLEGE, 256 (2004 Colloquium) (2006). Included in the Colloquium were articles by J. J. Paust, Military Commissions: Constitutional, Jurisdictional and Due Process Requirements at p. 289, and C. H. B. Garraway, Military Commissions—Kangareoo Courts? at 303.

13. Defenselink.mil/pubs/, January 18, 2007.

14. Ibid., Executive Summary, p. 1.Chapter 14 contains further details on Field Manual 2-22.3.

15. More detail is provided in Chapter 8.

Chapter Five

The Department of Justice Memoranda Relating to POWs, Detainees, and to Torture, 2002–2004

1. THE JANUARY 9, 2002 MEMORANDUM FOR WILLIAM J. HAYNES II, GENERAL COUNSEL, DEPARTMENT OF DEFENSE

This Memorandum dealt with the legal classification of persons who were apprehended in Afghanistan following their engagement with American military forces. On the basis of the Presidential Executive Order of September 25, 2001 it seemed reasonable to conclude that military personnel serving the Taliban government could claim POW status but that the terrorists composing the Al Qaeda forces could not. This view was not taken in the January 9, 2002, finalized on January 22, "Memorandum for William J. Haynes, II, General Counsel, Department of Defense" prepared by John Yoo, Deputy Assistant Attorney General, and Robert J. Delahunty, Special Counsel, Office of Legal Counsel, Department of Justice. In its final form it was signed by Jay S. Bybee, Assistant Attorney General. Mr. Yoo and Mr. Delahunty took the position that the laws of armed conflict, including the POW Convention, did "not protect members of the Al Qaeda organization, which as a non-State actor cannot be a party to the international agreements governing war. We further conclude that these treaties do not apply to the Taliban militia."[1] Thus began a saga that has resounded within the world-wide halls of justice and called attention to the rule of law.

The POW Convention is fairly specific concerning the types of persons entitled to POW status. Article 5 prescribes how the status of captives is to be determined. While there is agreement that members of the armed forces of a country, as well as members of organized militias or volunteer corps as units of the armed force do qualify. Al Qaeda were denied this status on the ground they were not a part of a national armed force. The interrogation of Afghanistan

65

detainees resulted from the need to determine whether those being held were lawful enemy combatants, e. g., Taliban, or unlawful enemy combatants, e. g., Al Qaeda. This was based on the proposition that Al Qaeda terrorists, like pirates and slave traders, were outside the law and could not qualify for the protections of the POW Convention.

The rationale of the Yoo-Delahunty Memorandum was that Al Qaeda "is merely a violent political movement or organization and not a nation-State. As a result, it is not eligible to be a signatory to any treaty. Because of the novel nature of the conflict, moreover, we do not believe that Al Qaeda would be included in non-international forms of armed conflict to which some of the provisions of the Geneva Convention might apply. Therefore, neither Geneva Conventions or the WCA [War Crimes Act of 1996] regulate the detention of Al Qaeda prisoners captured during the Afghanistan conflict."[2] This conclusion suggests that the laws and customs of war, including the POW Convention, with its Article 3(a) anti-torture provisions,[3] and the CAT, would offer little help to non-POW persons in detention. This in turn would mean that detainees, but not POWs, would be subjected to interrogation without regard to these two treaties dealing with "persons", or relevant federal statutes with their prohibitions against torture, defined as the imposition of "severe pain or suffering," as well as other humiliating and degrading treatment.

The authors of the Memorandum emphasized differences resulting from the size of the conflict with a distinction between "large-scale" and lesser situations. In their view Article 3 was applicable only to a "large-scale armed conflict between a State and an armed movement within its own territory and occurring within the territory of the high contracting Parties." They stated "[t]his limitation makes perfect sense if the Article applies to civil wars, which are fought primarily or solely within the territory of a single State. . . . The limitation makes little sense, however, as applied to a conflict between a State and a transnational terrorist group, which may operate from different territorial bases, some of which might be located in States that are parties to the Convention and some of which might not be."[4] Thus, it was concluded that Article 3 would apply only to a "large-scale" civil war within a given State.

It was evident that the authors of the Memorandum were endeavoring to demonstrate the uniqueness of facts and the inutility of trying to fit the existing facts into existing international law. It was based on an impossible effort to put "round pegs into square holes." The analysis failed to account for the fact that there was a de facto Taliban government in Afghanistan and that the involvement of the United States could not be considered to be a part of a civil war. It also overlooked the protections against torture and inhuman treatment contained in Article 3 of the POW Convention.

The effort to render irrelevant the laws and customs of war in this conflict caused consternation in the Department of State and among high-ranking legal advisors in the armed forces. The first response was that of William H. Taft, III, the Legal Advisor of the State Department. In his Memorandum of January 11, 2002, to Mr. Yoo, Mr. Taft stated that the POW Convention applied to the war in Afghanistan. This was based on the terms of the treaty, 50 years of United States compliance and practice, the confirming views of other parties, and the terms of Security Council Resolution 1193. The Department of Justice advice on how to deal with detainees was characterized as "seriously flawed," "untenable," "incorrect as well as incomplete," and "confused." Also noted was that the analysis of that Department was "contrary to the official position of the United States, the United Nations and all other States that have considered the issue."[5] Mr. Taft also advised Mr. Yoo "that if the United States took the war on terrorism outside the Geneva Conventions, not only could United States soldiers be denied the protections of the Convention—and therefore prosecuted for crimes, including murder—but President Bush could be accused of a 'grave breach' by other countries, and be prosecuted for war crimes."[6]

The issue reached a higher level when on January 25, 2002, Alberto R. Gonzales, Counsel to the President, advised President Bush that the POW Convention did not apply to "the conflict with Al Qaeda" and that there were "reasonable grounds" to conclude that it did not apply to the conflict with Taliban armed forces. This was based on the proposition that "terrorism renders obsolete [the Geneva Conventions'] strict limitations on the questioning of prisoners."

On January 26, 2002, Secretary of State Colin Powell wrote to Mr. Gonzales identifying the inadequacy and the dangers entailed in the above advice. He stated that the Gonzales advice did not "squarely present to the President the options that are available to him nor does it identify the significant pros and cons of each option."[7] One option identified by Secretary Powell was that the Geneva Convention did not apply to the conflict; the other option was that it did. In support of the latter he urged that "By providing a more defensible legal framework, it preserves our flexibility under both domestic and international law; it provides the strongest legal foundation for what we actually intend to do; it presents a positive international posture; preserves U. S. credibility and moral authority by taking the high ground; and puts us in a better position to demand and receive international support; it maintains POW status for U. S. forces; reinforces the importance of the Geneva Conventions; and generally supports the U. S. objective of ensuring its forces are accorded protection under the Convention."[8]

The Powell Memorandum was followed on February 2, 2002, by a Memoradum from Mr. Taft to Mr. Gonzales. Mr. Taft concluded that "A decision that the Conventions do not apply to the conflict in Afghanistan in which our armed forces are engaged deprives our troops there of any claim to protection of the Convention in the event they are captured and weakens the protections afforded by the Conventions in future conflicts."[9] The global and national self-interest perspectives of Mr. Powell and Mr. Taft were not fashionable in the White House at that time. The executive branch embarked on its long effort to establish a process for the interrogation and prosecution of unlawful enemy combatants or for releasing them.

President Bush responded to the conflicting advice from the foregoing with a directive on February 7, 2002, entitled "Status of Detainees at Guantanamo." It focused on policies to be implemented in light of the provisions of the POW Convention. The policy, as announced, would be "to treat all of the individuals detained at Guantanamo humanely and, to the extent appropriate and consistent with military necessity in a manner consistent with the principles of the Third Geneva Convention."[10]

It was determined that members of Al Qaeda, as a foreign terrorist group, were to be held in custody, and were not to receive POW benefits. Although the United States had not recognized the Taliban as the legitimate Afghan government, Afghanistan was a party to the Convention. The Memorandum stated that "the President has determined that the Taliban are covered by the Convention under the terms of the Geneva Convention. However, the Taliban detainees do not qualify as POWs."[11] On July 20, 2007 President Bush signed an Executive Order entitled "Interpretation of the Geneva Conventions Common Article 3 as Applied to a Program of Detention and Interrogation by the Central Intelligence Agency." Invoking his constitutional powers and several statutes, including the Military Commissions Act of 2006, he affirmed that "On February 7, 2002, I determined for the United States that the members of Al Qaeda, the Taliban, and associated forces are unlawful enemy combatants who are not entitled to the protections that the Third Geneva Convention provides to prisoners of war I hereby reaffirm that determination."[12] On February 7, 2002, it had been stated that the President "had determined that the Geneva Convention applies to the Taliban detainees, but not to the Al Qaeda detainees." Thus, a distinction was drawn between POW status and detainee status. The ultimate conclusion in 2002 was that "even though the detainees are not entitled to POW privileges, they will be provided many POW privileges as a matter of policy."[13]

The foregoing, with its admixture of international law and domestic policy, relates significantly to interrogation procedures. It allowed for the questioning of captured persons to determine who was a member of Al Qaeda. Once a person was found to be only a member of the Taliban that person would be accorded POW benefits, but not status, and would be subject to the limitations imposed on interrogation in the POW Convention, e. g., limited interrogation, while, if the individual were determined to be a member of Al Qaeda, further questioning could be conducted as a matter of law and policy. By calling for the humane treatment of individuals held in detention at Abu Ghraib and at Guantanamo the conclusion must be drawn that "individuals," when detained are to receive the protections against torture established in the POW Convention and in the 1984 CAT. The relevant provisions of the POW Convention and the CAT dealing with torture and humane treatment of detained persons are set forth in Chapter Two, Sections 1 and 2., supra.

The DOD and the Department of Justice were charged with the implementation of those policies. This led to a review of the meaning to be assigned to the term "torture". This resulted in a series of Memoranda prepared in the Department of Justice. The findings and conclusions, issued between August 1, 2002, and December 30, 2004, again excited a great deal of controversy. The Memorandum of August 1, 2002, written by John Yoo, Deputy Assistant Attorney General and Robert J. Delahunty, Special Counsel, Office of Legal Counsel, Department of Justice, which was known as the Bybee Memorandum was revoked on December 30, 2004. Prior to that date Mr. Gonzales had stated that the August 1, 2002 Bybee Memorandum had been the basis for President Bush's decision that the POW Convention did not apply to Al Qaeda detainees and that they were not entitled legally to the status of POWs under the Convention. During the period when the Bybee Memorandum was being implemented a great deal of damage was done to the U. S. system of military law, to identified U. S. military and civilian personnel charged and, in the case of military personnel, convicted of having breached statutory and treaty provisions as a result of various torture practices and other cruel, inhuman, and humiliating practices, to charges of misconduct of the Secretary of Defense, to the clouding of the long-time careers of very high level Army officers,[14] and to wide-spread international wonderment and dismay that the high level of misconduct that took place could occur in a country dedicated to the rule of law in world affairs.

2. THE AUGUST 1, 2002 MEMORANDUM FOR ALBERTO R. GONZALES, COUNSEL TO THE PRESIDENT RELATING TO TORTURE

This 50 page memorandum dealt with torture. It was entitled "Re: Standards of Conduct for Interrogation under 18 U.S.C. ## 2340-2340A," the Criminal

Torture Act of November 20, 1994.[15] It was signed by Jay S. Bybee, Assistant Attorney General. Its principal authors were John Yoo, Deputy Assistant Attorney General and Robert J. Delahunty of the Department of Justice. The memorandum was based on the assumption that the question had arisen "in the context of interrogations outside of the United States." Section 2340 defines the act of torture. Section 2340A makes it a criminal offense for "whomever outside the United States commits or attempts to commit torture . . ." The Memorandum focused on the meaning to be assigned to "torture," including the terms "excruciating and agonizing pain," as they were used in the POW Convention, in CAT, and in the implementing War Crimes Act of 1996.[16] The statutes contained penalties for violations.

Following the issuance of the Bybee Memorandum it was referred to by Attorney General Gonzales as the basis for the decision by President Bush that the Geneva POW Convention did not apply to Al Qaeda detainees being held outside the United States and they were not entitled legally to POW status. The Bybee Memorandum also referred to the Geneva Civilian Protection Convention, to CAT, including its RUDs, and national legislation implementing these agreements as we all national legislation relating to torture and torturers. The opinion was intended to "fine tune" the meaning of torture. It addressed only federal legislation. However, the statute implementing the CAT employed the same definition of torture as the one set out in Understanding II.(1)(a). The authors of the Memorandum advanced a special view that "severe" "excruciating and agonizing" pain under the Torture Victims Protection Act of 1991, the Criminal Torture Act of 1994, and the War Crimes Act of 1996 was "limited to pain 'equivalent in intensity to the pain accompanying serious physical injury, such as organ failure, impairment of bodily function, or even death." (Memo., p. 1).

Prior to the revocation of the Bybee Memorandum on December 30, 2004, it became necessary for the U. S. armed forces to translate the above opinion into language that could be understood and applied by interrogation and detention personnel dealing with detainees held at the Guantanamo Naval Base in Cuba, and later at the Abu Ghraib Joint Interrogation and Debriefing Center in Iraq.

The 2002 memorandum was divided into 5 parts: (1) the above statute, (2) the text, ratification history, and negotiating history of the Torture Convention, (3) the jurisprudence of the Torture Victims Protection Act,[17] dealing with civil remedies for torture victims "to predict the standards that courts might follow in determining what actions reach the threshold of torture in the criminal context," (4) international decisions regarding the use of sensory deprivation techniques, and (5) whether Section 2340A may be unconstitutional if applied to interrogations undertaken of enemy combatants pursuant to the President's Commander-in-Chief power.

The Memorandum summarized basic conclusions. With regard to Section 2340 the authors stated that for an act to constitute torture it "must inflict pain that is difficult to endure." (Memo, p. 1) Torture was identified as "severe pain." Physical pain amounting to torture must be "equivalent in intensity to the pain accompanying serious physical injury, such as organ failure, impairment of bodily function, or even death." (Memo, p. 1) " For purely mental pain or suffering to amount to torture under Section 2340, it must result in significant psychological harm of significant duration, e. g., lasting for months or even years." (Memo, p. 1.) " We conclude that the mental harm also must result in one of the predicate acts listed in the statute, namely: threats of imminent death; threats of infliction of the kind of pain that would amount to physical torture; infliction of such physical pain as a means of psychological torture; use of drugs or other procedures designed to deeply disrupt these senses, or fundamentally alter an individual's personality; or threatening to do any of these things to a third party." (Memo, p.1) It was concluded that the statute prohibited "only the most extreme acts," (Memo. 2) as evidenced by the fact that only the most extreme acts were reserved for criminal penalties for "cruel inhuman, or degrading treatment or punishment." (Memo.p. 1) Moreover "This confirms our view that the criminal statute penalizes only the most egregious conduct." (Memo, p. 2). " and that torture could be distinguished from cruel, inhuman, or degrading treatment." (Memo, p. 2) It was also observed that Congress in enacting the statute intended to "track" the Convention's definition of torture and the Reservations, Understandings, and Declarations that the United States submitted with its ratification.

The authors of the Memorandum also concluded regarding Section 2340A that it proscribed "acts inflicting, and that are specifically intended to inflict, severe pain or suffering, whether mental or physical. Those acts must be of an extreme nature to rise to the level of torture within the meaning of Section 2340A and the Convention." (Memo, p. 1). The authors also concluded that "certain acts may be cruel, inhuman, or degrading, but still produce pain and suffering of the requisite intensity to fall within Sections 2340A proscription against torture." (Memo, p. 7)

Also at issue was the meaning to be given to "specific intent to inflict severe physical or mental pain or suffering." As later explained by Mr.Yoo there was a need for analysis of these terms since the words were "rare in the federal code, no prosecutions have been brought under it, and it has never been interpreted by a court."[18] Following his research he concluded that the

"United States intentionally [had] defined torture strictly" and that this was consistent with the policies adopted by the Reagan and George H.W. Bush administrations.[19]

Following an assessment of the text of CAT it was concluded that Section 2340A was intended to "proscribe only the most egregious conduct. CAT not only defines torture as involving severe pain and suffering, but it makes it clear that such pain and suffering is at the extreme end of the spectrum of acts by reserving criminal penalties solely for torture. Executive interpretations confirm our view that the treaty (and hence the statute) prohibits only the worst form of cruel, inhuman, or degrading treatment or punishment." (Memo, p. 22). "CATs text, ratification history and negotiating history all confirm that Section 2340A reaches only the most heinous acts." (Memo, p. 22). Conduct causing harm to a detainee though coercive, but falling short "of only the worst" or "heinous acts," would not, according to the Memorandum, constitute torture. The authors concluded that "certain acts may be cruel, inhuman, or degrading but still not produce pain and suffering of the required intensity to fall within section 2340A protection against torture." (Memo, p. 1.)

The authors next looked to United States judicial interpretations for guidance as to the meaning of Section 2340A. The search revealed that there were no reported cases although one 2002 case referred to the fact that the "threat of imminent death was present and persistent." (Memo, p. 26).

In their more detailed analysis of the statute the authors identified critical terms. One was the specific intent ("specifically intended") provision of Section 2340. This meant that "the infliction of such pain must be defendant's precise objective." (Memo, p. 3). If a defendant acted on the basis that his conduct was only "reasonably likely to result from his actions, but no more, he would have acted with general intent." (Memo, p. 4). Further, a defendant's "good faith belief that his conduct would not produce the result the law prohibits negates specific intent." (Memo, p. 4). Support for these conclusions was based on federal court cases, a reference to Black's Law Dictionary, and a text book.

Another critical term of the statute was that acts amount to torture if they "cause severe physical or mental pain or suffering." Since the statute did not define the term "severe," the authors of the Memo examined cases holding that the statutory construction of a word called for "the ordinary meaning of the words used." (Memo, p. 5). They then referred to several dictionaries for guidance in interpreting "severe" concluding that the "adjective 'severe' conveys that the pain or suffering must be of such a high level of intensity that the pain is difficult for the subject to endure." (Memo, p. 5). For additional guidance they examined federal statutes dealing with health care where a person in the absence of immediate medical attention would be "(i) in serious jeopardy, (ii) serious impairment to bodily functions, or (iii) serious dysfunction of any bodily organ or part." The authors noted that under these statutes serious physical damage "must rise to the level of death, organ failure, or the permanent impairment of a significant body function." (Memo, p. 6). They concluded that "[t]hese statutes suggest that 'severe pain,' as used in Section 2340, must rise to a similarly high level—the level that would ordinarily be associated with a sufficiently serious physical condition or injury such as death, organ failure, or serious impairment of body functions—in order to constitute torture." (Memo, p. 6).

The authors provided a separate analysis of the expression "severe mental pain or suffering." They took into account that Section 2340 dealt with both "severe mental" and "severe physical" pain and suffering with "severe mental pain or suffering" being defined as "prolonged mental harm caused by or resulting from" a number of specific situations including in subsection (A) "severe physical pain or suffering." The analysis took into account references to "mental pain or suffering," and "physical pain or suffering." Attention was drawn to the fact that the expression "physical pain and suffering" was not used in the statute. It was concluded that the two statutory provisions were not "distinct" concepts. (Memo, p. 6, footnote 3.) This was explained: "Instead, it gives the phrase 'severe mental pain of suffering' a single definition. Because 'pain or suffering' is a single concept for the purposes of severe mental pain or suffering it should likewise be read as a single concept for the purposes of severe physical pain or suffering.'" (Memo, p. 6, footnote 3.) The authors added: "even if we were to read the infliction of severe physical suffering as distinct from severe physical pain, it is difficult to conceive of such suffering that would not involve severe physical pain. Accordingly, we conclude that 'pain or suffering' is a single concept within the definition of Section 2340." The terms used in Section 2340 were incorporated without change in Understanding (1) (a) deposited with the United Nations on October 21, 1994. If doubts were to be raised as to the meaning of the Understanding reference to the above would add to clarification

The authors of the Memorandum then provided an assessment of the term "prolonged mental harm" as it was used in Section 2340(2) of the statute, "harm caused by or resulting from predicate acts," identified in 2340(2), the legislative history of Sections 2340-2340(A), which was described as "scant," (Memo, p. 12), and then summarized the findings.

The "Conclusion" of the Mcmoramdum repeated the distinction between torture and acts that were of a lesser degree of magnitude and encompassed cruel, inhuman, or degrading treatment or punishment. The differences between physical and mental pain were again emphasized, including the duration of each, with severe mental pain requiring pain at the moment of infliction "but it also requires lasting psychological harm, such as seen in mental disorders like posttraumatic stress disorder." (Memo, p. 46).

The authors then essentially repeated the "block-busting" statement made on page 1 of the Memorandum: "Where the pain is physical, it must be of an intensity akin to that which accompanies serious physical injury such as death or organ failure." (Memo, p. 46). The page 1 statement reads: "[p]hysical pain amounting to torture must be equivalent in intensity to the pain accompanying serious physical injury, such as organ failure, impairment of bodily function, or even death." These were the "extreme" "worst," or "heinous" acts defined in Section 2340A. Short of "death," for example, as opposed to the "threat of imminent death" as employed in Understanding (1)(a) there were to be wide-ranging situations where "severity" would not reach the level of prohibited conduct. This conclusion arrived at in the Memorandum cannot be justified by the provisions appearing in Article 1 of CAT, in Understanding (1)(a) of the American reservations to CAT, nor to the language appearing in Section 2340A. By way of contrast the authors stated "Because the acts inflicting torture are extreme, there is significant range of acts that though they might constitute cruel, inhuman, or degrading treatment of punishment fail to rise to the level of torture." (Memo, p. 47). Article 16 of CAT was treated as the source for distinguishing between torture and "other acts of cruel, inhuman or degrading treatment or punishment which do not amount to torture as defined in Article 1". This was deemed to be consistent with other international law sources.

The authors' views were summarized. They stated: "We conclude that torture as defined in and proscribed by Sections 2340 and 2340A, covers only extreme acts, severe pain generally of the kind difficult for the victim to endure. Where the pain is physical it must be of an intensity akin to that which accompanies serious physical injury such as death or organ failure. Severe mental pain requires suffering not just at the moment of infliction but it also requires lasting psychological harm, such as seen in mental disorders, like post traumatic stress disorder. Additionally, such severe mental pain can arise only from the predicate acts listed in Section 2340. Because the acts inflicting torture are extreme, there is a sufficient range of acts that although they might constitute cruel, inhumane, or degrading treatment or punishment that fail to rise to the level of torture." (Memo, p. 46)

The vastness of this official advice to the President was identified in the last two sentences of the Memo. "Further, we conclude that under the circumstances of the current war against al Qaeda and its allies, application of Section 2340A to interrogations undertaken pursuant to the President's Commander-in-Chief powers may be unconstitutional. Finally, even if an interrogation method might violate Section 2340A, necessity or self-defense could provide justification that would eliminate any criminal liability." In retrospect the above appears to be directed more toward "winning" the war than adhering to the legal "niceties" contained in the several provisions of the relevant laws.

These ultimate statements did not follow the definition of torture in Article One of the CAT. They did not follow the views expressed by Department of State and Department of Justice officials in the Committee on Foreign Relations Committee hearings on RUDs to the Convention, to the terms of paragraph II.1(1)(a)(3) of the American Understanding to that agreement referring to "prolonged mental harm caused by or resulting from the threat of imminent death." They did not conform to the provisions of the Torture Victim Protection Act of 1991, and to the cases identified in the Memorandum.

3. THE MARCH 14, 2003 MEMORANDUM FOR WILLIAM J. HAYNES II, GENERAL COUNSEL, DEPARTMENT OF DEFENSE

On March 14, 2003 John C. Yoo, Deputy Assistant Attorney-General, submitted a memorandum classified as "Secret/noforn,"entitled "Re: Military Interrogation of Alien Unlawful Combatants Held Outside the United States"[20] to William J. Haynes II, General Counsel of the Department of Defense. The Haynes request called for an examination of "both domestic and international law that might be applicable to the conduct of those interrogations." (Memo. p. 1). The request was made concurrently with public disclosures of abuses occurring at the Abu Ghraib prison in Baghdad and following the relocation of detainees to the Guantanamo Naval Station.

The author's conclusions, focusing on the Fifth, Eighth, and Fourteenth Amendments to the Constitution, were stated in two places and different language was employed. Thus, at Memo (pp.1–2) the following appears:

"In Part I, we conclude that the Fifth and Eighth Amendments, as interpreted by the Supreme Court, do not extend to alien enemy combatants held abroad. In Part II, we examine federal criminal law. We explain that several canons of construction apply here. Those canons of construction indicate that federal criminal laws of general applicability do not apply to properly-authorized interrogations of enemy combatants, undertaken by military personnel in the course of armed conflict. Such criminal statutes, if they were misconstrued to apply to the interrogation of enemy combatants, would conflict with the Constitution's grant of the Commander in Chief power solely to the President."

"Although we don't believe that these laws would apply to authorized military interrogations, we outline the various federal crimes that apply to the special maritime and territorial jurisdiction of the United States: assault, 18 U.S.C. # 113 (2000); maiming, 18 U.S.C. # 114 (2000); and interstate stalking, 118 U.S.C. # 2261A (2000). In Part II.C, we address relevant criminal prohibitions that apply to conduct outside the jurisdiction of the United States: war crimes, 18 U.S.C. # 2441 (2000); and torture 18 U.S.C. # 2340A (2000 & West Supp. 2002)."

"In Part III, we examine the international law applicable to the conduct of interrogations. First, we examine the U. N. Convention Against Torture and Other Cruel, Inhuman, or Degrading Treatment or Punishment, April 18, 1988, 1465 U.N.T.S. 113 ('CAT') and conclude that U.S. reservations, understandings, and declarations ensure that our international obligations mirror the standards of 18 U.S.C. # 2340A. Second, we address the U. S. obligation under CAT to undertake to prevent the commission of 'cruel inhuman, or degrading treatment or punishment.' We conclude that based on the reservation, the United States' obligation extends only to conduct that is 'cruel and unusual' within the meaning of the Eighth Amendment or otherwise 'shocks the conscience' under the Due Process Clauses of the Fifth and Fourteenth Amendments."

"Third, we examine the applicability of customary international law. We conclude that as an expression of state practice, customary international law cannot impose a standard that differs from U. S. obligations under CAT, a recent multilateral treaty on the same subject. In any event our previous opinions make clear that customary international law is not federal law and that the President if free to override it at his discretion."

In Part IV, we discuss defenses to an allegation that an interrogation method might violate any of the various criminal prohibitions discussed in Part II. We believe that necessity or self-defense would provide defenses to a prosecution." (Memo, p. 2).

The Conclusion, as summed at the close of the Memorandum, (Memo. p. 81) uses these words: "For the foregoing reasons, we conclude that the Fifth and Eighth amendments do not extend to alien enemy combatants held abroad. Moreover, we conclude that different canons of construction indicate that generally applicable criminal laws do not apply to the military interrogation of alien enemy combatants held abroad. Were it otherwise, the application of these statutes to the interrogation of enemy combatants undertaken by military personnel would conflict with the President's Commander in Chief powers." (Memo, p. 81)

"We further conclude that CAT defines United States international law obligations with respect to torture and other cruel, inhuman, or degrading treatment or punishment. The standard of conduct regarding torture is the same as that which is found in the torture statement, 18 U.S.C. #2340-2340A. Moreover, the scope of United States obligations under CAT regarding cruel, inhuman, or degrading treatment or punishment is limited to conduct prohibited by the Eighth, Fifth, and Fourteenth Amendments. Customary international law does not supply any additional standards." (Memo, p. 81)

"Finally, even if the criminal prohibitions outlined above applied, and an interrogation method might violate those prohibitions, necessity or self-defense could provide justification for any criminal liability." (Memo, p. 81)

The March 14, 2003 Memorandum dealt with subjects of central importance that had been identified in the Department of Justice Memorandum of August 1, 2002 for the Counsel to the President and whose authors included Deputy Assistant Attorney General, John C. Yoo. With the open publication on March 3, 2008 of the March 14, 2003 Memorandum the question has arisen whether the March 14, 2003 Memorandum had, as had been the case with the August 1, 2002 Memo, been superseded by the December 30, 2004 Memo. The December 30, 2004 Memo explicitly disavowed the August 1, 2002 Memo. The December 30, 2004 Memo did not mention the March 14, 2003 Memo. The title of the August 1, 2002 Memo was "Standards of Conduct for Interrogation under 18 U.S.C. ##2340-2340A." The title of the March 14, 2003 Memo was "Military Interrogation of Alien Unlawful Combatants Held Outside the United States." However, both Memos dealt with 18 U.S.C. # 2340A and the interpretation by the authors that "severe" pain under the statute was pain "equivalent in intensity to the pain accompanying serious physical injury, such as organ failure, impairment of bodily function, or even death." (2002 Memo at 1, 2004 Memo at 2.)

The March 14, 2003 Memo in dealing with "The Conduct of Interrogations" (Memo, p. 1) concluded that United States reservations, understandings and declarations ensure that our international obligations mirror the standards of 18 U.S.C. #2340A." This was confirmed in the Conclusion to the Memo in these words: "The Standard of Conduct regarding torture is the same as that which is found in the torture statute, 18 U.S.C. ##2340-2340A." (Memo, p. 81.)

Foremost was the prohibition of conduct "specifically intended to inflict severe physical or mental pain or suffering." (18 U.S.C. 2340-2340A.) This presented the issue of a definition of "severe pain or suffering." The March 14, 2003 Memorandum, lacking a statutory definition of the term "severe," adopted the view that severe physical pain would have been the product of damage which "must rise to the level of death, organ failure, or the permanent impairment of bodily functions." (Memo, pp. 38–39) The March 14 position was summarized: "The victim must experience intense pain or suffering of the kind that is equivalent to the pain that would be associated with serious physical injury so severe that death, organ failure, or permanent damage resulting in a loss of significant body function will injury result." (Memo, p. 45) This construction was a principal reason for the revocation of the Bybee Memorandum dated August 1, 2002. This raises the question, now that the March 14, 2003 memo has become public information, whether a stance, in the form of a formal revocation, will be taken. In any event it would seem that the authority accorded to the March 14 memo, even though not expressly disavowed by the Department of Justice, may have been substantially diminished. The December 30, 2004 Memorandum did not find that the March 14, 2003 Memo had modified or set aside the August 1, 2002 Memo. One unverifiable statement has appeared that the Memorandum had been rescinded nine months after its issuance. Senator Patrick Leahy has been reported as stating it had been withdrawn by the Office of Legal Counsel. Mr. Yoo has been quoted as saying that it had been "recalled for 'appearances sake.'" [21] The author's written request to the Office of Legal Counsel seeking clarification whether the Memorandum had been withdrawn was not answered. The ACLU, which had relied on the Freedom of Information Act in order to obtain the release of the Memorandum, in response to the author's request as to the legal status of the Memorandum, replied it had no information on the subject.

Unfortunately, although CAT and supportive federal statutes prohibit the views contained in the two foregoing Memos respecting the meaning to be given to the expression "severe physical pain," the prospect that alien enemy combatants held abroad will have access to the federal courts to assert and to prove their allegations and complaints and secure redress can only be resolved through a holding by the U. S. Supreme Court that events occurring outside American territorial jurisdiction and control are governed by the U. S. Constitution.[22] If this were to occur federal statutes might be enacted terminating the functions of Military Commissions, and perhaps the Classified Information Procedures Act of October 18, 1988 (94 Stat. 2025, 102 Stat. 4396, Public Law 96-456) could be applied to the detainees much as it presently does for spies.

The references in the March 14, 2003 memo to other Department of Justice memos is illustrative of the concerns held at the indicated dates to the problems stemming from the wars in Afghanistan and Iraq. These included "Re: The President's Constitutional Authority to Conduct Military Operations Against Terrorists and Nations Supporting Them," September 25, 2001; "Re: Legality of the Use of Military Commissions to Try Terrorists," November 6,

2001; "Re: The President's Power as Commander in Chief to Transfer Captured Terrorists to the Control and Custody of Foreign Nations," March 13, 2002; "Re: Legal Constraints to Boarding and Searching Foreign Vessels on the High Seas," June 13, 2002; and "Re: Applicability of 18 U.S.C. # 4001(a) to Military Detention of United States Citizens," June 27, 2002.

Since the Memo of December 30, 2004 did not formally supersede the Memo of March 14, 2003, further authority was required to achieve that result. That occurred when Mr. Levin wrote to Mr. Haynes on February 4, 2005 noting its "withdrawal."

Deputy Assistant Attorney General Yoo attached the following disclaimer to his March 14, 2003 Memorandum: "By delimiting the legal boundaries applicable to interrogations, we of course do not express or imply any views concerning whether and when legally-permissible means of interrogation should be employed. That is a policy judgment for those conducting and directing the interrogations." Memo, p.1, fn 1.)

4. THE DECEMBER 30, 2004 MEMORANDUM FOR JAMES B. COMEY, DEPUTY ATTORNEY GENERAL RELATING TO TORTURE

The August 1, 2002 Memorandum was superseded in "its entirety" on December 30, 2004.[23] The new Memorandum deemed that earlier statements concerning the President's powers as Commander-in-Chief and potential defenses to liability were "unnecessary." A reconsideration of the statements made with respect to the Torture Victim Protection Act of 1991 required that they be "modified in some important respects . . ." especially regarding those 2002 "statements . . . limiting 'severe' pain under the statute to 'excruciating and agonizing' pain, id. at 19, or to pain 'equivalent in intensity to the pain accompanying serious physical injury, such as organ failure, impairment of bodily function, or even death,' id. at 1." (Memo. p. 2). In practical terms this meant that the Department of Defense would be obliged to take whatever action was necessary in order to insure that violence against detainees would have to be limited, whatever the means, well short of the consequences identified above. Nonetheless the 2004 Memorandum contained the following: "While we have identified various disagreements with the August 2002 Memorandum, we have reviewed this Office's prior opinions addressing issues involving treatment of detainees and do not believe that any of the conclusions would be different under the standards set forth in this memorandum." (Memo, p. 2, footnote 8.) Thus, the distinction between POWs and unlawful enemy combatants was retained.

Despite the disavowal of the August 1, 2002 Memorandum, the December 30, 2004 Memorandum displayed a startling similarity aside from the 2002 misreading of CAT's "only relevant" (Memo, p. 4). definition of torture. Thus, Part II of the new Memorandum discussed "(1) The meaning of 'severe,'" with reference to the testimony before the Senate Committee on Foreign Relations in 1990," " (2) The meaning of 'severe physical pain or suffering,'" "(3) The meaning of 'severe mental pain or suffering'" and "4. The meaning of 'specifically intended.'" The new Memorandum made liberal use of dictionary references and cited many cases, including those referred to in the first Memorandum.

The 2002 Memorandum closed with two additional references to specific intent. "First, specific intent must be distinguished from motive. There is no exception under the statute permitting torture to be used for a 'good reason.'" (Memo, p. 17.) Second, "specific intent to take a given action can be found even if the defendant will take the action only conditionally." (Memo, p. 17).

This interpretation was disavowed with the issuance of the Memorandum on December 30, 2004. The Office of Legal Counsel stated that it disagreed with the 2002 position limiting "severe pain under the statute to "'excruciating and agonizing pain'" "or to pain 'equivalent in intensity to the pain accompanying serious physical injury, such as organ failure, impairment of bodily function, or even death.'" In short, conduct leading to physical and mental pain falling well short of the ultimate harms identified above would produce a violation of the above treaties and federal legislation.

With the publication of the 2004 Memorandum the Department of Defense and military authorities began a serious and time-consuming search for new regulations that would meet the standards of the Constitution and international law. Court martial proceedings were initiated, and an effort was made to promulgate and enforce permissible military law, including Instructions, Orders, Rules, and Regulations controlling the procedures to be followed at interrogation and detention centers. As legal efforts, resulting from litigation initiated by detainees held as unlawful enemy combatants, got under way many in custody began to assert that they had been the victims of torture and that statements made by them had been coerced and should not be considered as incriminating.

Despite the need for a historically correct and strict interpretation of "torture," Mr. Yoo observed that the Congress had not precluded a country's right to rely on "self-defense and necessity" in arriving at its construction of the CAT provisions, even though it contained terms "to the contrary." Supporting this observation was the assertion of the highly disputed claim that in extreme wartime situations a Chief Executive can take actions going beyond the terms of national statutes. In his view his Memorandum identified constitutional options open to both the President and to Congress. His own view was that "[a] lawyer must not read the law to be more restrictive than it is just to satisfy his own moral goals, to prevent diplomatic backlash, or to advance the cause of international human rights."[24] In that part of the August 1, 2002, Memorandum dealing with the 1994 Federal torture statute, he concluded that "even if an interrogation method might violate Section 2340A, necessity and self-defense could provide justifications that would eliminate any criminal liability." Those persons, both lawyers and non-lawyers (frequently journalists), who were offended by these views, launched ad hominem attacks. Lawyers, by their calling, should be the first to know that they engage daily in making controversial judgments. Professionalism and the integrity of the bar require that respect must be given to controversial views. Without this fundamental condition basic Human Rights and duties would soon disappear. Only the hardiest would venture into a criminal court on behalf of an unpopular defendant.[25] However, professional standards do not immunize the ideas of lawyers from criticisms based on facts and opposing legal and policy outlooks. Yet, when a lawyer is also a university professor, overly hasty attacks on academic freedom and tenure appear to be highly regressive.

Commentators on the law of torture have relied heavily on the terms of the CAT. American commentators have also examined the relationship between the Convention and federal statutes. Almost without exception they have agreed that both allow no exceptions from their provisions. In explaining the function of the 2002 Memorandum Mr. Yoo stated that it "did not advocate or recommend torture; indeed it did not discuss the pros and cons of any interrogation tactic. Rather, the memo sought to answer a discrete question: What is the meaning of 'torture' under the federal criminal laws? What the law permits and what policy-makers choose to do are entirely different things."[26]

Critics of the Memorandum have focused on Mr. Yoo's contention that torture has not been practiced under Federal laws until the person being interrogated is essentially on death's doorstep. He has summarized the nature of the criticisms directed against that outlook. He wrote: "Critics have attacked the differences between the memo's conclusions and the definition of torture in the 1984 Convention Against Torture. They've attacked its discussion of possible defenses against prosecution and the scope of the commander in chief's power. Most of all, they have attacked the fact that it did not consider policy or moral issues."[27]

Central to the Memorandum was the fact that Al Qaeda was not a signatory to the POW Convention, were not covered by it, and operated by violating the laws of war. From a wider perspective, taking into account the law of war, Mr.Yoo asked how could a country "adapt to the decline of nation-states as the primary enemy in war?"[28] While supporting the POW and the Geneva

1949 Civilian Conventions dealing with a restricted use of violence for combatants and for protecting innocent civilians, he remained steadfast in his
view that, with regard to terrorists, "we must create a new set of rules."[29] He
did not alter his position that terrorists could not be treated as POWs. Referring to pirates and slave traders as being outside the protection of law, he
asked: "Why is it so hard for people to understand that there is a category of
behavior not covered by the legal system?"[30] In accepting the classification
of "unlawful enemy combatants" he stated that such persons "didn't deserve
the protection of the laws of war," which was based on the premise that a
"simple binary classification of civilians and soldiers isn't accurate."[31]

The controversy engendered by the classification of persons captured in
Afghanistan and Iraq and resultant detentions and interrogations led to efforts
in the DOD to promulgate more precise boundaries. One result was the publication in 2003 of a "Working Group Report on Detainee Interrogations in
the Global War on Terrorism: Assessment of Legal, Historical, Policy, and
Operational Conditions."[32] The cumulative effect of the Memorandums and
other policy statements prepared in the Departments of State, Defense, and
Justice and in the White House created uncertainty as to the meaning of the
POW and Torture Conventions and federal laws. This led to equivocal statements in the DOD, which resulted in a less than strict and integrated intellectual framework for high and low-level military personnel and for the civilians
accompanying the armed forces in the field.

This aspect of American warfare can be summarized as follows: With the
disclosure of interrogation methods employed at Abu Ghraib and the Guantanamo Naval Station in 2003 and 2004 popular demands were voiced for the
application of international law and national statutes. On June 22, 2004 the
White House released many detailed documents covering interrogation procedures. Governmental uncertainties relating to basic policies led to a review
in the Department of Justice. On December 30, 2004, it issued a new and
comprehensive "Memorandum for James B. Comey, Deputy Attorney General" prepared by Daniel Levin, Acting Assistant Attorney General. It "supersede[d] the August 2002 Memorandum in its entirety."[33] The 2004 Memorandum had been reviewed by the Criminal Division of the Department of
Justice. It had concurred with the analysis of this document. The Memorandum expressly disagreed with the August, 2002, Memorandum's statutory interpretation which had limited "severe" pain under 18 U.S.C. ##2340-
2340(A) to "excruciating and agonizing" pain . . ." or to pain "equivalent in
intensity to the pain accompanying serious physical injury, such as organ failure, impairment of bodily function, or even death."[34]

The 2004 Memorandum, after referring to the definition of torture in Article 1(1) of the CAT and the American RUDs deposited with the United Na-

tions, stated that the "criminal prohibition against torture that Congress codified in 18 U.S.C. ##2340-2340A generally tracks the prohibition in the CAT, subject to the U. S. understanding."[35] The Yoo Memorandum, being inconsistent with and departing from those provisions, was revoked. In arriving at that conclusion the 2004 Memorandum in part II examined the meaning to be given to four key phrases: (1) "severe," (2) "severe pain and suffering," (3) "severe mental pain or suffering," and (4) "specifically intended." In assessing the meaning of these terms the Memorandum made it clear that they applied to the CAT definition of torture and not to "other acts of cruel, inhuman or degrading treatment of punishment which do not amount to torture as defined in article 1."

5. CORRECTIVE LEGISLATION

The Military Commissions Act of 2006,[36] taking into account the foregoing Memoranda dealing with torture and with cruel, inhuman and degrading treatment or punishment, which had caused so much controversy following their releases, clarified the earlier interpretations by Department of Justice attorneys regarding statutory and treaty definitions through the adoption of new legislation.[37] It also raised the question of whether the RUDs to CAT continued to be the governing law of the United States relating to torture and to the meaning of cruel, inhuman, or degrading treatment or punishment. The 2006 statute in subchapter 950v. established important definitions and gave Commissions jurisdiction over such crimes as torture, cruel and inhuman or degrading treatment or punishment and set forth criminal penalties, extending in some situations to death.

The statute is repetitious. In Section 3 "Military Commissions," Chapter 47A, Section 11(A) described the crime of torture. It referred to the commission of an act "specifically intended to inflict severe physical or mental pain or suffering (other than pain or suffering incidental to lawful sanctions) upon another person within his custody or physical control for the purpose of obtaining information or a confession, punishment, intimidation, coercion, or any reason based on discrimination of any kind." Section 11(B) entitled "Severe Mental Pain or Suffering Defined," stated: "In this section, the term 'severe mental pain or suffering' has the meaning given that term in section 2340(2) of title 18." Section 12, dealing with cruel or inhuman treatment contained the terms of the punishable action and prescribed sentences. Section (B) contained definitions including that of "serious physical pain or suffering," as meaning "bodily injury that involves— '(I) a substantial risk of death; (II) extreme physical pain; (III) a burn or physical disfigurement of a serious

nature (other than cuts, abrasions, or bruises); or (IV) significant loss or impairment of the function of a bodily member, organ, or mental faculty.'" Further, "(ii)The term 'severe mental pain or suffering' has the meaning given
that term in section 2340(2) of title 18.'" Further, "(iii) The term 'serious
mental pain or suffering' has the meaning given the term 'severe mental pain
or suffering in section 2340(2) of title 18, except that—"(I) the term 'serious'
shall replace the term 'severe'" where it appears; and "(II) as to conduct occurring after the date of the enactment of the Military Commissions Act of
2006, the term 'serious and non-transitory mental harm (which need not be
prolonged)' shall replace the term 'prolonged mental harm' where it appears."

Section 13 dealt with "Intentionally Causing Serious Bodily Injury." In
part A, entitled "Offense," it is provided that "Any person subject to this
chapter who intentionally causes serious bodily injury to one or more persons,
including lawful combatants, in violation of the law of war shall be punished,
if death results to one or more of the victims, by death or such other punishment as a military commission under this chapter may direct, and, if death
does not result to any of the victims, by such punishment, other than death, as
a military commission under this chapter may direct." Part B defines "Serious Bodily Injury." In that paragraph the term "means bodily injury which
involves—(i) substantial risk of death; (ii) extreme physical pain; (iii) protracted and obvious disfigurement; or (iv) protracted loss or impairment of
the function of a bodily member, organ, or mental faculty."

These provisions were amended, supplemented, and repealed in Section
6 of the statute entitled "Implementation of Treaty Obligations." After
amending Section 2441 of title 18, U.S.C. referring to a grave breach of
common Article 3 of the 1949 Geneva Conventions, a new subchapter was
added entitled "(d) Common Article 3 Violations," dealing with prohibited
conduct including "(A).Torture.—The act of a person who commits or conspires to commit, an act specifically intended to inflict severe physical or
mental pain or suffering (other than pain or suffering incidental to lawful
sanctions) upon another person within his custody or physical control for
the purpose of obtaining information or a confession, punishment, intimidation, coercion, or any reason based on discrimination of any kind. (B)
Cruel or Inhuman Treatment.—The act of a person who commits, or conspires or attempts to commit, an act intended to inflict severe or serious
physical or mental pain or suffering (other than pain or suffering incidental
to lawful sanctions), including serious physical abuse, upon another within
his custody or control."

The statute then proceeds in (2) to effect definitions. "Severe mental pain
or suffering" is to be "applied for purposes of paragraphs (1)(A) and (1)(B)
in accordance with the meaning given that term in section 2340(2) of this ti-

tle." The term "serious bodily injury" is to be "applied for purposes of paragraph (1)(F) in accordance with the meaning given that term in section 113(b)(2) of this title." The term "serious physical pain or suffering" is to be "applied for purposes if paragraph (1)(B) as meaning bodily injury that involves—(i) a substantial risk of death; (ii) extreme physical pain; (iii) a burn or physical disfigurement of a serious nature (other than cuts, abrasions, or bruises; or (iv) significant loss or impairment of the function of a bodily member, organ, or mental faculty" which was also set forth in section 590v of the statute. In Section 6, Implementation of Treaty Obligations, in subparagraph (2) "Definitions" two important changes occur. The statue in paragraph (E) states that "the term 'serious mental harm or suffering' shall be applied for purposes of paragraph (1)(B) in accordance with the meaning given the term 'severe mental pain or suffering' (as defined in section 2340(2) of this title) except that—(i) the term 'serious' shall replace the term 'severe' where it occurs, and (ii) as to conduct occurring after the date of the enactment of the Military Commissions Act of 2006, the term 'serious and nontransitory mental harm (which need not be prolonged)' shall replace the term 'prolonged mental herm' where it appears." Contrary to the use of "severe mental pain or suffering as set forth in section 2340(2) that "(i) the term 'serious' shall replace the term 'severe' where it appears."

Section 6, Implementation of Treaty Obligations, in subsection number "(2) Retroactive Applicability," it is provided "The amendments made by this subsection, except as specified In subsection (d)(2)(E) of section 2441 of title 18, United States Code, shall take effect as of November 26, 1997, as if enacted immediately after the amendments made by section 583 of Public Law 105–118 (as amended by section 4002(e)(7) of Public Law 107-273)."

These changes materially modified, the terms of the first Understanding attached by the United States when it ratified CAT. Important changes were made in law and policy concerning definitions of torture and cruel, inhuman or degrading treatment or punishment. However, with respect to the latter the statute repeated the RUD provisions relating to the term "cruel, inhuman, or degrading treatment or punishment" as being controlled by the Fifth, Eighth, and Fourteen Amendments to the U. S. Constitution. The statute by reaffirming and republishing some of the statements contained in the RUDs, and not reconfirming all of the RUDs, but instead by promulgating substantial changes, raised the issue of which is to prevail, the unreconfirmed terms of the RUDs, as a part of the advice and consent legal impact of the RUDs, or whether they have been eliminated by the 2006 statute. As a general proposition, the priority assigned to opposing treaties and statues is that the last in point of time prevails. Whether this rule, in the event of litigation, will to be followed remains to be seen.

NOTES

1. Memorandum for William J. Haynes, II, General Counsel, Department of Defense, from John Yoo, Deputy Assistant Attorney General and Robert J. Delahunty, Office of Legal Counsel, Department of Justice, January 9, 2002, p. 1. See K. S. GREENBERG and C. J. PATEL, eds, THE TORTURE PAPERS: THE ROAD TO ABU GHRAIB (2005) for the Department of Justice memos referred to in this Chapter and for other relevant documents. M. DANNER, TORTURE AND TRUTH (2005).

2. Id., at pp. 1–2.

3. The Convention in dealing with the conditions of detention provides that "persons who have laid down their arms, including those in detention" are to be treated "humanely." To meet this standard Article 3(a) states that such persons are not to be subjected to "violence to life or person, in particular murder of all kinds, mutilation, cruel treatment and torture . . ." Article 3(c) outlaws "outrages upon personal dignity, in particular, humiliating and degrading treatment." The Convention also refers to the circumstances under which POWs are to be released.

4. Supra, note 1 at p. 8.

5. Department of State Memorandum, pp.3–4 (January 26, 2002).

6. Ibid. Compare: J. Mayer, Outsourcing Terror, 81 The New Yorker, No. 1, p. 112 (February 14 & 21, 2005), H. BALL, BUSH, THE DETAINEES, AND THE CONSTITUTION (2007), J. GOLDSMITH, THE TERROR PRESIDENCY (2007), J.J. PAUST, BEYOND THE LAW, THE BUSH ADMINISTRATION'S UNLAWFUL RESPONSES IN THE WAR ON TERROR (2007), J. J. Paust, Above the Law: Unlawful Executive Authorization Regarding Detainee Treatment, Secret Renditions, Domestic Spying, and Claims of Unchecked Executive Power, 2007 Utah Law Review 345 (2007).

7. Supra, note 5 at pp. 3–4.

8. Ibid.

9. "Gonzales and the Geneva Convention, Attorney General Confirmation Hearings," A Human Rights First Report, p. 12, n.d.

10. Department of State Fact Sheet, p. 1 (February 7, 2002).

11. Ibid.

12. The White House, Office of the Press Secretary, July 20, 2007, p. 1.

13. Ibid.

14. A. COCKBURN, RUMSFELD, HIS RISE, FALL AND CATASTROPHIC LEGACY (2007), M. Hersh, The General's Report, Annals of National Security, 83 The New Yorker, No. 17, p.58 (June 25, 2007).

15. For detail, see Chapter 3, #2.

16. For detail, see Chapter 3, #3.

17. 28 U.S.C. # 1350 note (2000). For detail, see Chapter 3, # 1.

18. Los Angeles times, B11, July 6, 2004.

19. Ibid.

20. It was declassified by the Department of Defense on March 31, 2008, and openly published on April 1, 2008.

21. The ACLU, which obtained access to the Memo has responded to my inquiry that it possesses no information on the recall of the Memo. A similar inquiry to the Office of Legal Counsel of the Department of Justice has been unanswered.

22. See, Boumediene v. Bush, Chapter Nine, where it was held that 58 Guantanamo Bay detainees were entitled to the habeas corpus privilege.

23. Memorandum for James B. Comey, Deputy Attorney General, Re: Legal Standards Applicable Under 18 U.S.C. ## 2340-2340A, December 30, 2004, p. 2. For an assessment of the differences between the August 21, 2002 and the December 30, 2004 memos see M. Lederman, Understanding the Office of Legal Counsel Torture Memos (Parts I, II, III, and Coda), January 7, 2005, in Balkinization (Balkin.com.).

24. Supra, note 14.

25 For a stirring defense of counsel who braved public animosity by lawyering for alleged communists during the McCarthy era, see J. A. Ball, President, State Bar of California, Freedom of the Bar, Journal of the State Bar of California, p. 109 (1957). Following the release of the March 14, 2003 Yoo memorandum relating to the interrogation of Guantanamoa Bay detainees he found himself again in the center of a firestorm of generally adverse criticism. To maintain the highest standards of legal professionalism in a political universe requires probity of the highest order.

26. Supra, note 17.

27. Ibid.

28. Los Angeles Times, B11, February 1, 2005.

29. J. Mayer, Supra, note 6.

30. Ibid. For a more detailed analysis, see JOHN YOO, THE POWERS OF WAR AND PEACE: THE CONSTITUTION AND FOREIGN AFFAIRS AFTER 9/11 (2005); JOHN YOO, WAR BY OTHER MEANS, AN INSIDER'S ACCOUNT OF THE WAR ON TERROR (2006). Compare, J. J. Paust, Executive Plans and Authorizations to Violate International Law, 43 Col. J. Trans. L., 811 (2005). Other appraisals include J. MARGULIES, GUANTANAMO AND THE ABUSES OF PRESIDENTIAL POWER (2006), R. A. POSNER, NOT A SUICIDE PACT; THE CONSTITUTION IN A TIME OF NATIONAL EMERGENCY (2006). Professor Yoo's role as a former Assistant Attorney General took a new turn on January 4, 2008, when a suit against him was filed in the United States District Court for the Northern District of California. Entitled Jose Padilla and Estela Lebron v. Yoo the plaintiffs charged that as a result of his legal memo relating to interrogation Mr. Padilla had been held in confinement between June 9, 2002 and January 5, 2006, including solitary confinement for almost two years, during which confinement Mr. Padilla had been incarcerated in "extreme isolation," subject to "sensory deprivation," subjected to "threats of physical abuse and death," and had been given "chemical" dosages against his will.

31. Supra, Note 6.

32. Wsj.com/public/resources/documents,military__0604.pdg.

33. Memorandum, p. 1.

34. The 2004 Memorandum made it clear that it did not "address the many other sources of law" that may apply to detention and interrogation, including the "Geneva Conventions; the Uniform Code of Military Justice, 10 U.S.C. # 801 et seq.; the

Military Extraterritorial Jurisdiction Act, 18 U.S.C. ## 32661-3267; and the War Crimes Act, 18 U.S.C. #2441, among others." Memorandum, p. 2, fn. 6.

35. Ibid., at 5.

36. Pub. L. 109-366, 120 Stat. 2600. Other aspects of the statute are treated in detail in Chapter 8.

37. Chapter 8, section 2, deals with the other important provisions of the Military Commissions Act.

Chapter Six

Department of Defense and Army Investigations of Violations of the Laws of War in Iraq, 2003–2005, and Corrective Actions

1. INTRODUCTION

By April-May, 2003, stories began to circulate that detainee torture and cruel and inhumane treatment was taking place at the Abu Ghraib Prison (Baghdad Central Confinement Facility) and that the responsible persons were military personnel assigned to the 800 Military Police Brigade and to the 205 Military Intelligence Brigade as well as civilian employees of the Army. The prison housed those detainees that could qualify as prisoners of war, while others awaited classification as lawful alien enemy combatants, with others being non-combatant civilians, including many common criminals who had been incarcerated during the regime of Saddam Hussein. Viewed from a legal perspective the lawful members of the Iraqi armed forces were entitled to the protection of the 1949 Geneva POW Convention, while the rights of civilians were governed by the 1949 Geneva Civilian Convention. All fell within the definitions contained in the 1984 CAT. They were also subject to relevant federal laws, including those designed to insure the protections set forth in the two treaties, subject to the reservations, understandings, and declarations attached by the United States to the CAT at the time of its ratification. Pending the effective lifetimes of the Department of Justice memorandums identified in the preceding Chapter the detainees would be subject to the indicated views regarding POWs and torture, together with the lesser offenses, identified in the international agreements.

2. WHAT HAD GONE WRONG?

As the results of the investigations were made known it soon became apparent that a great deal had gone wrong and that a vast amount of blame could be properly distributed to many active participants running all the way from the White House to the rawest recruit serving in Iraq. The cumulative effects of the Department of Defense and the Army disclosures leave no doubt as to the specific transgressions by members of the armed forces. Although it was not the function of the several investigative reports to identify the misadventures stemming from White House decisions, it was evident that the decision to wage war against Iraq had been taken before the armed forces fully understood how they were going to achieve military superiority in a variety of situations including plans for coping with the administration of victory once Saddam Hussein had been removed from office. Extremely wide ranging and important issues had not been sufficiently considered, one of which a valid approach to the management, including imprisonment, of captured personnel so that they could not take up arms again against the United States, and so that intelligence gathering could be obtained in a timely fashion so that future enemy plans and operations might be neutralized. This factor was well summarized by General Douglas MacArthur: "In no other profession are the penalties for employing untrained personnel so appalling or so irrevocable as in the military." The violations by American forces and civilian contract personnel in Iraq of the laws and customs of war, and the attempts to bring American behavior within the required legal norms, diverted the energies that were required to control guerilla activities, contributed to the heavy financial costs required to "win the peace," and reduced to a very low level the positive image that the United States has endeavored to uphold and sustain respecting its commitment to the rule of law in world affairs.

3. FINDINGS AND RECOMMENDATIONS

All of the investigative committees searched for instances of torture. They inquired into the circumstances where it had been employed. They identified degrees of fault and made proposals for corrective action. The Department of Defense and the Army embarked on separate inquiries. In 2003 Secretary Rumsfeld appointed a committee of prominent persons with Mr. James R. Schlesinger, a former Secretary of Defense as chairman. It included Harold Brown, who had also served as Secretary of Defense. In its report dated August 24, 2004, the panel pointed to "tensions between military necessity" and national security.[1] In its view there was a need for a "sharper moral compass." It concluded that "abuses" were "not a part of authorized interrogation nor were they even directed at intelligence targets." Conditions surrounding the abuses were identified. They included poor training, insufficient staffing, inadequate oversight, confused lines of authority, the presence of evolving and unclear policies, delays in the arrival of additional troops, hazards resulting from the need to defend against daily attacks, and a "generally poor quality of life."[2] The most serious finding was that acts of torture represented "deviant behavior and a failure of military leadership and discipline."[3] The focus of the report was on operations in the field. It did not condemn the Secretary of Defense although in some quarters charges were being levied that there had been a failure, starting at the top, in the "chain of command."

Continuing concerns based on public reports of abuses at the military prisons in and around Baghdad resulted in the appointment by the Department of Defense of General Paul Kern to probe the entire situation. On August 26, 2004, relying on information supplied by the chief investigators, Lt. Gen. Anthony R. Jones and Maj. Gen. George E. Fry, whose inquiries had focused on the activities of the Military Police Brigade and the Military Intelligence Brigade, as well as on civilians supporting these two units in the field, reported that there had been "serious misconduct" coupled with a "loss of moral values."[4]

Responsible Army commanders located in Iraq had expressed concerns respecting alleged abuses conducted engaged in by personnel of the 800th MP Brigade. The Commander of the Combined Joint Task force, Lieutenant General Ricardo S. Sanchez, received approval on January 24, 2003 to engage in such investigations beginning on November 1, 2003. The investigations conducted by Lieutenant General David D. McKiernan began on that date and covered suspected detainee abuse, detainee escapes, accountability lapses, and more broadly as to the fitness and performance of the Brigade.

Early questions arose as to the methods that were being employed during interrogations. From August 31, 2003 to September 9, 2003 a team headed by Major General Geoffrey D. Miller, who had been in charge of such matters at the Guantanamo Naval Air Station detention facility conducted an inspection and rendered a report. It used as its base line the interrogation procedures and authorities employed at that facility. They allowed for the "conditioning" of detainees by the military police prior to questioning by military intelligence personnel. Major General Miller in referring to has experience at the Guantanamo Naval Air Station had conclude that "It is essential that the [Military Police] guard force be actively engaged in setting the conditions for successful exploitation of the internees."[5] A strict line identifying the separate functions of the military police and intelligence had not been maintained. It was reported that when the Miller recommendations were reviewed by General Sanchez that the latter stated that General Miller's appraisal was not necessarily correct since the 1949 Geneva POW Convention was fully applicable in Iraq. It is a fact that all high level military officials have maintained that position and also that army commanders have been more aware of the requirements of the POW Convention than to the controversial interpretations and ultimate disavowal of the views expressed as to the meaning of "torture" as contained in the August 1, 2002, Department of Justice Memorandum dealing with CAT.

Shortly after receipt of the Milller report General Sanchez had directed that a team, headed by Major General Donald J. Ryder, consisting of military police, legal, medical, and automation experts make an assessment of the Brigade. Working from October 16, 2003 to November 6, 2003 it made a report dealing with detention and corrections operations. Unsatisfactory operational situations were identified.

Remaining dissatisfied with the effectiveness of the 800th Military Police Brigade and the torture that had occurred there General Sanchez on January 31, 2004, appointed Major General Antonio M. Taguba, to conduct an "Article 15-6 Investigation of the 800th Military Police Brigade." Its detention and internment operations were to be scrutinized. Four specific tasks were identified. He was to inquire into all facts and circumstances surrounding recent allegations of detainee abuse including maltreatment at the Baghdad Central Confinement Facility. He was to look into detainee escape and accountability lapses as reported by Combined Joint Task Force Seven regarding the Abu Ghraib Prison. Thirdly he was to investigate the training, standards, employment, command policies, internal procedures, and command climate in the Brigade. Finally, he was to make specific finding of fact concerning all aspects of the investigation, and to make recommendations for corrective action.

After having concluded that the Brigade's detainee operations raised issues of accountability, care, and well being of Enemy POWs, retained persons, civilian detainees, other detainees, and Iraqi criminal prisoners, Major General Taguba stated that there "is a general lack of knowledge, implementation, and emphasis of basic legal, regulatory, doctrinal, and command requirements within the 800 MP Brigade and its subordinate units."[6] This negative appraisal led to the recommendation that the unit's Commanding General be reprimanded for "failing to ensure" that the unit's personnel "knew, understood, and adhered to the protections afforded to detainees in the Geneva Convention Relative to the Treatment of Prisoners of War."[7] A substantial number of the soldiers who had engaged in acts of torture were court martialed with sentences based in the gravity of the offenses. The Report, with its 106 annexes, recited details of important interviews. References were made to unit personnel who had performed their duties with exemplary competence.

The final "Conclusion" of the Report stated "several" unit personnel "have committed egregious acts and grave breaches of international law . . . Key senior leaders [in both of the Brigades] failed to comply with established regulations, policies, and command directives in preventing detainee abuses . . . during the period August 2003 to February 2004."[8] The Report referred to corrective action, namely, "Approval and implementation of the commendations of this AR 15-6 Investigation and those highlighted in previous assessments are essential to establish the conditions with the resources and personnel to prevent future occurrences of detainee abuse."[9]

The publication of the Report produced other constructive results. One was the issuance on March 23, 2005 of a Joint Chiefs of Staff "Joint Doctrine for Detainee Operations." Then, on September 6, 2006, the DOD issued the long-awaited Field Manual 2.23-3 entitled "Human Intelligence Collector Operations." It was expected that before Intelligence and Military Police units were certified as "battle ready" by the Department of Defense and the Army that affected personnel would have been highly trained in the indicated subject matter. These documents provide detailed guidance. It was expected that careful training and constant reminders of their importance would lead to u better record of compliance with the solemn obligations accepted by the United States when it ratified the relevant 1949 Geneva Conventions and the 1984 CAT.[10]

Another important inquiry was conducted by Vice Admiral Albert B. Church, III, the Navy's Inspector General. He was appointed by Secretary of Defense Donald Rumsfeld in May, 2004. His public Report was issued on March 3, 2005. It was a comprehensive review of interrogation and detention practices and procedures, employed by the Armed Forces in Iraq and at Guantanamo. Included in the report was an extended review of medical activities, including identified derelictions. Included was proof of lack of effective medical administrative processes for ill and wounded persons. In March, 2008, a more complete, but not an entire, report became public as a result of legal action initiated by the ACLU. As a result documentation identifying dismal and vivid portrays of unlawful military practices, including torture and lesser violations became available.

The initial Church Report acknowledged the applicability of the Geneva POW Convention, while noting that lawful interrogations may be "offensive by their very nature" because of the "natural tensions" surrounding the process.[11] The Report referred to combat zone orders specifying approved questioning procedures. It also confirmed earlier determinations by the Commanding General of the Iraq forces in September, 2003, which had failed to countermand policies and instructions which had been issued at lower levels within the command. The Report took note of a revised interrogation policy issued in May, 2004, which had retained some of the earlier approved techniques, with the addition that under no circumstances would exceptions be approved.[12] But it was added that both directives "contained certain ambiguities."[13] The Church Report concluded that the ultimate fault of the interrogation-detention process was not the inadequacy of high-level directives but rather the unbridled misconduct of military police and intelligence personnel in Iraq.

As a result of ACLU efforts a redacted version of the Church Report became available at the end of March, 2008. It revived the allegations that had been made in the journal Lancet of August, 2004, which had expressed the view that military health care personnel should take the lead in preventing Human Rights abuses. Attention had been drawn to general Assembly Resolution 37/194 of December 18, 1982, where principle 2 stated: "It is a gross contravention of medical ethics, as well as an offense under applicable international instruments, for health personnel, particularly physicians, to engage, actively or passively, in acts which constitute participation in, complicity in, incitement or attempts to commit torture or other cruel, inhuman or degrading treatment or punishment." Important article were published in the New England Journal of Medicine in 2004 and 2005 reminding physicians of responsibilities in time of armed conflict.[14]

Revelations supported by factual proofs have demonstrated that American military personnel, and civilian employees of the armed forces, have engaged in violations of the laws and customs of war through torture and the use of cruel, inhuman or degrading treatment or punishment.[15] The facts in individual cases have resulted in disciplinary actions against active duty personnel in the form of court-martials and reductions in rank. A second approach has been suggested by a large number of international lawyers. They have called for the criminal prosecution of President Bush and very high ranking cabinet and sub-cabinet officials who have embraced the need to win the war on terror through the employment of measures falling within the definition of torture or illegal cruel, inhuman and degrading treatment or punishment. Notably included in this category are lawyers who have prepared legal briefs in which interpretations have been put forward concerning the operational definition of "torture" as it was set forth in CAT. Among the selected defendants was John C. Yoo, the author of the Department of Justice Memo dated January 9, 2002.[16] A third approach, employed with some success in difficult situations, such as apartheid in the Republic of South Africa, has been to focus on reconciliation rather than punishment. This approach has avoided strict reference to legal principles and unsympathetic legalisms in favor of policies of accommodation. If the United States is intent on improving its image as supportive of the world rule of law, and this requires a certain amount of harmony at home, it should be remembered that the architects favoring a wide-open definition of "torture" have lost to wiser counsels and have in many instances experienced public disavowal.

NOTES

1. Final Report. http.//www.defenselink.mil/transcripts/2004/tr20040824-secdef 1221.html.

2. Ibid.

3. Ibid.

4. Los Angeles Times, A1, August 26, 2004.

5. Article 15-6 Report, 8.

6. Id. at 22.

7. Id. at 44. The Report referred to other deficiencies on the part of the Commander. These included misrepresentations relating to her visits to subordinate units, failure to impose disciplinary sanctions for misconduct on the part of officers and non-commissioned officers, failure to take action relating to the "ineffectiveness" of a subordinate commander and staff officers, failure to disseminate reports on results and recommendations relating to escapees and obtaining unit personnel understanding of them, failure to ensure and enforce basic soldier standards throughout her command, and failure to provide sufficient training so that the members of her command could achieve basic proficiency in assigned tasks. Ibid.

8. Id. at 50.

9. Ibid.

10. For a more general appraisal, taking into account historic Supreme Court cases, see CARL Q. CHRISTOL, INTERNATIONAL LAW AND U. S.FOREIGN POLICY, 2nd Revised Edition, 2006, pp. 377–379.

11. Executive Summary, Department of Defense. Detention Operations and Detainee Interrogation Techniques, Hearing, Senate Armed Services Committee, p.1, March 10, 2005.

12. Id. at p. 8.

13. Ibid.

14. 351 New Eng. J. Med. 414 (2005); 32 New Eng. J. Med. 3 (2005).

15. J. JAFFER and A. SINGH, eds., ADMINISTRATION OF TORTURE: A DOCUMENARY RECORD FROM WASHINGTON TO ABU GHRAIB AND BEYOND (2007); K. S. GREENBERG and J. L. DRATEL, eds., THE TORTURE PAPERS: THE ROAD TO ABU GHRAIB (2005).

16. Among the authorities who have advanced this approach is Prof. J. J. Paust in THE BUSH ADMINISTRATION'S UNLAWFUL RESPONSES IN THE "WAR" ON TERRORISM (2007) where he has argued that there was "a common plan to violate customary and treaty-based international law in the interrogation of detainees." In testimony before the Subcommittee on the Constitution, Civil Rights and Civil Liberties House Judiciary Committee on May 6, 2008, Professor Marjorie Cohn stated

that President Bush approved of the policy of coercive interrogation authored by the National Security Council Principals Committee consisting of Vice-President Cheney, National Security Advisor Rice, Secretary of Defense Rumsfeld, Secretary of State Powell, CIA Director Tenet, and Attorney General Ashcroft. She also asserted that Mr. "Yoo and the other Justice Department lawyers who wrote the enabling memos are also liable for the same offenses." Testimony, p. 3.

Chapter Seven

Civilian Employees of the United States Go to War

1. INTRODUCTION

With the capture and detention of Iraqi military personnel at Abu Ghraib the interrogation capabilities of the Army came under severe strain. It turned to civilian employees possessing the required language skills and an understanding of interrogation procedures. When it became evident that the wars in Afghanistan and Iraq would require the defeat of guerilla movements, the protection of civilians, and the safeguarding of the governmental infrastructure, the United States entered into contracts, principally with Blackwater, USA, CACI International, Inc., and Titan Corporation. As a result private corporations sent thousands of civilian employees to Afghanistan and Iraq where they provided necessary support for the armed forces, for the Department of State and for other departments and agencies. They provided personnel, goods, and services.

The employees consisted of American nationals, Iraqi nationals, and the nationals of many other countries. They were engaged to provide security services, assistance to the newly forming government of Iraq, technical competence in the fields of engineering, rebuilding of water and sanitation facilities, bringing oil production back on its feet, sanitation services, medical, transportation, and police activities, providing food and laundry services to military personnel, and because of the need to communicate with captured military personnel a supply of interrogators and interpreters. This raised the pressing legal question of what law was to govern the relations among all of the parties. When Iraqi prisoners were tortured or subjected to cruel, inhumane, and demeaning treatment or punishment applicable laws and institutions were called into play.

The misconduct of civilian employees first came to light with the torture and other crimes practiced by the civilian interrogators at Abu Ghraib. The world became aware of the misbehavior of Department of State contractors in September, 2007, with the news that 17 Iraqi civilians had been gunned down by employees of Blackwater, USA, which held a contract with the Department of State to furnish security for its employees.

2. JURISDICTION OVER CIVILIANS AND THE PROSECUTORIAL FUNCTION

Jurisdiction over civilians who have attached themselves to or who have been employed by American departments and agencies has been created by several statutes for different governing bodies. So that their presence would not interfere with military operations by U. S. forces the terms of the Uniform Code of Military Justice, Section 802, Article 2 of Sub-Chapter 1(General Provisions) provides that it applies "[i]n time of war [to] persons serving with or accompanying an armed force in the field."

The commission of crimes by American citizens accompanying an armed force in the field has long presented American armed forces with prosecutorial problems. This was addressed in the Military Extraterritorial Jurisdiction Act (MEJA) of 2000.[1] It entered into force on November 2, 2000 following the signature of President Clinton. Section 3261 entitled "Criminal Offences Committed by Certain Members of the Armed Forces and by Persons Employed by or Accompanying Members of the Armed Forces Outside the United States" provides that "whoever engaged in conduct outside the United States that would constitute an offense punishable by imprisonment for more than 1 year if the conduct had been engaged in within the special maritime and territorial jurisdiction of the United State—(1) while employed by or accompanying the Armed Forces outside the United States; or (2) while a member of the Armed Forces subject to chapter 47 of title 10 (the Uniform Code of Military Justice) shall be punished as provided for that offense."

The MEJA extended Federal law to govern criminal acts committed by military contractors also accompanying the Armed Forces overseas.

Having given Federal District courts jurisdiction in felony matters the statute also provided that concurrent jurisdiction would still remain "with respect to offenses or offenses that by statute or by the law of war may be tried by a court-martial, military commission, provost court, or other military tribunal."

In an analysis of Section 3261 it was noted that persons "employed by the Armed Forces" means "a DOD civilian employee, including a non-appropriated fund instrumentality employee, a DOD contractor or subcontractor at any level, or an employee of such contractor or subcontractor . . ." The definitions used the term DOD contractors or subcontractors. Consequently, individuals, or organizations under contract with other parts of the U. S. government were not covered by this Act."[2]

When it became public knowledge that civilian contractors were engaged in the Abu Ghraib abuses, Attorney General Ashcroft announced that the Department of Justice was considering applying the statute. When it became evident that some of the contractors were employees of the CIA, with other contractors working for the Department of Interior, it was decided that the MEJA was not applicable.[3]

3. ARMY REPORTS ON ABUSES BY CIVILIAN EMPLOYEES IN IRAQ

In March, 2004, Army Major General Antonio M. Taguba filed a report with the DOD based on an inquiry he had made of the interrogation procedures employed at Abu Ghraib. In it he found that that "Numerous incidents of sadistic, blatant, and wanton criminal abuses were inflicted on several detainees . . . systematic and illegal abuse."[4] The Report led to the investigation of two private military contractors, namely, CACI International Inc. and Titan Corporation, with the former supplying at least one interrogator, and the latter at least two translators. According to the Report one CACI interrogator "made a false statement to the investigation team regarding the locations of his interrogations, the activities during the interrogations, and his knowledge of abuses."[5] A second interrogator was charged with misleading investigators when he denied witnessing misconduct. It was also determined that he did not have the required Army security clearance. The military investigations concluded that "[i]n general, U. S. civilian contract personnel [CACI and Titan], third country nationals, and local contractors do not appear to be properly supervised within the detention facility at Abu Ghraib."[6]

On August 24, 2004, a lengthy report was made to the Army by Major General George R. Fay and Lt. Gen. Anthony R. Jones. It confirmed 44 incidents of abuse that took place at Abu Ghraib involving Army intelligence personnel, military police, and employees of the CACI and Titan contractors. Both firms on the basis of independent reviews denied the allegations. The Fay-Jones report asserted that 35 percent of the interrogators provided by CACI "lacked formal military training as interrogators" for work which the Pentagon should be allowed to outsource, and then only in extreme and pressing

situations. "The report also charged the Army with failure to investigate properly the backgrounds of many of the contract employees."[7]

While the Justice Department was reviewing these facts several private actions were commenced on behalf of tortured and abused persons. In one case
it was charged that the violations came within the purview of the Alien Tort
Claims Act allowing aliens to sue the United States for certain violations of
international law occurring abroad. A second suit was begun, sponsored by
the Center for Constitutional Rights, charging violations of the 1970 RICO
statute. The suit alleged violations of the 1949 Geneva Conventions, the 8th,
5th, and 14th Amendments to the Constitution, and other Federal laws and international law. The possible prosecution of CACI contractors was muddied
by the fact that they had become Federal employees as a result of a Department of Interior contract calling for the supply of information technology
rather than under the terms of the 2000 MEJA. This required an assessment
by Federal prosecutors of whether reliance on Section 2340A of Title 18 of
the United States Code dealing with torture could be sustained. The Fay-
Jones inquiry concluded that it remained unclear who, if anyone in the
Army's contracting or legal team, approved of the employment of civilians by
the Department of Interior. In the pending lawsuits all of the plaintiffs alleged
that the private firms knowingly collaborated with Army personnel in the
prison misconduct and abuses.

Several facts stand out. A court martial would possess jurisdiction over interrogators and translators employed by civilian firms when those employees
accompanied armed forces in the field. Although the military forces could set
the conditions for such employment activities, on several occasions it was reported that civilian employees in Iraq gave instructions and directions to military personnel. Further, the Graham Amendment to Section 552 of the Uniform Code of Military Justice reading "declared war or a contingency
operation" would be applicable, if by any stretch of the imagination a court
were to determine that the conflict was not a "war." Alleged misconduct by
DOD contractors and their subcontractors would still be subject to the UCMJ.

4. THE 2001 FEDERAL ASSAULT STATUTE

On a special set of facts the Federal Assault Statute, as amended late in 2001,[8]
contained a new description of the Special Maritime and Territorial jurisdictional area of the United States. The area was identified as "the premises of
the United States diplomatic, consular, military or other United States government missions or entities in Foreign States, including buildings, parts of
buildings, and land appurtenant or ancillary thereto used for purposes of those

missions or entities, irrespective of ownership." Allegations have been made that the CIA in order to avoid the application of the foregoing to their investigation and detention activities has avoided such areas, including abandoned U. S. property, or other foreign government owned property. However, if CIA personnel were deemed to be "accompanying the Armed Forces outside the United States," as set forth in the 2000 MEJA, acts of torture or similar harsh investigative processes would provide the basis for prosecutions.[9]

5. THE DOD INSTRUCTION NO. 3020.41, OCTOBER 3, 2005

Seeking to regularize an overarching governing structure for "Contractor Personnel Authorized to Accompany the U. S. Armed Forces" the DOD issued Instruction No. 3020.41. Broad in scope it applied to contractors and employees of contractors and their subcontractors at all tiers within DOD contexts. Included in its coverage were third country nationals and host nation personnel, who were authorized to accompany U. S. Armed Forces, when they were employees of U.S. military agencies. Such persons were referred to as "contingency contract personnel."

They were to be supplied with appropriate Geneva Convention identifica tion cards. Section 6 of the Instruction emphasized legal requirements. It provided that every function or service obtained by the contracting process was to be reviewed "on a case-by-case basis in consultation with the servicing legal office to ensure compliance with relevant laws and international agreements." The effective date was updated on January 29, 2007.

6. CIVILIAN EMPLOYEES OF THE DEPARTMENT OF STATE

The Department of State having the large responsibility of dealing with the government of Iraq so that it might once again become a self-sufficient instrument of government entered into contracts with the three firms identified above. They, along with their subcontractors, employed American nationals, Iraqi nationals, and the nationals of many other countries. They were hired to provide security services, assistance to the newly forming government, technical competence in the fields of engineering, rebuilding of water and sanitation facilities, bringing oil production back onto its feet, medical services, transportation services, and police administration. In the course of providing security services the employees of Blackwater USA, apparently without provocation opened small arms fire on Iraqi civilians, killing 17. Decedents in 2007 instituted a case entitled Estate of Himoud Saed Atban v. Blackwater USA in the Federal District

Court for the District of Columbia seeking compensation. The civilian employees were also contracted to provide food and laundry services to military personnel, and, because of the need to communicate with captured military personnel a supply of interrogators and interpreters.[10]

In order to exercise control over civilian employees the Department of
State created a Diplomatic Security Service designed to provide rules for the
use of force by civilian employees. It was entitled "Mission Firearms Policy."
The policy was constructed on the premise that there had to be a zero toler-
ance respecting State department officials in Iraq. The rules have been identified as being "more aggressive than those used by the military for its contract forces."[11] Following the September killings the Department of State and
the Department of Defense reached an accord in which both parties agreed to
a higher degree of coordination, benefiting both entities. The military, in particular, was promised that their tactical operations would not be interfered
with by Blackwater employees. It was reported that the Department of State
granted immunity to the affected employees in order to obtain a full statement
of the facts surrounding the event. In the event that the employees were
charged in an American district court for violations of federal laws, the question of the validity of the grants would have to be examined.

Additionally, the Department of State has given notice that closer attention
would be given to the use of force by its employees, that investigations would
be instituted earlier, that a plan for compensating victims would be studied,
that cultural-sensitivity programs would be initiated for its civilian employees, that it would seek contracts with firms from Arabic-speaking countries,
and that it would coordinate more closely with the government of Iraq in the
licensing of contractor firms.[12]

7. CONCLUSION

The early absence and delayed presence of clear DOD rules and regulations
governing the structural relationship of the private contract employees who
engaged in interrogations and translations, including legal limitations applicable to their activities at Abu Ghraib, marked the inadequacy of advanced
military planning. When combined with torture and cruel and inhuman conduct, and detentions and interrogations by military personnel, these facts resulted in universal condemnations and disapprovals of this phase of the
American war effort. Existing law left no doubt where the ultimate authority
resided. In the course of time suitable legislation was enacted and new rules
and regulations were promulgated. Both military personnel and the affected
civilians were prosecuted.

With the complexities attendant on long-term, far-distant, highly divergent and unwieldy military operations, involving very heavy reliance on civilian contractors, and with civilians going to war in support of Department of State nation-building efforts, and military special needs, the time has come for new national and international rules governing such relationships and activities. While future rules might take the form of international agreements, they could also be the product of decision making by national governments. These rules and regulations would be applicable to the highest level of DOD officials as well as to the military forces in the field.

Since extended wars frequently result in guerilla activities and this will require the employment of large numbers of contract civilians for service as interrogators and translators, this will necessitate the preparation for teaching of instructional materials so that the front-line operational personnel will possesses the required skills and competence required in such activities.[13] The International Committee of the Red Cross might be authorized to make occasional inspections and to receive and publicize reports on the levels of achievement and compliance.

The time has long since passed for those who initiate and engage in war with the employment of both military personnel and civilians to suppose that their responsibilities are limited. They must proceed with abundant caution to insure that the basic rules of humanity are in place, are understood, are being fully implemented, and are enforced

NOTES

1. 18 U.S.C. Chapter 212, 18 U.S.C. 3261, Pub. L. No. 106-523, 114 Stat. 2488. L. A. Dickinson, Accountability of Private Security Contractors under International Law and Domestic Law, 11 ASIL Insights, No. 31, December 26, 2007.

2. G. R. Schmitt, Amending the Military Extraterritorial Jurisdiction Act of 2002; Rushing to Close an Unseen Loophole, DA-PAM 29-50-385. The Army Lawyer, June 1, 2005.

3. Ibid, p. 2.

4. Quoted in S. M. Hersh, The General's Report, 83 The New Yorker, No.17, p, 58, June 25, 2007.

5. v. P. Chatterjee and A. C. Thompson, Private Contractors and Torture at Abu Ghraib, http://www.corpwatch.org/article.php?id=11285m May 7, 2004.

6. Ibid.

7. D. Phinney, Private Contractors Face Legal Action for Crimes in Abu Ghraib, http://www.corpwatch.org//article.php?id=11524, p. 1, September 15, 2004. A revealing role of military contractors in Iraq can be found in J. Scahill, Blackwater: The Rise of the World's Most Powerful Mercenary Army, (2007). At p. 157 he quotes the

Taguba report as concluding that an interrogator at CACI and a translator employed by Titan "were either directly or indirectly responsible for the abuses at Abu Ghraib," noting that "both companies denied the allegations."

8. 18 U.S.C. 113, 18 U. S. C. 7.

9. A former CIA contractor was found guilty in August, 2006, in a Federal District court in Raleigh, N. C. for the abuse of a detainee in Afghanistan. At the time of his sentencing in February, 2007, he was the only U. S. civilian to have been charged with torture or other abuses taking place in Iraq or Afghanistan. 101 AJIL No. 2, p. 507, April 2007.

10. J. K. Elsea and N. M. Serafino, Private Security Contractors in Iraq: Background, Legal Status, and Other Issues, CRS Report to Congress, CRS, June 21, 2007, p. 1. The case of Saleh v. Titan and CACI International, Inc., seeking monetary damage for injuries suffered during interrogations at Abu Ghraib was filed in the Federal District Court for the Southern District of California in 2004. It was transferred to the Federal District Court for the District of Columbia in 2007. Several of the causes of action met the requirements for trial, which had not been resolved early in 2008.

11. R. J. Hillhouse, Don't Blame Blackwater, Christian Science Monitor, Nov, 2, 2007, p. 9.

12. Los Angeles Times, A8, October 24, 2007.

13. S. PERCY, MERCENARIES, THE HISTORY OF A NORM IN INTERNATIONAL RELATIONS (2007).

Chapter Eight

The Role of Congress: Laws and Procedures for the Trial of Unlawful Detainees

1. THE DETAINEE TREATMENT ACT (DTA), DECEMBER 30, 2005

Congressional responses dealing with the capture, classification, and detention of enemy combatants were designed to close gaps in existing statutes and executive orders. It was an affirmative response to the view that the world had become a more dangerous place. Gathered together in one place were a variety of issues involving terrorism, detainees, and torture that had emerged during the Afghanistan and Iraq wars. Of critical significance were provisions dealing with the writ of habeas corpus and the jurisdiction of federal courts. While each of these subjects could be separated for special discussion, I have elected to assess them within the context of the December 30, 2005 enactment.[1] Later legislation and the responses of courts will be addressed as they arise. Thus, Section 1002 called for the application of uniform standards for the interrogation of persons being detained by the federal government. Only the techniques "authorized by and listed in the United States Army Field Manual on Intelligence Interrogation" were to be employed.

The Army began to rewrite FM-34-52 in 2004 following the Abu Ghraib prison abuse scandal. The new directive, Army Field Manual 2-22.3, "Human Intelligence Collector Operations" had been the object of a very extensive and detailed consideration. In November, 2005, it was scheduled for release, but combat commanders asked for a delay so that there could be additional reviews. At issue was the detailing of the acceptable interrogation procedures falling short of torture and the accompanying crimes, and whether the procedures were to be set forth in a classified annex so that prisoners would not know what they were.

On September 5, 2006, the DOD issued its Defense Directive 2310.01E, entitled "The Department of Defense Detainee Program," setting forth principles governing detainee activities.[2] At the same time the U. S. Army published the new field manual, FM 2-22.3 , entitled "Human Intelligence [HUMINT] Collector Operations" specifying techniques that must be followed during detentions and interrogations of enemy combatants.[3]

The DOD Defense Directive, referring to DOD "policy," required that "[a]ll detainees shall be treated humanely and in accordance with U. S. law, the law of war, and applicable U. S. policy." The terms of the Directive were to apply as minimum requirements, and without regard to a detainee's legal status, the standards set forth in Common Article 3 of the 1949 Geneva Conventions, "as construed and applied by U. S. law . . . in the treatment of detainees, until their final release, transfer out of DOD control, or repatriation." The Directive mandated the registration of and accounting for all detainees, thereby making it impossible for the secret holding of "ghost detainees" during a period of torture. It also called for cooperation with the International Committee of the Red Cross during American engagements in armed conflicts.

Section 5-74 of the new Field Manual contained two major provisions. First, it extended the guarantee of being "treated humanely" set forth in the Detainee Treatment Act of 2005 and DOD Directive 2310.01E, "Department of Defense Detainee Program" to "[a]ll captured or detained personnel, regardless of status . . ." This broad and unqualified language conveys the view that this provision applies to such persons without regard to their classification as lawful alien enemy combatants or unlawful alien enemy combatants, which terms, with their legal consequences, were used and the consequences understood in the Department of Defense at that time. Second, the provision referred to more than to "humane treatment." The protection, stated in the negative, was: "no person in the custody or control of DOD, regardless of nationality or physical location, shall be subject to torture or cruel, inhuman, or degrading treatment or punishment, in accordance with and as defined in US law."

The new Field Manual was designed to prevent the use of torture and associated misconduct in military facilities. Section 5-75 specifically prohibited in connection with intelligence interrogations the placing of hoods or sacks over the heads of detainees, applying beatings, electric shock, burns, or other forms of physical pain, the use of military working dogs, and "waterboarding." Other prohibitions were listed including the deprivation of necessary food, water, or medical care. It stated that interrogations "may only be conducted by personnel trained and certified in the interrogation methodology, including personnel in MOSs 97E, 351M (351E), or select others as may be approved by DOD policy. Interrogations are always to be conducted in accordance with the Law of War, regardless of the echelon or operational environment in which the HUMINT collector is operating."[4] The foregoing provision in identifying areas of military specialization reserved for military personnel allowed to engage in interrogations is, in so far as it goes, quite clear. However, the following quoted language seems to open the door for non-military personnel to engage in interrogations. This raises the entire issue of civilian contractors, whether the Field Manual applies to them, and the nature of the relationship between the DOD and such civilian contractors, including the terms of the Uniform Code of Military Justice relating to persons accompanying the armed forces in the field, applicable Army rules and regulations, and any specially permitted contractual relations between the two parties.

HUMINT interrogations apply to the gaining of reliable information to satisfy intelligence requirements. Questioning is restricted to "a captured or detained person." The interrogations must be consistent with applicable law and policy. These include "US law; the law of war; relevant international law; relevant directives including DOD Directive 3115.09; 'DOD Intelligence Interrogations, Detainee Debriefings, and Tactical Questioning'; DOD Directive 2310.01E; 'The Department of Defense Detainee Program'; DOD instructions; and military execute orders including FRAGAOS." Detailed debates within the DOD whether the HUMINT should be applicable to both detainees and to POWs (EPWs) was resolved in favor of its dual application.[5]

The issue of "command responsibility" was addressed in the Field Manual. Section 5-54 states that "(c) compliance with laws and regulations, including proper treatment of detainees, is a matter of command responsibility." Commanders have an affirmative duty to ensure their subordinates are not mistreating detainees or their property." Consideration was given to requests from non-DOD agencies to conduct interrogations in Army facilities. Section 5-55 provides that "(I)n all instances, non-DOD agencies must observe the same standards for the conduct of interrogation operations and treatment of detainees as do Army personnel."

During the Abu Ghraib debacle it was revealed that military police personnel had used guard dogs on captives as a part of the process of readying them for interrogation. This conduct became the subject of universal condemnation. The new Field Manual in Section 5-59 did not prevent the Military Police from using dogs for security needs. However, it provided expressly that "(for) purposes of interrogation, military working dogs will not be used." The Manual listed a number of actions that were prohibited as interrogation techniques. Section 5-75 included: forcing a detainee to be naked, perform sexual acts, or pose in a sexual manner; placing hoods or sacks over the head of a detainee; placing duct tape over eyes; applying beatings, electric shock, burns, or other forms of physical pain; waterboarding; inducing hypothermia or heat injury; conducting mock executions; and depriving a detainee of necessary food, water or medical care. The drafters of the new Field Manual expressed much concern over the practice referred to as "separation." In Appendix M-2 this was described as "involv(ing)" the removal of a "detainee from other detainees and their environment, while still complying with the basic standards of humane treatment and prohibitions against torture or cruel, inhuman, or degrading treatment or punishment, as defined in the Detainee Treatment Act of 2005 and addressed in GPW Article 3 (Common Article III)." "Separation" was distinguished from "segregation," with the latter referring to purposes unrelated to interrogation, such as hospitalization or to protect the security of the detainee. Described as "the only restricted interrogation technique that may be authorized for use," it amounted to (although these words were not used) "solitary confinement." The announced purpose of "separation" was to "deny the detainee the opportunity to communicate with other detainees in order to keep him from learning counter-resistance techniques or gathering new information to support a cover story; decreasing the detainee's resistance to interrogation."(Appendix M-1, p. 347.) The special nature of this technique was identified with the caution that "Separation will only be used during the interrogation of specific unlawful enemy combatants for whom proper approvals have been granted in accordance with this appendix."

The foregoing does not constitute an all-encompassing list of procedures constituting torture or cruel, inhuman, or degrading treatment or punishment prohibited in CAT or the foregoing Directive or Field Manual. Other manifestations may be employed in the future. The rank and file of military personnel require great clarity as to the boundaries between permitted and prohibited conduct. The Directive and the Field Manual have contributed materially to that need.

Section 5.76 called for the preparation of interrogation plans by intelligence-gathering personnel. Before submitting a plan for approval the preparer was asked to respond to two questions. The first: "If the proposed approach technique were used by the enemy against one of your fellow soldiers, would you believe the soldier had been abused?" The second: "Could your conduct in carrying out the proposed technique violate a law or regulation? Keep in mind that even if you personally would not consider your actions to constitute abuse, the law may be more restrictive." The response was that if both questions were answered in the affirmative then the contemplated action should not be conducted. Staff Judge Advocate officers could be consulted before actions were undertaken.

The standards of interrogation set forth in the new Field Manual apply to all U.S. military services and to all DOD personnel, including contractors conducting interrogation on behalf of the armed forces in DOD facilities. They do not apply to the CIA.[6]

Section 1003 of the Detainee Treatment Act was entitled "Prohibition on Cruel, Inhuman, or Degrading Treatment or Punishment of Persons Under Custody or Control of the United States Government." It provided that "No individual in the custody or under the physical control or the United States Government regardless of nationality or physical location shall be subject to cruel, inhuman or degrading treatment or punishment." These were understood as those encompassed in the Fifth, Eighth, and Fourteenth Amendments "as defined" in the 1984 RUDs to CAT.

Section 1004 offered legal protections, both civil and criminal, to designated U. S. government personnel who had been engaged "in specific operational practices, that involve detention and interrogation of aliens who the President or his designees have determined are believed to be engaged in or associated with international terrorist activity . . ." The authorized defense was that the described person, as an officer, employee, member of the Armed Forces, or other agent "did not know that the practices were unlawful and a person of ordinary sense and understanding would not know they were unlawful." The statute also allowed an accused to plead that he was relying in good faith on the advice of counsel. The government was authorized to pay the costs of counsel and other incidental charges arising out of the court proceedings

Section 1005 of the Detainee Treatment Act dealt with "Procedures for Status Review of Detainees Outside the United States." Specific reference was made to Combatant Status Review Tribunals and to Administrative Review Boards and their existing procedures produced by DOD orders were approved. The Order creating a "Designated Civilian Official" was also enacted into law. The decisions of the Tribunals and Boards were to be reported periodically to Congress. The procedures of the two entities were to include assessments, to the extent practicable, as mandated by 1005(b)(1)(A) "whether any statement derived from or relating to such detainee was obtained as a result of coercion; and (B) the probative value (if any) of such statement."

Section 1005(e) of the statute, entitled "Judicial Review of Detention of Enemy Combatants," took a new and highly controversial position on the issuance of writs of habeas corpus. The then existing provision, Section 2241 of title 28, U.S.C., was amended by adding at the end: "Except as provided in section 1005 of the Detainee Treatment Act of 2005, no court, justice, or judge shall have jurisdiction to hear or consider—(1) an application for a writ of habeas corpus filed by or on behalf of an alien detained by the Department

of Defense at Guantanamo Bay, Cuba; or (2) any other action against the
United States or is agents relating to any aspect of the detention by the Department of Defense of an alien at Guantanamo Bay, Cuba, who—(A) is currently in military custody; or (B) has been determined by the United States
Court of Appeals for the District of Columbia Circuit in accordance with the
procedures set forth in section 1005(e) of the Detainee Treatment Act of 2005
to have been properly detained as an enemy combatant."[7]

Section 1005(e)(2)(A) dealt with the "Review of Decisions of Combatant
Status Revision Tribunals of Propriety of Detention." It assigned to the
United States Court of Appeals for the District of Columbia "exclusive juris-
diction to determine the validity of any final decision of a Combatant Status
Review Tribunal that an alien is properly detained as an enemy combatant."
This power was limited in subparagraph (B). Such claim had to be "brought
by or on behalf of an alien—(i) who is, at the time a request for review by
such court is filed, detained by the Department of Defense at Guantanamo
Bay, Cuba; and (ii) for whom a Combatant Status Review Tribunal has been
conducted, pursuant to applicable procedures specified by the Secretary of
Defense." The scope of the review was established in subparagraph (C) (i)
and (ii). In (i) it was limited to the consideration of whether a CSRT's determination met the standards and procedures specified by a Secretary of Defense for CSRTs "(including the requirement that the decision of the Tribunal
be supported by a preponderance of the evidence and allowing a rebuttable
presumption in favor of the Governments evidence). In (ii) whether the use of
such standards and procedures "make the determination . . . consistent with
the Constitution and laws of the United States." The court's jurisdiction with
respect to the claims of an alien were to cease "upon the release of such alien
from the custody of the . . . DOD pursuant to paragraph (D).

Section 1005(e)(3) gave the appeals court exclusive jurisdiction to determine the validity of any final decision rendered pursuant to Military Commission Order No.1 dated August 31, 2005, or any successor military order.
If that final decision dealt with a capital case or a case in which the alien was
sentenced to a term of imprisonment of 10 years or more, the appeal was a
matter of right. In any other case the availability of an appeal was to be determined at the discretion of the court. A problem was posed by the selection
in different orders and statutes of the terms "enemy combatant" and "alien unlawful enemy combatant." If there were a factual finding that a person, being
held as a Guantanamo Bay detainee, under Military Commission Order No.
1, as an "enemy combatant" would this finding also allow for a holding that
the indicated person was an "alien enemy unlawful combatant" pursuant to
the 2006 MCA? The question arises if "any successor military order" would

be applicable which resulted in the finding by a successor CSRT that the detainee could properly be reclassified as an "alien unlawful enemy combatant." The alternative would be new legislation adopting either the foregoing view or requiring an entirely new proceeding. If the initial inquiry were deemed to have adhered to the requisite procedures required of CSRTs it could be concluded that the findings of the initial CSRT proceeding could be relied on in the successor inquiry to establish or not establish that the detainee was an "alien unlawful enemy combatant." This would avoid the need for further legislation.

Subparagraph (C) (i) and (ii) fixed a limitation on appeals. The appeals court could only exercise jurisdiction in an appeal brought by or on behalf of an alien who was, "at the time of the proceedings pursuant to the military order [No. 1, or successor] . . . detained . . ." by the DOD at Guantanamo, and "(ii) for whom a final decision has been rendered pursuant to such a military order."

Subparagraph (D) identified the scope of review. In (i) and (ii) the court of appeals was limited to a consideration of "whether the final decision was consistent with the standards and procedures specified in the military order referred to in subparagraph (A); and to the extent the Constitution and laws of the United States are applicable, whether the use of such standards and procedures to reach the final decision is consistent with the Constitution and laws of the United States."

Section 1005(f) stated that "Nothing in this section shall be construed to confer any constitutional right on an alien detained as an enemy combatant outside the United States."

Section 1005(g) defined the United States, "when used in a geographic sense," to encompass the territory defined in section 101(a)(38) of the Immigration and Nationality Act, and "in particular, does not include the United States Naval Station, Guantanamo Bay, Cuba." In adopting this provision The President and Congress reasserted that the United States occupied the Naval Station resulting from the 1898 leasehold agreement and that the United States could not claim sovereignty over the area. The statute was a repudiation of the Supreme Court's 2004 holding in Rasul v. Bush that in habeas corpus matters the jurisdiction of the United States extended to "aliens held in territory over which the United States exercises plenary and exclusive jurisdiction, but not 'ultimate sovereignty.'"[8]

Section 1005(h) fixed the effective date of the legislation, namely "the date of the enactment of this Act." It was signed on December 30, 2005. Section 1005(h) also fixed the date for the review of CSRTs and Military Commission Decisions. It provided with respect to any claim whose review is governed by paragraphs (2) and (3) of subsection (e) that such paragraphs "shall apply with respect to any claim that is pending on or after the date of the enactment of this Act."

Section 1006 of the act provided for the Training of Iraqi Forces Regarding Treatment of Detainees. They were to receive training "regarding the international obligations and laws applicable to the humane detention of detainees, including protections afforded under the Geneva Conventions and the Convention Against Torture." The instruction was to be carried out by DOD personnel and "contractor personnel" of the DOD. So that the instruction would be effective the DOD was instructed to provide an Arabic and other translations of the US Army Field Manual on Intelligence Interrogation. The Secretary of Defense was instructed to submit copies of regulations, policies, and orders to the Armed Service Committees of the Congress. The first report was due not less than 30 days following their issuance, with an annual report to be submitted in due course.

A number of the provisions of the statute immediately attracted adverse criticism both at home and abroad. Highlighted was the withdrawal from the federal courts of the power to issue writs of habeas corpus. The writ, considered to be the guardian of individual rights against arbitrary governmental misdeeds and mistakes, has long been a coveted foundation stone basic to individual freedom and liberty. The withdrawal of such a protection should, it was argued, almost never be contemplated, and the threats of unlawful alien enemy detainees, committed to acts of terrorism, though very grave in their consequences, still remained an insufficient reason to change the rules. The statute with its provisions for review of CSRT and Military Commission holdings by the United States Circuit Court for the District of Columbia, it was argued, although not preventive in nature, allowed for a sufficient consideration of the administrative holdings of CSRTs and the criminal convictions of Military Commissions so that a fair outcome, though delayed, would result ultimately. This, of course, provided no solace to the uncertain prospect of a court of appeals ruling. A further fact must be taken into account. The number of detainees held at Guantanamo, many for a period up to five years, has varied from a high of about 600 to around 400. By mid-2007 the figure was down to about 350. Only a relatively few had been accorded a habeas corpus hearing. Would petitions for a writ from so many persons inundate the courts in those judicial districts where the filings are most likely to occur, so that, assuming that case loads otherwise would remain constant, judicial procedures could not take place in a timely manner? That this is not a casual matter can be reflected in the fact that in many districts the courts are already heavily burdened with exceedingly heavy case loads leaving little room for additional cases and the timely resolution of them. The Padilla litigation is a case in point. The filing of motions, counter-motions, and judicial rulings, as well as the prosecution and defense of the case-in-chief, has consumed months at the trial court level. At the end it may well be the longest case in a Federal District Court in Florida. There has been a shortage in judicial appointments and confirmations resulting from Congressional rejections of new nominations to these tribunals. In those judicial districts where there remains a tremendous backlog in immigration-related cases, resulting from more aggressive border patrol efforts, the problem has reached a crisis level.[9] A further, and companion concern dealt with vesting the DOD with the authority to determine, though administrative processes, what disposition should be made of detainees. Do the procedural and substantive standards applicable to Military Commissions meet the standards of civilized justice? Was the required impartiality to be the hallmark only of judges engaged in the judicial process?

2. THE MILITARY COMMISSIONS ACT (MCA), OCTOBER 17, 2006

The Military Commissions Act of October 17, 2006,[10] was a further response to the strengthening view that the world, as a result of vigorous terrorist activities, was becoming a more dangerous place. The statute, despite serious efforts to resolve Executive and Congressional differences during its finalization, has been the subject of numerous criticisms. The vote in the House of Representatives was 253 in favor against 168. 219 Republicans and 34 Democrats voted for it while 160 Democrats and 7 Republicans plus one Independent, who voted "no." In the Senate the vote was 65 to 34, with 53 Republicans and 12 Democrats voting in favor, while 32 Democrats, one Republican and one Independent, voted "no." Influential Senators, while favoring the statute, have expressed doubts regarding the habeas corpus provisions and have proposed important amendments. In the Senate, where the debate centered on the habeas corpus provision, a motion to remove that section failed by a vote of 48 to 51. The debate has been described as "impassioned," and "deeply partisan." Senator Leahy stated that the administration had lost its "moral compass," and Senator Specter regarded the habeas corpus provision as "patently unconstitutional" and predicted that the Supreme Court would "clear it up."

The White House has refused to depart from its decision that Guantanamo and Bagram detainees be classified and prosecuted under military law and procedures and that reference of detainee problems to Article III Constitutional Courts must be highly restricted pursuant to the terms of the statute.

The Department of Defense charged with the enforcement and administration of the Act has moved slowly in the issuance of rules and regulations on procedural, investigative, and trial procedures. Perhaps the most serious charge that was levied was that detainees were held for extended periods and were faced with the prospect of indeterminate imprisonment.

Other serious criticisms were directed at the characteristics of military commissions and the absence of requirements that commissions comply in every respect with constitutional safeguards, the absence of constraints on measures employed in maintaining custody and control over the detainees, the procedures allowing for counsel to confer with detainee clients at Guantanamo, evidence and burden of proof in Commission hearings, the possibility that evidence resulting from torture or other forms of coercion might influence the decisional process, that appellate procedures might be flawed, and, in general, the fact that the detainees were subject to a lesser standard of justice than that available to American citizens or residents in the United States. Critics, influenced by Human Rights considerations, and fearful that guarantees contained in the Third Geneva Convention were being diluted, including its non-application to persons classified as "detainees," were challenged by those who contended that Al Qaeda was experiencing very substantial growth and that threats to national security were increasing. This was coupled with the retention in custody of those persons holding key intelligence contacts and who constituted ongoing threats to national security. The MCA amended the U. S. War Crimes Act. In doing so it specified that violations of the crimes set forth in Common Article 3 of the Geneva Convention were also crimes under American law

Despite these charges and counter-charges, sight should not be lost of the fact that the statute provided the government with a foundation upon which to build its governmental processes. The statute contained important definitions, identified in considerable detail unlawful conduct, sought to clarify the relation between the provisions of the statute with the guarantees set forth in the Uniform Code of Military Justice, contained statute of limitation provisions, extended the prohibitions under Federal law on cruel, inhuman, or degrading treatment or punishment to encompass all those in the custody or under the physical control of the United States, without regard for nationality or physical locations, and resulted in numerous Department of Defense directives designed to guarantee to all detainees common rights when faced by prosecution including a 238 page "Manual for Military Commissions" issued on January 18, 2007.

The Military Commissions Act was designed to negate many of the important holdings in the Supreme Court decision in Hamdan v. Rumsfeld. In responding to the Court's conclusion that the 2001 Presidential military commission did not meet the requirements of the 1949 Geneva Convention or the provisions of the UCMJ for a "competent tribunal," the 2006 statute endeavored to structure the new Military Commission so that it would meet the required criteria. The statute, while moving more closely to the general standards required for trials in Article III courts, did not grant to alien enemy detainees in U. S. custody at the Guantanamo Naval Station the right to claim and to use the writ of habeas corpus. The terms of the statute were so favorably received by the Bush administration that the President did not attach a typical signing statement in which claims of executive powers under the constitution were reserved. However, Section 2 of the statute may have supplied a reason. It reads: "The authority to establish military commissions under chapter 47A of title 10, United States Code, as added by section 3(a), may not be construed to alter or limit the authority of the President under the Constitution of the United States and laws of the United States to establish military commissions for areas declared to be under martial law or in occupied territories should circumstances so require."

The statute was divided into 10 sections containing over 200 provisions in 38 pages. The sections, in addition to number 2, dealt with Military Commissions, Amendments to Uniform Code of Military Justice, Treaty Obligations not Establishing Grounds for Certain Claims, Implementation of Treaty Obligations, Habeas Corpus Matters, Revisions to Detainee Treatment Act of 2005 Relating to Protection of Certain United States Government Personnel, Review of Judgments of Military Commissions, and Detention Covered by Review of Decisions of Combatant Status Review Tribunals of Propriety of Detention.

Each section was divided into subchapters, with Section 3 dealing with Military Commissions, containing General Provisions in Subchapter I, Composition of Military Commissions in Subchapter II, Pre-Trial Procedure in Subchapter III, Trial Procedure in Subchapter IV, Sentences in Subchapter V, Post-Trial Procedure and Review of Military Commissions in Subchapter VI, and Punitive Matters in Subchapter VII.

The General Provisions, Subchapter I, contained important definitions. Thus, #948a(1) defined "unlawful enemy combatant " to mean "(i) a person who has engaged in hostilities or who has purposefully and materially supported hostilities against the United States or its co-belligerents who is not a lawful enemy combatant (including a person who is part of the Taliban, al Qaeda, or associated forces); or (ii) a person who before, on, or after the date of the enactment of the Military Commissions Act of 2006, has been determined to be an unlawful enemy combatant by a Combatant Status Review Tribunal or another competent tribunal established under the authority of the President or the Secretary of Defense. #948a(2) defined "lawful enemy combatant" to mean "(A) a member of the regular forces of a State party engaged in hostilities against the United States; (B) is a member of a militia, volunteer corps, or organized resistance movement belonging to a State party engaged in such hostilities, which are under responsible command, wear a distinctive sign recognizable at a distance, carry their arms openly, and abide by the law of war; or (C) a member of a regular armed force who professes allegiance to a government engaged in such hostilities, but not recognized by the United States." #948a(3) defined "alien" as "a person who is not a citizen of the United States."

The provisions of the Act are so specific and detailed that it is not possible to identify all of them. For those selected for commentary reference will be made to the enumeration employed in the statute. The authors of the legislation were concerned over the relationship of the statute to Article 3 of the 1949 Geneva Conventions. Thus, in sub-section #948b. (f) it was provided that "A military commission established under this chapter is a regularly constituted court, affording all the necessary 'judicial guarantees which are recognized as indispensable by civilized peoples' for purposes of common Article 3 of the Geneva Conventions." The statute added in sub-section #948b.(g) that "No alien unlawful enemy combatant subject to trial by military commission under this chapter may invoke to Geneva Conventions as a source of rights."#948c. identified the persons subject to military commissions, namely, "Any alien unlawful enemy combatant is subject to trial by military commission under this chapter." The importance of this precise formulation, as opposed to the terms employed in the definitional provisions, has, as has been noted, served as the basis for protracted litigation following the initial holdings of the Military Commission.

Sub-section #948d., dealing as it does, with the jurisdiction of military commissions deserves mention. 948d.(a) provides that "A military commission under this chapter shall have jurisdiction to try any offense made punishable by this chapter or the law of war when committed by an alien unlawful enemy combatant before, on, or after September 11, 2001." 948d.(b) provided that Military Commissions under this chapter "shall not have jurisdiction over lawful enemy combatants. Lawful enemy combatants who violate the law of war are subject to chapter 47 of this title. Courts-martial established under this chapter shall have jurisdiction to try a lawful enemy combatant for any offense made punishable under this chapter."

#948d.(d) dealt with punishments. Under its terms "A military commission under this chapter may, under such limitations as the Secretary of Defense may prescribe, adjudge any punishment not forbidden in this chapter, including the penalty of death when authorized under this chapter or the law of war."

The Composition of Military Commissions, Subchapter II, in sub-sections 948h. through 948m. made provision for the organization and staffing of military commissions. The Pre-Trial Procedure, Subchapter III, in 948q. identified the requirements for charges and specifications. Section 948r. bore the title "Compulsory self-incrimination prohibited; treatment of statements obtained by torture and other statements." Sub-section 948r.(b) provided that "A statement obtained by the use of torture shall not be admissible in a military commission under the chapter, except against a person accused of torture as evidence that the statement was made." Sub-section 948r. in paragraphs (c) and (d) distinguished between statements obtained before the enactment of the Detainee Treatment Act of December 30, 2005 and those made after its enactment. Both subparagraphs took into account a disputed claim relating to "the degree of coercion" experienced by a detainee and the admission of such a statement before a military commission. In the first time frame such a statement would be admissible "only if a military judge finds that (1) the totality of circumstances renders the statement reliable and possessing sufficient probative value; and (2) the interests of justice would be best served by admission of the statement into evidence." In the second time frame the same conditions would be applicable. Added to them was the provision that "(3) the interrogation methods used to obtain the statement do not amount to cruel, in human, or degrading treatment prohibited by section 1003 of the Detainee Treatment Act of 2005."

The Trial Procedures, Subchapter IV, in sub-sections 949a. through 949o. made reference to rules, unlawfully influencing action of military commissions, duties of trial counsel and defense counsel, sessions, continuances, challenges, oaths, former jeopardy, pleas of the accused, opportunity to obtain witnesses and other evidence, defense of lack of mental responsibility, voting and rulings, number of votes required, military commission to announce action, and record of trial.[11]

The Sentences, Subchapter V, in sub-sections 949s. through 949u. identified prohibitions against cruel and unusual punishments, referred to maximum limits, and prescribed were confinements could take place. 949t., dealing with maximum limits, provided that "The punishment which a military commission under this chapter may direct for an offense may not exceed such limits as the President or Secretary of Defense may prescribe for that offense."

The Post-Trial Procedure and Review of Military Commissions, Subchapter VI, in sub-sections 950a. through 950j. dealt with error of law; lesser included offenses, review by the convening authority, appellate referral; waiver or withdrawal of appeal, appeal by the United States, rehearings, review by Court of Military Commission Review, review by the United States Court of

Appeals for the District of Columbia Circuit and the Supreme Court, appellate counsel, execution of sentence; procedure for execution of death sentence, and finality of proceedings; findings and sentences. 950i. fixed the procedures for the execution of a death sentence. In paragraph (b) it is provided that "If the sentence of a military commission under this chapter extends to death, that part of the sentence providing for death may not be executed until approved by the President. In such a case, the President may commute, remit, or suspend the sentence, or any part thereof, as he sees fit." The President pursuant to 950i.(c)(2) may not act until the legality of proceedings is final with finality being determined only after the judgment had been considered by the United States Court of Appeals for the District of Columbia, and, where possible only after the United States Supreme Court had completed its review.

Sub-section 950j. (b) was the first of two sub-sections of the statute dealing with habeas corpus jurisdiction-stripping provisions. It was identified under the heading of "Provisions of Chapter as Sole Basis for Review of Military Commission Procedures and Actions." A more detailed reference to 950j. appears below in connection with the provisions found in Section 7 of the Statute, which also contained jurisdiction-stripping provisions.

The Punitive Matters, Subchapter VII, in sub-sections 950p. through 950w. dealt with statement of substantive offenses, principals, accessory after the fact, conviction of lesser included offense, attempts, solicitation, crimes triable by military commission, and perjury and obstruction of justice; contempt. These sub-sections provide evidence of the wide sweep of the legal concepts and tools, particularly in the area of criminal law, that have been been brought to bear on those persons, identified as "alien unlawful enemy combatants," who have engaged in acts of terrorism against the United States. Taking into account the criticisms directed against some of the statute's provisions, the Military Commissions Act of 2006 constituted an impressive legal edifice bringing together a coherent approach to the punishment of those persons who using uncivilized methods have consciously dared to destroy and disrupt the well-being of Americans. The statute, on the whole, is a civilized response to those who have no attachment to a sense of community and the needs of a functioning society.

Sub-section #950p., a statement of substantive offenses, referred in paragraph (a) to "purpose." It states: "The provisions of this subchapter codify offenses that have been traditionally triable by military commissions. This chapter does not establish new crimes that did not exist before its enactment, but rather codifies those crimes for trial by military commissions." In paragraph (b) "effect," the following appears: "Because the provisions of this subchapter (including provisions that incorporate definitions in other provisions of law) are declarative of existing law, they do not preclude trial for crimes that occurred before the date of the enactment of this chapter."

#950v., "Crimes triable by military commissions," constitutes the practical heart of the statute. In paragraph (a)" Definition and Construction," the term "military objective" is defined as consisting of "(A) combatants; and (B) those objects during an armed conflict—(i) which by their nature, location, purpose, or use, effectively contribute to the opposing force's war-fighting or war-sustaining capability; and (ii) the total or partial destruction, capture, or neutralization of which would constitute a definite military advantage to the attacker under the circumstances at the time of the attack." In this paragraph a "protected person" is identified. The term means "any person entitled o protection under one or more of the Geneva Conventions, including—(A) civilians not taking an active part in hostilities; (B) military personnel placed hors de combat by sickness, wounds, or detention; and (C) military medical or religious personnel." This paragraph also provided a definition of "Protected Property." It also, under the heading of "Construction," referred to the "intent" specified in certain offenses identified in the following subparagraph (b). The statute stated that the specified intent "preclude[d] the applicability of such offense with regard to—'(A) collateral damage; or (B) death, damage , or injury incident to a lawful attack."

In #950v paragraph (b) "Offenses" the statute identified twenty-eight triable under the chapter "at any time without limitation." Among the offenses were torture, cruel or inhuman treatment, and intentionally causing serious bodily injury. In describing the elements of these crimes references were made to relevant legislation and to the RUDs attached by the United States in its ratification of CAT.[12]

950w. added to the powers of a military commission. Reference was made to perjury and obstruction of justice, and provided for the use of the contempt power. This paragraph also required the Secretary of Defense within 90 days of the enactment of the statute to submit to the Senate Committee on Armed Services and to the House of Representatives "a report setting forth the procedures for military commissions prescribed under chapter 47A of title 10, United States Code."

Section 4 of the Act dealt with amendments to the Uniform Code of Military Justice. They referred to the applicability of the Code to lawful enemy combatants and added to the Code the crime of conspiracy so that the Code would be consistent with the Act.

Section 5 was entitled "Treaty Obligations Not Establishing Grounds for Certain Claims." The Section referred to habeas corpus rights in a generalized prohibition applicable to persons seeking to invoke the jurisdiction of American courts. Paragraph (a) provided: "No person may invoke the Geneva Conventions or any protocols thereto in any habeas corpus or other civil action or proceeding to which the United States, or a current or former officer, employee, member of the Armed Forces, or other agent of the United States is a party as a source of rights in any court of the United States or its States or territories." Paragraph (b) listed all four of the 1949 Conventions as being included.

The statute contains many references to the Geneva Conventions. Section 948b(g) of the MCA states that [n]o alien unlawful enemy combatant subject to trial by military commission under this chapter may invoke the Geneva Conventions as a source of rights." The identity of the commission is not further specified but it appears to refer to the MCA commission.

Section 6 dealt with the "Implementation of Treaty Obligations." In subsection (a) reference was made to the "Implementation of Treaty Obligations." Subsection (b) referred to the "Revision of War Crimes Offense Under Federal Criminal Code." Subsection (c) dealt with the "Additional Prohibition on Cruel, Inhuman, or Degrading Treatment or Punishment." Section 6 was designed to tie together statutory and treaty provisions found in other enactments and agreements so that a consistent Statute would result. To achieve this goal Section 6.(a)(1) began by providing that "The acts enumerated in subsection (d) of section 2441 of title 18, United States Code, as added by subsection (b) of this section, and in subsection (c) of this section, constitute violations of common Article 3 of the Geneva Conventions prohibited by United States law." Section 6.(a)(2) continued the process of clarifying international commitments. Thus, entitled "Prohibition on Grave Breaches," this section stated: "The provisions of section 2441 of title 18, United States Code, as amended by this section fully satisfy the obligation under Article 129 of the Third Geneva Convention for the United States to provide effective penal sanctions for grave breaches which are encompassed in common Article 3 in the context of an armed conflict not of an international character. No foreign or international source of law shall supply a basis for a rule of decision in the courts of the United States in interpreting the prohibitions enumerated in subsection (d) of section 2441."

Section 6.(a)(3) contains several interesting and important provisions that relate to the separation of powers principle. While the reference in this statute is only to the Geneva Conventions, Congress acknowledged that the President, under the Constitution and under this section "has the authority for the United States to interpret the meaning and application of the Geneva Conventions and to promulgate higher standards and administrative regulations for violations of treaty obligations which are not grave breaches of the Geneva Conventions." However, out of an abundance of caution, the Congress in Section 6.(a)(3)(D) stipulated that "Nothing in this section shall be construed to affect the constitutional functions and responsibilities of Congress and the judicial branch of the United States." If there were something employed by Congress, and in this instance acting also on behalf of the judiciary, identified as a "legislative signing statement," the foregoing might well serve as a model.

Section 6(b) is entitled "Revision to War Crimes Offenses under Federal Criminal Code." It provided that "Section 2441 of title 18, United States Code, is amended—(A) in subsection (c), by striking paragraph (3) and inserting the following new paragraph (3): '(3) which constitutes a grave breach of common Article 3 (as defined in subsection (d)) when committed in the context of and in association with an armed conflict not of an international character; or'" and which added a new subsection(d) which incorporated common article 3 prohibitions. Included were torture, cruel or inhuman treatment, performing biological experiments, murder, mutilation or maiming, intentionally causing serious bodily injury, rape, sexual assault or abuse, and taking hostages.

Definitions of acts constituting torture and cruel or inhuman treatment were set forth in Section 6(b) (1)(2). Cross references identified other provisions of the Act for the meaning to be given to definitional terms. If changes were stipulated, they were identified. For example, with regard to paragraph "(E) the term 'serious mental pain or suffering' shall be applied for the purposes of paragraph (1)(B) in accordance with the meaning given the term 'severe mental pain or suffering' (as defined in section 2340(2) of this title), except that—(i) the term 'serious' shall replace the term 'severe' where it appears, and (ii) as to conduct occurring after the date of the enactment of the Military Commissions Act of 2006, the term 'serious and non-transitory mental harm (which need not be prolonged)' shall replace the term 'prolonged mental harm' where it appears."

The Section also dealt with the retroactive applicability of the amendments. Those, excepting as specified in subsection (d)(2)(E) of section 2441 of title 18, United States Code, were to take effect as of November 26, 1997, as if enacted immediately after the amendments made by section 583 of Public Law 105-118 (as amended by Section 4002(e)(7) of Public Law 07-273).

Section 6(c) sought to clarify and render consistent the restrictions dealing with the prohibition on cruel, inhuman, or degrading treatment or punishment appearing in the Constitution, federal statutes, and ratified treaties, including the RUDs attached by the United States to the CAT. The first limitation stated that "No individual in the custody or under the physical control of the United States Government, regardless of nationality or physical location, shall be subject to cruel, inhuman, or degrading treatment or punishment." The second limitation provided that "In this subsection, the term 'cruel, inhuman, or degrading treatment or punishment' means cruel, unusual, and inhumane treatment or punishment prohibited by the Fifth, Eighth, and Fourteenth Amendments to the Constitution of the United States, as defined in the United States Reservations, Declarations and Understandings to the United Nations Convention Against Torture and Other Forms of Cruel, Inhuman or Degrading Treatment or Punishment done at New York, December 10, 1984."

Section 7 of the Act contained the Act's second reference to habeas corpus matters. Of vast historical and value-laden significance any change in its meaning or availability was bound to touch on raw nerves. Since the principle is anchored in the Constitution and is considered to be of hallmark significance to the rule of law as implemented in America's judicial process, any modification that would reduce its availability and application would be most likely to evoke outrage and criticism. While it is true that the first statute granting courts the power over habeas corpus dates back to the founding of the Republic and that it has been modified from time to time, with the last change prior to the enactment of the War Commissions Act of 2006, which had been made in the Detainee Treatment Act of December 30, 2005, the adoption of Section 7 was seen as an excessive restriction on judicial powers and an extension of presidential powers. This occurred in the backdrop of constant calls for government secrecy, wire-tapping, an unpopular war where civil and political rights and liberties were already under siege which was, in the minds of many, being unnecessarily diminished, and where political dialogue often proceeded without taking into account the facts supplied by a reliable science and technology.

Evidence of such malfeasance was found in the provisions of Section 7. It amended Section 2241, title 28, United States Code, "by striking both the subsection (e) added by section 1005(e)(1) of Public Law 109-148 (119 Stat. 2742) [being the Detainee Treatment Act of December 30, 2005] and the subsection (e) added by section 1405(e) of Public law 109-163 (119 Stat. 3477) and inserting the following new subsection (e)(1): "No court, justice, or judge shall have jurisdiction to hear or consider an application for a writ of habeas corpus filed by or on behalf of an alien detained by the United States who has been determined by the United States to have been properly detained as an enemy combatant or is awaiting such determination." By this it is made clear that habeas corpus restrictions apply to all alien enemy combatants, not just to those held at the Guantanamo Naval Station. A new subsection (e)(2) extended the foregoing prohibition. It provided: "(2) Except as provided in paragraphs (2) and (3) of section 1005(e) of the Detainee Treatment Act of 2005 (10 U.S.C. 801 note) no court, justice, or judge shall have jurisdiction to hear or consider any other action against the United States or its agents relating to any aspect of the detention, transfer, treatment, trial, or conditions of confinement of an alien who is or was detained by the United States and has been determined by the United States to have been lawfully detained as an enemy combatant or is awaiting such determination."

Section 3 of the statute dealing with Military Commissions contains Subchapter VI entitled "Post-Trial Procedure and Review of Military Commissions." That Subchapter in subsection 950(j)(b) under the heading "Finality [of] proceedings, findings, and sentences" was the first of the statute's references to the non-availability of the writ of habeas corpus, stating: "Except as otherwise provided in this chapter and notwithstanding any other provision of law (including section 2241 of title 28 or any other habeas corpus provision), no court, justice or judge shall have jurisdiction to hear or consider any claim or cause of action whatsoever, including any action pending on or filed after the date of enactment of the Military Commissions Act of 2006, relating to the prosecution, trial or judgment of a military commission under this chapter, including challenges to the lawfulness of procedures of military commissions under this chapter." Subsection 950(j)(b) was relied on by the government in Hamdan/Khadr v. Gates, the 2007 Supreme Court case number 07-1156.[13]

Section 7 of the MCA established the effective date for that provision. It was to be the date of the Act's enactment and was to apply to "all cases without exception, pending on or after the date of the enactment . . . which relate to any aspect of the detention, transfer, treatment, trial, or conditions of detention of an alien detained by the United States since September 11, 2001." The effective date of the amendment appears to be the date of the presidential signature, i. e., October 17, 2006 rather then September 25, 2006 when the bill was adopted by the Congress.

It is a basic principle of United States law that a criminal statute has no retroactive force. Prior to September 25, 2006 members of Congress were aware that the Bush administration planned to limit the role of habeas corpus in detainee cases. On September 25 the Senate Committee on the Judiciary met to consider that possibility. Both Senators Specter and Leahy expressed the view that the denial of the writ to Guantanamo detainees was unconstitutional. (S. Hrg. 109-658, Serial No.J-109-113.D.) Senator Specter stated that the procedures for the governance of a Commission were almost non-existent and would result in prejudice to "those who may be charged with serious war crimes." Senator Leahy considered that the statutory terms of 950j.(b) "would perpetuate the indefinite detention of hundreds of individuals against whom the government has brought no charges and presented no evidence . . . [and that the] government has made very limited use of military commissions." He was also concerned that the statutory provision would be employed by enemies of the

United States "as a pretext for torture and indefinite detention without judicial review of Americans abroad."

A. PROPOSALS FOR THE REPEAL OF THE HABEAS CORPUS-STRIPPING PROVISIONS

Motivated by such considerations the two Senators introduced S. 4081 entitled "A bill to restore habeas corpus for those detained by the United States," more formally identified as the Habeas Corpus Restoration Act of 2006. The broad and preliminary contours of the bill were considered on September 25, 2006, with Senators Specter, Leahy, and Coryn stating their views. They were joined by a small but impressive number of witnesses, with additional submissions for the record. Senator Coryn stated that the purposes and provisions of the two statutes were to provide detainees with fair opportunities to demonstrate that they were not a threat to the United States, and cited the presence of Administrative Review Boards, Combatant Status Review Tribunals, Military Commissions, and the right to appellate review by the Court of Appeals for the District of Columbia, concluding that this combination provided Due Process for detainees "in a way that does not jeopardize this legislation . . ." In his view the process allowed for meaningful reviews and was "intended to satisfy the absence of ability to petition for a writ of habeas corpus." (Congressional Record P.S. 10064, September 25, 2006). He also observed that the statutory provisions met and exceeded the requirements for dealing with POWs in Article 5 of the 1949 Geneva Convention.

On December 5, 2006 Senator Specter publicly reviewed the status of existing habeas corpus legislation and the effect of the repeal of the habeas corpus provisions in the 2006 MCA. He referred to the two separate provisions in the statute. He identified the effect of each. The first constituted "A new paragraph in the habeas corpus statute, 28 U.S.C. Sec. 2241(e), that would bar any alien detained by the United States as an enemy combatant from filing a writ of habeas corpus. The new paragraph was to apply to all pending cases 'without exception' thereby barring all pending habeas corpus applications pending on behalf of Guantanamo Bay detainees." (Congressional Record: December 5, 2006 (Senate) Page S11197-S11199).

He then referred to Section 950j(b) of the MCA characterizing it as "[a]n entirely new habeas corpus limitation that barred any habeas corpus review of military commission procedures. Had this bill been passed before the Hamdan v. Rumsfeld case was decided, the Supreme Court would not have had jurisdiction to review and reject the military commission procedures that were at issue." He described the result that would be produced by the proposed statute, namely, it "would strike these two provisions from the law in their entirety, thereby restoring the right of aliens detained within U. S. territorial jurisdiction (including at Gitmo) to challenge their detention via file (sic) writs of habeas corpus." He added: "Because the Military Commission Act already completely repealed and superseded the habeas corpus limitations created by the Graham Amendment to the Detainee Treatment Act of 2005, the bill would restore the state of play before the DTA."

He concluded by referring to the "actual effect" of the bill. It would prevent the application of the MCA in federal courts with its denial of jurisdiction to hear 196 habeas corpus applications currently pending on behalf of detainees at the Naval Station. "This bill would restore jurisdiction and allow those cases to be decided on their merits. It would also allow habeas corpus challenges to military commission procedures."

He challenged the position taken by Senator Coryn with Senator Specter urging that the availability of CSRTs did not constitute an adequate and effective remedy for habeas corpus. He referred to the Supreme Court case of Swain v. Pressley (430 U. S. 372 (1977)) which had determined that "the substitution of a collateral remedy is neither inadequate nor ineffective to test the legality of a person's detention does not constitute a suspension of the writ of habeas corpus."

Senator Leahy considered the two habeas corpus provisions of the MCA to be ill-advised and vague. Referring to his belief that the government could detain any noncitizen declared to be an enemy combatant he called attention to the filing by the government in a Virginia Federal District Court case in which the government urged that the "Military Commissions Act allows the Government to detain any noncitizen declared to be an enemy combatant without giving that person any ability to challenge his detention in court." (Congressional Record: December 5, 2006 (Senate) Page S11197-S11199).

Despite the strong opposition to the jurisdiction-stripping provisions of the MCA, and the fact that those provisions would not have been enacted if three Senators had opposed the stripping provisions the issue has not been brought to a new vote in the Senate. Many senators are awaiting a propitious time to get approval of a habeas corpus provision referred to as the Habeas Corpus Restoration Act. On June 7, 2007 the Senate Judiciary Committee voted 11 to 8 in support of the measure. Many influential members of the House of Representatives have also called for the repeal of the present provision. Pending any future Supreme Court decision, the statute has been enforced.[14] Then, on June 12, 2008 the Supreme Court in Boumediene v. Bush, in a 5-4 opinion, held that persons identified as unlawful alien enemy combatants held at the Guantanamo Naval base were entitled to have access to the constitutional privilege of habeas corpus.[15]

NOTES

1. Pub. L. 109-359.

2. http://www.defense link.mil.pubs/> Critical parts appear in 100 ASIL, No.4, 943, October 2006. An earlier Memorandum, dated June 3, 2005, had been issued by the Assistant Secretary of Defense to all very high level DOD officials and to military commanders entitled "Medical Program Principles and Procedures for the Protection and Treatment of Detainees in the Custody of the Armed Forces of the United States." It called for the use of accurate and complete medical records, identified treatment purposes, allowed for the disclosure of medical records in stipulated situations, mandated the reporting of possible violations, including circumstances in which it was suspected that a detainee had received "inhumane treatment," and required that health care personnel involved in the treatment of detainees or other health care matters receive appropriate training in applicable policies and procedures regarding the care and treatment of detainees.

3. http://www.fas.org/irp/doddir/army/fm2-22-3.pdf.>

4. FM 2-22.3, Section 1–20, p. 18.

5. Ibid., Section 5-50, p. 89.

6. See Infra, Chapter 12.

7. 119 Stat. 2742.

8. 542 U. S. 466, 124 S. Ct. 2686 (June 28, 2004).

9. Taking Arizona as an example, with many immigration prosecutions, the Federal District Court case load between September 1996 and December 2006 increased by 94 percent. For the court in Tucson the case load jumped 112 per cent in the same period. In 1996 there were 1,800 criminal felony filings, and in 2006 there were more than 3,500. For Arizona the average number of sentencings per federal judge in 2006 was about 100 per year. But, by 2007 each of the five Tucson judges averaged 604 per year. Public defenders have indicated that the system was "overwhelming," with concerns for sub-standard legal representation. The log-jam in judicial appointments, if broken, or the creation of new judgeships, would also require the employment of additional staff so that the work of the court could be done. While the courts with numerous immigration cases and those confronted with requests for the issuance of the writ of habeas corpus are dissimilar in many respects, the common theme is one of effective legal counsel and prompt access to the courts. Christian Science Monitor, May 7, 2007, p.11.

10. Pub. L. 109-366, 120 Stat. 2600. The Military Commissions Act was reviewed by four authors in Agora, 101 AJIL, No. 1, 35, January 2007 and by three more in Agora (continued) in 101 AJIL, No. 2, 322, April 2007. In the April Agora J. M. Beard in "The Geneva Boomerang: The Military Commission Act of 2006 and U. S. Counterterror Operations," refers to choices of descriptive terms. He states "The term 'law of war' is referenced throughout the MCA and was applied by the Supreme Court in Hamdan as it was incorporated in the U. C. M. J. It is commonly used interchangeably with 'international law of armed conflict,' 'jus bello,' and 'international humanitarian law.' While 'law of war' is not defined in the MCA, Department of Defense

(DOD) regulations define it as "that part of international law that regulates the conduct of armed hostilities' and further specify that the term 'encompasses all international law for the conduct of hostilities binding on the United States or its individual citizens, including treaties and international agreements to which the United States is a party, and applicable customary international law.' DoD Law of War Program, DoD Directive 2310.01E, sec.3.1. (May 9, 2006). p. 58, f. 5."

11. Ibid.

12. This section is dealt with in Chapter 5, section 4.

13. Infra, Chapter 8, F.

14. Undoubtedly the views expressed by Alexander Hamilton in the 84th Federalist Paper, May 28, 1783, will be referred to. Grouping the need to protect the writ of habeas corpus with the prohibition of ex post facto laws and prohibitions on the granting of titles of nobility, he wrote that they provided a greater security to liberty and republicanism than any other constitutional provisions. He added: :"For the State to take away a man's life, to confiscate his estate, by violence and without accusation in trial and the practice of arbitrary imprisonments have been the most formidable instruments of tyranny." Bad as these were he added the views of Sir William Blackstone that a secret confinement in "gaol" "where sufferings are unknown or forgotten, is a less public, a less striking, and therefore a more dangerous engine of arbitrary government." He concluded by quoting Blackstone: "The writ of habeas corpus is the BULWARK of the British Constitution." (Capitals in original.)

15. See Chapter 9.

Chapter Nine

The Courts Become Engaged in and Are Confronted by Serious and Somewhat Novel Problems in the Context of the Separation of Powers Principle—Leading Cases

1. INTRODUCTION

Courts, both American and foreign, have been asked to rule on terrorist activities and torture. In American courts the detainees held at the Guantanamo Naval Station have laid claim to constitutional guarantees such as access to Federal District courts through writs of habeas corpus and via allegations of violations of provisions of the Fifth and Eighth Amendments. These cases have been based on claims of torture and the other lesser included offenses practiced on the detainees while in custody. In several cases where an alien, charged with terrorist acts, was captured in the United States and not held at Guantanamo, prosecutions have been instituted in Federal District Courts. In one case (Jose Padilla), where a U. S. citizen was arrested in the United States and not held at Guantanamo, based on charges of terrorist activity in Afghanistan, initial custody and control was vested in military authorities, and it was not until it was ruled that he could claim the benefit of the Constitution that his case was transferred to a Federal District Court. The Bush administration has taken the position that wherever possible military proceedings should replace civilian courts in determining the disposition of alien detainees. Thus, a system of Administrative Review Boards, Combat Status Review Tribunals, and Military Commissions was created to determine the rights and duties of the Guantanamo Bay detainees. When the first Military Commission established by Executive Order on November 13, 2001 was declared unconstitutional it was replaced by the version identified in the 2006 Military Commissions Act. Military authorities were slow in implementing the Commissions, but they are now functioning.

American courts have now been asked to respond to plaintiffs' cases in which detainees, such as Jose Padilla, through a tort action commenced by his mother, seek to hold high ranking Department of Defense officials financially responsible for the practices causing harm to him while in military detention.

A third class of cases are those instituted in foreign jurisdictions alleging that the Secretary of Defense and Army officers exercising command responsibilities had caused or allowed torture and the other included offenses to be practiced on them while in detention. These cases are criminal cases.

A. Rasul v. Bush, President of the United States (June 28, 2004, 124 S. Ct. 2686); Al Odah v. United States (June 28, 2004, 124 S. Ct. 2686)

A brief reference to these cases was made in Chapter Three. It will be recalled that the exercise by the United States at the Guantanamo Naval Station of complete jurisdiction and control, as agreed to in the lease agreement of 1903, was treated in Rasul v. Bush as the equivalent of national sovereignty.

By 2008 appeals had been perfected to the United States Supreme Court in six major detainee cases. Rasul v. Bush and Al Odah v. United States were decided in 2004. A companion case, Hamdi v. Rumsfeld (124 S. Ct 2633) was also decided in 2004. The fourth, Rumsfeld v. Padilla (124 S. Ct. 2711) was decided the same year. Hamdan v. Rumsfeld (126 S. Ct. 2749) was decided in 2006. Boumediene v. Bush and its companion case, Al Odah v. United States, were decided in 2008. Each case dealt with serious legal problems that resulted from the activities of terrorists, both within the United States and abroad, and in which both U. S. citizens and aliens were engaged.

These important cases, along with those following below, were the first to reach the Supreme Court, dealing with the wars in Iraq and Afghanistan. All centered around constitutional provisions, statutory enactments, executive orders, customary international law, and international agreements to which the United States is a party. Raised for consideration was their application to aliens held by United States military personnel, captured outside the United States, and referred to as unlawful military combatants. They were the detainees held at the Guantanamo Naval Base. Another series of cases dealt with alleged terrorists, consisting of both aliens and U. S. citizens, captured within the United States. Other cases dealt only with U. S. citizens captured while fighting for Al Qaeda in Afghanistan.

Shahfig Rasul, a Kuwati national, along with 13 others, including David Hicks, an Australian, were captured in Afghanistan. Believed to be terrorists engaged in hostile military activities they were removed to the Naval Base. Seeking release and relying on petitions for writs of habeas corpus filed on their behalf by relatives, who were described as "best friends," they were not successful in obtaining the writs in the District Court in the District of Columbia.[1] The trial court held that it did not have jurisdiction. Authority to grant the writs was based on 28 U.S.C. Section 2241–2243. The applicants also raised 28 U.S.C. Section 1331, the federal question statute, the Tort Claims Act, 28 U.S.C. 1350, and the Administrative Procedures Act, 5 U.S.C. Sections 555, 702, and 706.

The claims of the detainees were that they were not combatants, had never engaged in acts of terrorism, no charges of wrong-doing had been made despite lengthy detentions, consultation with counsel had not been permitted, meetings with family members had not been allowed despite requests, and that they had been treated harshly. No allegations were made respecting torture or inhuman and cruel acts by the captors. The trial court based its holding on the Supreme Court case of Johnson v. Eisentrager, (339 U.S. 763 , 1950) which had ruled that aliens held outside the sovereign territory of the United States were not entitled to habeas corpus relief. That decision was deemed to be controlling since Eisentrager was a German citizen, captured in China by American soldiers, and after having been convicted in a military commission for violations of the laws and customs of war, had been jailed in an American military prison located in Germany. The trial court stated that the 1903 lease arrangement did not create a de facto sovereignty in favor of the United States. It concluded that the detainees' situation was no different than the one confronting Eisentrager. The matter was then appealed to the Circuit Court for the District of Columbia. It upheld the ruling of the lower court stating that "the 'privilege of litigation' does not extend to aliens in military custody who have no presence in 'any territory over which the United States is sovereign.'"[2]

When the Rasul case reached the United States Supreme Court it held that the Guantanamo detainees had the right to challenge the legality of their detention in federal courts. The holdings of the two lower courts were reversed. Distinctions were made. First, it was observed that Rasul petitioners were "not nationals of the countries at war with the United States" while the defendants in the Eisentrager case had been "alien enemies," namely "subjects of a foreign state at war with the United States." Second, the Eisentrager petitioners had been tried and convicted in a Military Commission that had been properly established and their convictions had been reviewed and approved by the military authority which had established the Commission. Third, the Eisentrager prisoners had never been in the United States while the Rasul petitioners had been held in custody for two years. The majority, while accepting the general proposition that the laws of the United States should not have extraterritorial application, this was deemed inapplicable since for all practical purposes the Naval Base was within the territorial jurisdiction of the United States. Fourth, the majority declined to follow the Eisentrager holding since subsequent decisions had overruled the statutory predicate to its holding. The question was whether statutory provisions relating to habeas corpus, which had not been modified since the Eisentrager decision, required that habeas corpus petitioners be physically present within the territory where the Federal District Court was located. Since the petitioners were being held at the Naval Base it was concluded that the lower court had dismissed the petition for the writ on statutory rather than constitutional grounds. It was deemed that when the Eisentrager case had been decided that the court had ruled that the Constitution, independent of ensuing legislation, did not guarantee access to the federal court system. Thus, Justice Stevens in summarizing the Eisentrager holding stated that that court had looked "only to the question of the prisoners' constitutional entitlement for judicial review." He also stated that the only mention of a statutory entitlement was "a passing reference" to its absence. Justice Stevens concluded that there was little reason to think that Congress intended the statute's territorial coverage to vary depending on the citizenship of a detainee. Further, the fact that that the petitioners were being held in a military prison was "immaterial." In the Rasul case the views expressed in the Eisentrager case on the unavailability of habeas corpus were disavowed. In Rasul the Supreme Court based its ruling on the application of 28 U.S.C. section 2241, not the Constitution.

The majority, consisting of Justices Stevens, Souter, Kennedy, Ginsburg, and Breyer, observed that the detainees might have valid causes of action for non-habeas claims. In doing so they would have to meet the burden of proof that the Federal Tort Claims Act or the federal question statute were relevant.

Justice Kennedy, while supporting the results announced by the majority, objected to the controlling reasons. He would have followed the "framework" of the Eisentrager decision in approaching the habeas corpus issue. He preferred that the Rasul case be considered "against the backdrop of the constitutional command of separation of powers . . ." and that there was a "realm of political authority over military affairs where the judicial power may not enter." He accepted the proposition that the Naval Base was "a United States territory," and concluded that the indefinite detention of the detainees and the absence of "any legal proceeding to determine their status . . ." required judicial intervention.

A dissenting opinions was written by Justices Scalia in which Chief Justice Rehnquist and Justice Thomas joined. Justice Scalia, relying on constitutional rather than statutory grounds, would have applied the Eisentrager ruling. He argued that the Court of Appeals had decided the case by referring to statutory requirements rather than the Constitution. He relied on the canon of constitutional avoidance to support a statutory interpretation, which if invoked, would, in his view present constitutional difficulties. He also emphasized, because of the existence of many Federal District Courts the practical difficulties that would be experienced if trials were to be conducted within the United

States. Reference was made to the availability of witnesses and their pre-trial availability. He suggested that Congress could remedy the problem by establishing a district court sitting at the Naval Station. This was consistent with his view that the Supreme Court had wrongfully become a decision maker when that role had been conferred by the Constitution on Congress. His outlook was captured in this sentence: The majority ruling "was a novel holding [and] contradicted a half-century of precedent on which the military undoubtedly relied . . . an irresponsible overturning of settled law in a matter of extreme importance to forces currently in the field . . ."

The DOD responded on July 7, 2004, with the issuance of a Memorandum to the Secretary of the Navy entitled "Order Establishing Combatant Status Review Tribunal." Applying "only to foreign nationals held as enemy combatants in the control of the Department of Defense at the Guantamamo Bay Naval Base," it created a forum, with identified procedures, to normalize investigations into continuing detentions of such persons.

B. Hamdi v. Rumsfeld; Al Odah v.United States (June 28, 2004) 124 S. Ct. 2633

Yaser Esam Hamdi was a U. S. citizen by birth. As a youth he was taken by his parents to Saudi Arabia. He fought with Taliban military forces in Afghanistan until captured. He was then removed to the United States as an alleged enemy combatant and held in a military prison. On June 11, 2002, his father obtained a Federal District Court order requiring access to counsel by Hamdi and that a Public Defender was to have unmonitored access to his client. The government appealed the ruling regarding access to counsel. The appeals court denied unmonitored access to counsel.

In August, 2002, the trial court examined a governmental declaration designed to show that the accused was an enemy combatant. The judge determined that the declaration failed to demonstrate that the accused fell into that category. On January 8, 2003, the Court of Appeals ruled against Mr. Hamdi and remanded the matter to the trial court . It held that Mr. Hamdi should be accorded counsel. In doing so it cited precedents holding that federal courts must accord "great deference" to a President's "wartime detention decisions." The court then rejected the governments proposal that in the absence of a judicial ruling that "any American citizen alleged to be an enemy combatant could be detained indefinitely without charges or counsel on the government's say so." It was ruled that if Mr. Hamdi were an "enemy combatant" then his detention would be lawful. At the same time the court observed that "detention of enemy combatants serves critical functions." The target was to obtain foreign military information and the knowledge of conspiracies. The detainee was prevented from engaging in terrorist activities and from returning to a field of battle.

Of greater importance was the presentation of separation of powers issues. The Court of Appeals cautiously observed that "the review of executive branch decisions premised on military determinations made in the field carries an inordinate risk of a constitutionally problematic intrusion into the most basic responsibilities of a coordinate branch." And, " [t]he constitutional allocations of war powers affords a President extraordinarily broad authority as Commander in Chief and compels courts to assume a deferential posture in reviewing exercises of this authority."

To Mr. Hamdi's contention that his ongoing detention was unlawful since "the relevant hostilities have reached an end," the court responded: "Whether and when it would be open to this Court to find that a war though merely formally kept alive had in fact ended, is a question too fraught with gravity even to be adequately formulated when not compelled,"[3] With the nation engaged in large scale military activities special significance was given to the separation of powers principle.

In approaching the question of counsel for Mr. Hamdi the appeals court asked if he were subject to prosecution during his detention. Finding that he had not been charged with a crime the appeals court decided he was not entitled to counsel. The court stated: "As an American citizen, Hamdi would be entitled to the due process protections normally found in the criminal justice system, including the right to meet with counsel, if he had been charged with a crime. Hamdi's citizenship rightfully entitles him to file this petition to challenge his detention, but the fact that he is a citizen does not affect the legality of his detention as an enemy combatant." The holding that he was entitled to access to habeas corpus proceedings, but not allowed to have counsel, produced a great outcry with much sentiment favoring an appeal to the United States Supreme Court.[4]

In December 2003 the case took on a new direction. The Public Defender representing Mr. Hamdi had asked the Supreme Court to rule on whether his client could be imprisoned without access to counsel and in the absence of charges against him. On the day prior to the government's response it withdrew from is position relating to the right to counsel and agreed to such representation. This was conditioned by the claim that such representation was "not required by domestic or international law and should not be treated as precedent."[5] The government added that it was acting only "as a matter of discretion and military policy," and that there was "no general right to counsel under the laws and customs of war" and that it had the power to detain alleged combatants "at least for the duration of the conflict" without having to file charges against them.[6] In supporting these conclusions the government urged the need to interpret such matters in the light of the wartime detention of combatants, including U. S. citizens, rather than normal criminal prosecutions. The powers of the Commander in Chief were urged as imposing restrictions on those due process rights guaranteed in the constitution. This position was announced after Mr. Hamdi had been interrogated and was based on the proposition that counsel should not be allowed to interfere with intelligence gathering activities.

On appeal to the United States Supreme Court Mr. Hamdi raised questions based on the Due Process requirements of the 5th and Fourteenth Amendments, the 1949 Geneva POW Convention, and the provisions of the 2001 Authorization for the Use of Military Force Resolution (AUMF).[7] That statute had not made specific reference to the "detention" of persons captured in Afghanistan. It had granted to the President broad powers of enforcement.

The plurality opinion, written by Justice O'Connor, joined by Chief Justice Rehnquist and Justices Kennedy and Breyer, with concurrences and dissents in part by Justices Souter and Ginsburg, held that "Due Process demands that a citizen held in the United States as an enemy combatant be given a meaningful opportunity to contest the factual basis for that detention before a neutral decision maker" such as a "military tribunal." In arriving at this result she acknowledged that "Congress [had] authorized the detention of combatants in the narrow circumstances alleged here." This was in response to the government's argument that since Mr. Hamdi was an "enemy combatant" that he could be held "indefinitely—without formal charges or proceedings—unless and until it makes the determination that access to counsel or further proceedings is warranted." In responding to the President's decision that alleged terrorists could be confined for interrogation without fixed time limits, Justice O'Connor stated "It would turn our system of check and balances on its head to suggest that a citizen could not make his way to court with a challenge to the factual basis for his detention by the government." She added: The Constitution "most assuredly envisions a role for the three branches when individual liberties are at stake." In responding to the view that that Mr. Hamdi could be detained indefinitely she held that detentions terminated with the cessation of hostilities. Behind this determination was a concern that such persons might return to the field of battle or again take up arms against the United States.

She ruled that proceeding by way of a petition for a writ of habeas corpus to a Federal District Court was the proper procedure for invoking that court's jurisdiction. While noting that in principle Congress could suspend the writ, pursuant to the terms of the Constitution (invasions or rebellions), that Congress in the enactment of the Patriot Act had not suspended it.

Justice Scalia concluded that there had not been a military exigency making "resort to the traditional criminal process impracticable." Thus, he favored an ordinary criminal trial or an indictment based on treason. He stated that the place where Mr. Hamdi had been arrested, not on a foreign field of battle, was irrelevant when the captured person was a citizen of the United States.

Justice Thomas referred to the "war powers" of the President as they related to national security needs of the country. Emphasizing the importance of the separation of powers principle he stated that the "war powers" of the President could not be "balanced away" by the Court. This was based on the view that members of the Court lacked the ability and the background to weigh competing concerns correctly. He also stated that granting detainees access to the writ of habeas corpus was erroneous.

Following the decision the government, fearing that sensitive intelligence information might be compromised in further judicial proceedings, decided to terminate such proceedings. It struck a deal with Mr.Hamdi in which he agreed to return to Saudi Arabia where his parents were living, subject to his renouncing his U. S. citizenship. He promised not to sue the United States, not to return to the United States for 10 years, agreed to remain in Saudi Arabia for the next 5 years, and to advise the United States of any foreign travels for 15 years.

C. Padilla v. Rumsfeld (June 28, 2004) 542 U. S. 426

Jose Padilla was born in Brooklyn. As a civilian he was arrested by the F.B.I. in Chicago in May, 2002, following a flight from Cairo. He has been held in custody, first in military prisons, and since January, 2006, in a Florida federal jail, pending the outcome in 2007 of his trial in a Federal District court. Mr. Padilla during May, 2002, had been under surveillance following contacts with an Al Qaeda official in Pakistan. At his arrest the government stated that during his contacts with terrorists that he had learned how to construct a nuclear "dirty bomb" designed to spread radiation without a nuclear explosion. The government announced that Mr. Padilla had plans to steal radioactive materials in the United States so that he could perfect his plan.

However, no charges were brought. His detention was based on prior associations with terrorists with whom the United States was at war and on the belief he was a security threat. It was the government's position that his involvement in terrorist activities violated the laws and customs of war and that he was an unlawful enemy combatant.[8] On June 9, 2002 President Bush designated Mr. Padilla as an enemy combatant and referred to his having been "closely associated with Al Qaeda" while the "United States was at war."

Mr. Padilla obtained counsel who filed a petition for a writ of habeas corpus in the Federal District Court in New York City, naming as defendant Secretary of Defense Donald Rumsfeld. His theory was that he should be charged formally with violations of American laws and international law or released. If charged he would claim all of his constitutional rights to a fair trial.

On December 4, 2002 the court determined that the President possessed the authority to classify Mr. Padilla an unlawful enemy combatant under the laws of war and could be detained. However, it ordered the government to submit evidence to substantiate that finding. Continued custody was supported by the need to keep him from rejoining the enemy, that detention was an important tool in the war against terrorism, and that interrogation while in custody would provide intelligence information that could aid military and anti-terrorist operations. The trial court held that the writ of habeas corpus had been validly invoked to contest the detention and that Mr. Padilla had the right to consult with counsel in his application for the writ.

In its holding the District Court rejected Mr. Padilla's argument that the President as Commander in Chief had exceeded his authority in establishing a class of persons identified as unlawful enemy combatants.

The issue of Mr. Padilla's right to counsel can be addressed at two levels. First, counsel was allowed to appear in court to support the petition for the writ. Second, it was held that, because of his terrorist status, he was not entitled to counsel in determining his innocence or guilt. A distinction was made between the basic right of citizens to have counsel, and that of terrorists as members of groups with international roots and intent on using their typical violent measures. It was contended that terrorists could not be treated as ordinary criminals. To support this distinction the court would be obliged to accept that extreme measures were characteristically employed by terrorists.

The President had another option. He could have, because the United States had concluded that it was engaged in an existing "war" against terrorists, determined that Mr. Padilla was a POW. As such, he would be detained without any access whatever to a Federal District Court and released automatically when the war was over. Such an approach would have to demonstrate that Mr. Padilla had been engaged in a lawful military activity.

The case was certified on April 10, 2003, to the Court of Appeals for review. The principal issue was whether the President was permitted under the Constitution and by law to direct military authorities to detain illegal enemy combatants. At issue, also, was whether a terrorist type of detainee could consult with counsel, and, if so, under what circumstances.

The Court of Appeals announced its decision on December 18, 2003.[9] The majority held that the "detention was not authorized by Congress, and absent such authorization, the President did not have the power under Article II of the Constitution to detain as an enemy combatant an American citizen seized on American soil outside a zone of combat." The court ruled that the 1972 Federal Non-Detention Act established the conditions for detentions of U. S. citizens on American soil and that the 2001 War Powers Act did not create an exception, citing Youngstown Sheet & Tool Co. v Sawyer.[10] That decision had prevented President Truman from seizing steel mills during the Korean War. On the basis of that decision the majority held that the President did not have an inherent power to detain Mr. Padilla. Mr. Hamdi did not benefit from this ruling since he had been apprehended in Afghanistan. In February, 2004, the Pentagon granted Mr. Padilla further permission to consult, on a monitored basis, with counsel.

Secretary Rumsfeld appealed to the United States Supreme Court. On June 28, 2004, by a vote of 5-4, it reversed and remanded the decision of the lower court.[11] The majority consisted of Chief Justice Rehnquist, and Justices O'-Connor, Kennedy, Scalia, and Thomas. Dissenting Justices were Stevens, Souter, Ginsburg, and Breyer. This distribution is worthy of note since remaining issues in the other detainee cases will be decided by a new court as a result of the death of the Chief Justice, the resignation of Justice O'Connor, and the appointment of Court of Appeals Justice Roberts as Chief Justice. The latter, while serving on the appeals court, joined in a unanimous opinion in the case of Hamdan v. Rumsfeld in 2005,[12] which involved a Guantanamo detainee alleged to be an illegal enemy combatant.

In the Padilla case the following issues were presented to the Supreme Court: the authority of the President to classify a person as an "enemy combatant," and the rights of such person, the powers of the President as Commander in Chief, the use of force authorized by Article II of the Constitution, the detention of persons for a very long time, the Fifth Amendment dealing with Due Process, and whether Mr. Padilla in seeking habeas corpus relief in the Federal District Court in New York City had filed his petition in the wrong place and against the wrong person since at the time of the filing he was being detained in a military prison in Charleston, South Carolina. Of further relevance was whether a detainee could build a case on the terms of Section 2241 of Title 28 of the Federal Code which deals with the exercise of habeas corpus rights.

The majority held that the New York court did not have jurisdiction since Mr. Padilla was being held in South Carolina. This resulted in a reversal requiring Mr. Padilla to start anew naming his immediate custodian, the military commandant in South Carolina as the defendant, not the Secretary of Defense, and filing the action in South Carolina. The Court did not rule on the question whether the President could detain the accused on the basis of his military powers. Having ruled on the narrow issue of jurisdiction, the appeal was dismissed without prejudice.

The dissenting justices focused on the historic scope of habeas corpus. Justice Stevens described the case as "exceptional," and declared that the Court should not "suffocate the writ in stifling formalities" or "hobble its effectiveness." Owing to the extended detention of Mr. Padilla Justice Stevens noted that the "stakes in this case are those of a free society." He also called attention to the fact that during the detention the government would be engaged in "unlawful procedures to extract information."

Counsel for Mr. Padilla on July 2, 2004, filed a petition for the writ in the Federal District Court in Charleston. In this fresh start (Padilla v. Hanft, United States Navy Commander, Consolidated Naval Brig) the trial judge in a habeas corpus action ruled on February 28, 2005, that President Bush had exceeded the authority vested in him by federal statutes and the Constitution. He ordered that Mr. Padilla be released or that criminal charges be lodged against him or that he be held as a material witness.

The government then appealed to the Court of Appeals for the Fourth Circuit. On September 9, 2005, it unanimously reversed the trial court.[13] The appeals court, taking into account the facts before it, relied heavily on the Patriot Act (AUMF) whereby the President was "authorized to use all necessary and appropriate force against those nations, organizations, and persons . . . in order to prevent any future acts of international terrorism against the United States by such nations, organizations, or persons." It noted that the AUMF did not vary depending on the "locus of capture." It also observed that courts do not have the ability to weigh national security interests even though this increases the power of the executive branch and diminishes the role of Congress. Justification for the detention of Mr. Padilla was based on the need to prevent the return of combatants to the battlefield during the conflict. This rationale mirrored that identified by Justice O'Connor in Hamdi v. Rumsfeld which condition she identified as "a fundamental incident of waging war." The Court of Appeals in addressing the length of detention stated that the power to detain was "not a power to detain indefinitely. Detention is limited to the duration of the hostilities as to which the detention is authorized . . . Because the United States remains engaged in the conflict with a Al Qaeda in Afghanistan, Padilla's detention has not exceeded in duration that authorized in the AUMF."

The Court of Appeals rejected four arguments advanced on behalf of Mr. Padilla. First, an effort was made to distinguish his case, since he had been captured in Afghanistan, from that of Mr. Padilla, who had been arrested in the United States. The court deemed that the locus of the capture was irrelevant. Second, it was urged that the military detention was neither necessary nor appropriate since the accused might have been prosecuted in a civilian tribunal, where there was a possibility that he would qualify for bail. The response was that such a trial might not achieve the purpose of detention, i.e., preventing his return to the scene of battle. Further, it was considered that detention in a civilian jail would impede efforts to gather intelligence and might allow the accused to communicate with confederates with resulting harm to national security. Third, it was argued that the AUMF did not contain a clear statement authorizing detention. The court, after examining the terms of the statute and the holding in the Hamdi case, concluded that the statute was sufficiently clear and precise. Fourth, counsel for the accused asked the court to apply the holding set forth in Ex parte Milligan,[14] which had set aside a conviction in a military tribunal at a time and place where civilian courts were functioning. The appeals court found no difficulty in distinguishing Mr. Milligan, a newspaper editor, and Mr. Padilla.

In its summary the appeals court emphasized the fact that the accused had participated with Al Qaeda and the Taliban forces in fighting against the United States. Also, Mr. Padilla's purpose in returning to the United States was emphasized. He had "entered the United States for the avowed purpose of further prosecuting that war by attacking Americans and targets on our own soil . . ."

On October 2, 2005 counsel for Mr. Padilla asked the United States Supreme Court to issue a writ of certiorari. This was denied on April 3, 2006, thereby accepting the President's decision to hold Mr. Padilla for military prosecution.[15] Voting to deny certiorari were Chief Justice Roberts and Justices Stevens, Kennedy (who filed a concurring opinion), Scalia, Thomas, and Alito. Voting in favor of issuing the writ were Justices Souter, Ginsburg, and Breyer.

The majority in effect sidestepped the substantive issues relating to governmental authority over citizens detained since 9/11 by considering the appeal to be moot. This resulted from Mr. Padilla's being transferred to civilian custody. Their concern was reflected in their announcement that he would receive the "protections guaranteed to all federal criminal defendants." Justice Kennedy, joined by the Chief Justice and Justice Stevens, stated that they considered the denial of the writ as "a proper exercise of [the Court's] discretion in light of the circumstances of the case." He characterized the government's mootness argument as being based on the premise that Mr. Padilla, now having been charged with crimes and released from military custody, had received the principal relief he had sought. He noted that Mr. Padilla had responded by asserting that the case had not been mooted by the government's voluntary actions because there remained the possibility that he could be redesignated and retried as an enemy combatant. Without responding to these

contentions Justice Kennedy stated that there were "strong prudential considerations disfavoring the exercise of the Court's certiorari power." This outlook was based on "fundamental issues respecting the separation of power,
including consideration of the role and function of courts . . . , [which coun-
seled] against addressing those claims when the course of legal proceedings
has made them, at least for now, hypothetical. This is especially true given
that Padilla's current custody is part of the relief he sought, and that its lawfulness is uncontested."

The three dissenting justices asserted that it was high time and profoundly
important for the court to rule on the power of the executive branch to hold a
United States citizen in custody following his characterization as an enemy
combatant. Sharing Justice Kennedy's concern they noted that despite the
present prosecution in a civilian tribunal that there was nothing preventing the
executive branch from returning to the road that it had previously constructed
and defended.

Before the Supreme Court had ruled the government filed a motion in the
Court of Appeals for the 4th Circuit in the case of Padilla v. Hanft asking it
to order that Mr. Padilla be released from military custody and turned over to
civilian authorities for prosecution in the Federal District Court for the southern district in Florida.[16] The government also asked the Court of Appeals to
withdraw its ruling of September 9, 2005. Both motions were denied. Justice
Luttig on December 21, 2005, speaking on behalf of a unanimous court,
wrote an opinion highly critical of positions advanced by the Bush administration. He began by noting that the Supreme Court had not ruled on the September 9 decision. That was not to occur until January 1, 2006, when it overruled the Court of Appeals decision of September 9, 2005. He pointed out that
the alleged offenses being prosecuted in Florida were considerably different
and far less serious than those for which he had been held in military custody.
More specifically, the Florida indictments did not mention the acts of Mr.
Padilla upon which the government purportedly based its military detention
decision. These were the facts that the Court of Appeals had relied on in deciding that the President had the authority to detain Mr. Padilla, namely, his
having taken up arms against the United States in Afghanistan and his return
to the United States to blow up buildings as Al Qaeda prosecuted its war of
terrorism in the United States.

Justice Luttig then announced the reasons for not vacating the September
9 decision.[17] Since that date the government both in motions and in press
releases "has given rise to at least the appearance that the purpose of these
actions may be to avoid consideration of our decision by the Supreme
Court." Second, "aside from the need to protect the appearance of regular-
ity in the judicial process, we believe that the issue presented by the gov-

ernment's appeal to this court and Padilla's appeal to the Supreme Court is of sufficient national importance as to warrant consideration in the Supreme Court, even if that consideration concludes only in a denial of certiorari." Further, even though "the various facts it has asserted are not necessarily inconsistent or without basis, its actions have left not only the impression that Padilla may have been held for these years, even if justifiably, by mistake — an impression we would have thought the government could ill afford to leave extant." He added that "these impressions [of expediency] have been left, we fear, at what may ultimately prove to be substantial cost to the governments credibility before the courts, to whom it will one day need to argue in support of a principle assertedly of like importance and necessity to the ones that it seems to abandon today." It is not an exaggeration to say that no part of the Bush administration's campaign against terrorism has drawn a greater and longer challenge than the long-term detention of enemy combatants, both citizens and aliens.

1. *United States v. Jose Padilla, et. al. Federal District Court of Florida , Case No. 06-11585 (2005)*

This was followed by a series of legal maneuvers in which the government, despite its long effort to hold Mr. Padilla in military custody so that he might ultimately be tried by a Military Commission, reversed its position announcing that he would be prosecuted in a Federal District Court. This occurred on November 20, 2005, when President Bush instructed the Secretary of Defense to release Mr. Padilla to the Attorney General for criminal proceedings and to terminate his classification as an "enemy combatant." It was not, however, until January 1, 2006, that the Supreme Court granted the request of the government to transfer Mr. Padilla from military custody to a civilian jail in Florida. He was the first citizen arrested in the United States and designated by President Bush as an "enemy combatant" to face criminal charges in a civilian court. Also charged by the Florida grand jury were Adham Amin Hassoun, Kifah Wael Jayyousi, Mohamed Youssef, and Kassem Daher.

Prior to January 1, 2006 a grand jury had been impaneled in Florida and testimony had been received as to Mr. Padilla's alleged transgressions. The date of his first indictment was November 22, 2005. A variety of other charges including participation in a conspiracy with Mr. Padilla were brought against the other defendants named above. Counsel for Mr. Padilla presented a motion to the trial judge, Judge Marcia Cooke, asserting that the indictments were overlapping and repetitive and that Mr. Padilla could be subjected to double jeopardy. The motion was based on the indictments referred to above.

Count one dealing with "murder, kidnapping, or maiming outside the United States" was based on 18 U.S.C. 956(a)(1) and 18 U. S. C. #2. These involved a conspiracy to commit illegal violent acts outside the United States. Counts two and three, relating to a conspiracy to provide material support in furtherance of a # 956(a) violation and actually providing material support provision of material support and resources, were based on 18 U.S.C. 2339(A)(a). Material was defined as "property, tangible or intangible, or service, including training, expert advice or assistance in safekeeping of false documents, [use of] communications equipment, facilities, weapons, lethal substances, explosives, [and their] transportation." The conspiracy provision of count two, was based on 18 U.S.C. # 371. It criminalized conspiracies to commit offenses against the United States. According to Judge Cooke "Count two charges defendants with conspiring to commit the substantive offenses alleged in count three which in turn has as its object the offenses alleged in count one." She accepted the argument of the defendants that "the three counts essentially seek to punish them thrice for the same offense by alleging the same set of facts to prove what are, in their estimation, three indistinct charges." Accepting this line of reasoning the trial judge held that the indictments were "multiplictous" thereby allowing for double jeopardy. This interlocutory holding was appealed by the government to the Court of Appeals which reversed it and remanded the holding to the District Court with the instruction to "reinstate" count one of the current indictment. This was based on the view that a defendant "might violate one section without violating the other." It was the view of the appeals court that each indictment was based on a separate statutory prohibition and that none allowed for the merger of the different charges "into another lesser included offense." The early indictments of Mr. Padilla were superseded. At the time the trial jury was impaneled and sworn the indictments covered 31 pages with references to violations of ten federal statutes.

A trial date was set for January 22, 2007. This led to an extended filing of pretrial motions raising jurisdictional questions with Mr. Padilla seeking a dismissal of the case. This was to be accomplished through a ruling that coercive interrogations, including the use of torture in obtaining responses, flawed the government's case and were inadmissible in a civilian court. The defense claimed that torture had been employed overseas by the C.I.A. on a foreign terrorist, Zayn Abu Zubayday, an Al Qaeda member, who had then implicated Mr. Padilla. On September 6, 2006, President Bush stated that the C.I.A. had used "an alternate set of procedures," without detailing what they may have been. It was also Mr. Padilla's contention that his confessions had been coerced and had resulted from his having been held in solitary confinement and under harsh circumstances. The defendant's case was based on the proposition that Mr. Padilla was entitled to his day in court and that for more than 3½ years he had not been charged with a crime, for nearly two years he was prevented from consulting a lawyer, friends, or family, and that he had not been advised of his right to remain silent. Counsel for Mr. Padilla have asserted that prior to his arrest he had been searched and that the government had confiscated $10,000, his cell phone, and a phone book. Further, the government had moved Mr. Padilla from a jail in one jurisdiction to another in a different jurisdiction making it impossible for him to obtain judicial oversight. His counsel raised the question of whether the detention and the interrogations had so clouded his mind that from a mental point of view his confessions were untrustworthy and that he was so incapacitated that he should not be obliged to defend himself in court. His counsel described his ailment as "post-traumatic stress disorder," which was so grave that Mr. Padilla was not competent to stand trial and was not able to aid in his own defense. In a brief filed with the Federal District Court in Miami Mr. Hamdan's Public Defender stated that the "government's interrogation strategies and isolation techniques with regard to Mr. Padilla during his incarceration at the brig are at the outer limits of civilized propriety."[18] In responding to the mental stress experienced by the accused the government's technical experts identified his mental condition at the time of trial as "constituting an anxiety syndrome and antisocial personality disorder."[19] In the expert's opinion these conditions were not so severe as to interfere with some basic capabilities to assist in his defense.

This was followed in February, 2007, by testimony by two forensic psychology experts called by Mr. Padilla. Following their testing of the accused they concluded that he revealed a "strong indication of cognitive impairment" and a 98% probability of brain injury.[20] Both reported that Mr. Padilla feared that his Public Defenders were part of a government plot against him. A third expert, a clinical psychologist, testified that Mr. Padilla "suffered from a form of Stockholm syndrome in which a captive identifies with his aggressors because of a perception that they control your fate. When you are helpless and dependent on an all powerful group, it takes away your anxiety when you line up with them."[21] It was this expert's opinion that Mr. Padilla would not contradict the government for fear of reprisals. The government's further response was that the facts upon which the civilian trial was to proceed had been obtained independently of those that were obtained during his military detention and that there was no connection between the facts derived from the military detention and those arrived at independently and through the use of other means and at other times.

Following his indictment counsel for the accused again asked the trial judge, Marcia Cooke, to dismiss three of the charges on the ground they were virtually identical and could subject defendants to double jeopardy or over-lapping convictions and punishment for essentially the same act. She granted the motion relating to conspiracy to "murder, kidnap, and maim." On appeal to the 11th Circuit Court of Appeals in Atlanta this holding was reversed, with the court stating that "although they appear to be nested within one another, each stands alone from the others." Judge Cooke also ordered that the accused must undergo a mental competency examination. This occurred after Mr. Padilla's counsel had charged that while in custody he had been subjected to stress positions, to noise, to extreme temperatures, to noxious fumes, to forced hypothermia, had been given mind-altering drugs, and whose Koran was removed from his cell from time to time. During his incarceration Mr. Padilla was subject to constant (24-hours a day) video surveillance during which time he was experiencing extreme isolation while held in a window-less 9-foot by 7-foot cell. However, at one point the videotaping was sus-pended for 72 hours. His counsel asked for an account of the interrogations during that period. According to his counsel the interrogations consisted of "outrageous government conduct," amounting to torture, and that because of such behavior the case should be dismissed. The prosecution denied the alle-gations of torture alleging that no evidence had been presented. The prosecu-tion added that Mr. Padilla's correct remedy would be to sue his military in-terrogators in federal court for civil damages or to seek government prosecution of the alleged torturers. Judge Cooke endeavored to keep the is-sues of torture and mental competence separate, with the latter confined to Padilla's state of mind at the time of the district court proceedings thereby avoiding inquiries into his mental state while in military custody.

On February 28, 2007, Judge Cooke ruled that Mr. Padilla was fit to stand trial. She added that the ruling did not prejudice a reconsideration in the event that the trial disclosed that the defense's claim that Mr. Padilla had been the subject of "outrageous government conduct" amounting to torture and that a causal relationship could be established between torture and a mental condi-tion which would not make him fit to stand trial.

As counsel engaged in trial preparation the government disclosed that it possessed a "Mujahideen Data Form" allegedly completed by Mr. Padilla, but signed by him as "Abu Abdullah al Mujahir," one of the aliases used by Mr. Padilla, in July, 2000, prior to attending an Al Qaeda training facility in Afghanistan. Both sides presented arguments relating to its authenticity, with the government saying it would rely on a C.I.A employee, but stated that his identify could not be made known for security reasons.

Motions were made to Judge Cooke. She ruled, for example, that Mr. Padilla had not been deprived of a speedy trial saying that the federal case commenced with the Miami indictment. On the other hand, she ruled against the admission of evidence obtained in interrogations conducted during his military custody. In response to the government's contention that Mr. Padilla had become a willing recruit to engage in a violent Islamic holy war and his response that the government had entrapped him into becoming a jihads soldier, Judge Cooke in April, 2007, ruled that entrapment was a matter of proof and would be resolved in the course of the trial. Ultimately it was decided that the pretrial publicity depicting Mr. Padilla as a potential nuclear bomber had not prevented a fair trial. Finding a jury in Miami believed to be impartial proved to be time consuming. Almost everyone had heard of Mr. Padilla. Early in May, 2007, a panel was selected composed of five blacks, four whites, and three Latinos with a broad array of jobs, political leanings, and assumptions about terrorist activities. Seven were men; 5 were women. Both sides accused the other of trying to obtain a "stacked" jury. Alternates, having an equally diverse background, were also selected.[22] On May 18, 2007, the jury was reconfigured with its consisting of five Latinos, four whites, and three African Americans. The trial finally began on May 14, 2007.

The government endeavored to prove that Mr. Padilla voluntarily associated himself with other terrorists with common plans to imperil the security of the United States. The conspirators, other than Mr. Padilla, had engaged in rather modest, but nonetheless effective means to recruit and compensate terrorists. It was charged that by their conduct they had implemented their several goals. The defense sought to negate such charges, and attempted to persuade the jury that Mr. Padilla has already suffered more than was merited, particularly because the charges against him in final analysis were quite thin. Judge Cooke made it clear to counsel that she had separated the conspiracy charges from the initial dirty bomb allegations.

The case of Jose Padilla has served as a reminder of 9/11. Following that attack scholars in the field of terrorism revealed that terrorists, often under the guidance of Al Qaeda constituted a real threat in many parts of the world. These revelations by experts constituted a real surprise to many Americans. A system of colored-coded alerts has served as a reminder of the threats. Disclosures that many people living in the United States, both citizens and aliens, who have benefited from the privileges enjoyed in America, but who have engaged in acts of terrorism, has been hard to believe. This has been particularly true in the case of aliens in the United States possessing Arabic backgrounds. As residents in the United States they have enjoyed those democratic guarantees never available to them in the countries of their origins.

Their acts have demonstrated a lack of gratitude and appreciation for their new-found privileges. For American citizens, long schooled in a preferred way of life, such conduct has been particularly hard to understand. Their disruptive conduct, to the extent of violations of the law, has led to prosecutions.

Jose Padilla and his co-conspirators fit this description. They have obliged the United States to find a lawful procedure for their trials. The government's strategy and tactics in these cases has been far from its best and brightest in the history of American jurisprudence. Counsel for Mr. Padilla have summed the situation as "The treatment of Mr. Padilla, a natural born citizen of he United States, is a blot on this nation's character, shameful in its disrespect for the rule of law, and should never be repeated."[23]

In approaching this task the United States was obliged to select the forum for prosecutions. In the case of Mr. Padilla the first choice was a military tribunal. The second choice was a Federal District court, a civilian tribunal. This followed the example of the prosecution of John Walker Lind, an American citizen, for terrorism. He, by contrast, had been apprehended in Afghanistan. His prosecution ended in a plea bargain negotiated by a highly-experienced American criminal lawyer. Arrived at when 9/11 was fresh in the minds of the public and the parties, a lengthy jail term was agreed to. As the Padilla case moved into its final stages, and with its disposition of the accused still unresolved, speculation arose as to his possible sentence—which could be the death penalty—and , if it were less than the death penalty, whether it would be commensurate with that of Mr. Lindh. Such speculation was based on different situations. Even in similar ones the question had to be whether there had been, or even could be, a base for a fair and impartial determination. The scales of justice sometimes find true, but variable facts, hard to resolve.

The Padilla case, based on the early impulse to establish an operational distinction between military and civilian tribunals for detainees, resulted in military custody. However, the logical next step of prosecution did not take place for over 3 years since an appropriate military tribunal did not exist and plans for a Military Commission had not materialized. This required a reconsideration of the strategy and tactics for the identification of the tribunal to be given jurisdiction in the prosecution. As Supreme Court cases began to impose limits on the executive branch options began to diminish. Expediency prevailed. Mr. Padilla went to trial in the Federal District court in Miami.

During the period of Mr. Padilla's military incarceration the factual bases, as reflected in the civilian indictments, were very materially modified. The original arrest was based on the proposition that he was engaged in acquiring nuclear components so that a dirty bomb could be activated and exploded in the United States. At the time of his trial these had been superseded with charges of terrorist activity and conspiracy with other persons (aliens) to cause death to persons and destruction of property. Because of the superseding indictments the trial judge warned government lawyers not to refer to the dirty bomb episode.

During his military custody Mr. Padilla had been subjected to intense interrogation under a variety of coercive conditions. Whether these measures had risen to the level of torture was never decided. Judge Cooke ruled that there could not be any reference by counsel for the accused to the fact that he had been interrogated while being detained as an "illegal enemy combatant." At issue was the meaning to be assigned to the word "torture," and this entailed reference to federal legislation, the CUDs to the CAT, the numerous instructions, rules, regulations, and Field Manuals detailing what was considered to be acceptable practice and what was not to be permitted.

In bench rulings Judge Cooke had the benefit of numerous amicus briefs filed on behalf of the accused by academics, special interest groups engaged in the protection of civil and political rights and liberties, and Human Rights. These were intended to provide legal and intellectual support to the Public Defender. Counsel drawn from the Departments of Justice and Defense and the armed forces were able to demonstrate their special expertise in these matters. They also benefited from amicus briefs.

Of course, the final outcome depended on more than legal briefs, especially in a jury trial. The litigation skills reflected in verbal presentations, and a knowledge of court room procedures, played important roles. Opening and closing statements on the part of counsel were intended to highlight key points. Counsel for the Arabic coconspirators emphasized that funds allegedly had been collected and dispersed only for humanitarian purposes. Convictions carried the death sentence. All defendants were convicted. Judge Cooke was scheduled to announce the sentences on December 5, 2007. The sentencing was postponed. In the meantime speculation has developed as to what punishments fit the crimes. Opinion has centered on a term of years, time off for brig time, and a reduction of time served as a result of the treatment they experienced while in custody.

In the sentencing briefs filed with the court quite disparate views found expression. The government emphasized that the accused had been trained as an Al Qaeda "killer". Further, "Padilla's contribution to the charged conspiracies was unique, and uniquely fanatical and dangerous." Counsel for the accused stated that the government had "offered no evidence of any sinister motive" and that "there is no evidence that Mr. Padilla ever sought to harm an innocent person." On January 22, 2008, Mr. Padilla was sentenced to a period of imprisonment of 17 years and 4 months. The federal sentencing guideline, with its "terrorism enhancement" provision required a minimum of 360 month's imprisonment. Judge Cooke referred to the long period of solitary confinement and the fact that no one was harmed in rejecting the application of the "terrorism enhancement" provisions.

The ramifications of this trial extended far beyond the federal courthouse in Miami. Daily accounts flooded the worldwide media, with editorials and opinions, scholarly and otherwise, being widely disseminated. The trial attracted international attention since in many parts of the world the case was viewed from the perspective of America's conformity with the precepts of the world rule of law. Undoubtedly, in due course, the decision of the trial court and probably the opinions of appellate tribunals, will be summarized in the report of the United States representative to the United Nations Committee Against Torture. This will be reviewed by the members and observations will be forthcoming, allowing the United States respond to what it may consider to be misunderstandings or misperceptions.

A separate, but closely related, subject will be the impact of this case on the Combatant Status Review Tribunals cases and the Military Commission cases involving the classification and the disposition of alien enemy combatants in custody at the Guantanamo Naval Station.

2. *LeBron v. Rumsfeld, et al., Federal District Court of South Carolina 07-cv-94, (February 9, 2007)*

On February 9, 2007, Estalla LeBron, mother and next of friend of Jose Padilla, filed a civil action against Secretary Rumsfeld and 59 other United States federal officials for abuses occurring during his military detention. Filed in a Federal District Court in South Carolina, prior to the outcome of the criminal proceeding in Florida, against highly placed governmental officials including Mr. Rumsfeld, the new Secretary of Defense, Robert Gates, former Attorney-General John Ashcroft, former Deputy Secretary of Defense Paul Wolfowitz, and the former head of the Defense Intelligence Agency, Lowell Jacoby, they were charged with having personally ordered or approved of orders of detention and interrogation during the time Mr. Padilla was in military custody and control.

At issue were fundamental principles contained in the Constitution, treaties, statutes, and common law rights, including procedural and substantive due process, right to be free from cruel and unusual punishment, right to freely exercise one's religion, right to access information, right to associate with family members, their right to associate with him, right of access to legal counsel and to courts, the right to be free from compelled self-incrimination, right to be free from torture and other cruel, inhuman, humiliating and degrading treatment, from treatment that shocks the conscience, right against arbitrary and unreasonable seizure and detention, and ones right to be free from governmental conspiracies intended to deprive him of his rights, privileges, and immunities under the law. The case immediately attracted the attention of a world-wide audience interested in the measures taken regarding the war on terrorism and the status occupied by world rule of law principles in the United States.

The complaint alleged that Mr. Padilla had suffered and continued to suffer "serious mental and physical harm" as a result of defendants' conduct and were exacerbated by the fear that he would again be detained as an enemy combatant, which the government had acknowledged. Seeking to vindicate plaintiffs' constitutional rights and to ensure that neither Padilla or any other person be treated in the same way in the future, they requested a declaration that the conduct of defendants was unlawful and violated plaintiffs' rights, an injunction against his re-detention as an enemy combatant, money damages of $1 against each defendant, and such other relief as may be just and appropriate. A jury trial was requested by plaintiffs.

D. Hamdan v. Rumsfeld (June 29, 2006) 126 S. Ct. 2749

Salim Ahmed Hamdan , following his apprehension in Afghanistan and his detention at Guantanamo, challenged the Presidential Order of November 13, 2001 creating military commissions. He was a Yemeni national and driver for Osama Bin Laden and believed to be an active participant in Al Qaeda. He was classified by the DOD as an alien enemy combatant. Following a hearing before a military commission in April, 2004, he was charged with conspiracy to commit war crimes. They included attacks on civilians, destruction of civilian property, terrorism, participation in the activities of Osama Bin Laden, the delivery of weapons to Al Qaeda training camps, and having received instructions on the methods of terrorism in one of the camps. He was also identified as an "unprivileged belligerent."

In December, 2003, the government appointed counsel to advise him of the rights accorded him in commission inquiries. In April, 2004, a petition for a writ of habeas corpus was filed for him in the Federal District Court sitting in the District of Columbia. He asserted that the Presidential Order of November 13, 2001 required congressional approval and had not met the requirements of The Detainee Treatment Act of December 30, 2005, that the creation of a military commission violated the Uniform Code of Military Justice and, as a prisoner of war he was entitled to the benefits of Common Article 3 of the 1949 Geneva POW Convention with its absolute prohibition on the "cruel treatment and torture" of detainees held in the conflict with Al Qaeda. He maintained that the military commission was not a body meeting the requirements of Article 5 of the Convention when it called for trials before a "competent tribunal." He challenged the impartiality of the commission members that had reviewed his case, and argued that the case should have been heard in a courts-martial proceedings governed by the Uniform Code of Military Justice. He considered that he would have had more extensive rights in a courts-martial than in a commission hearing . He also asserted that Congress had not suspended judicial review of some cases pending on December 30, 2005.

Hamdan v. Rumsfeld,[24] one of three considered almost simultaneously in the District Court of the District of Columbia, was assigned to Judge James Robertson. All three involved petitions for writs of habeas corpus. Judge Robertson ruled on November 8, 2004, that Hamdan was entitled under Article 5 of the Convention to have his case resolved by a "competent tribunal" rather than the military commission. After examining the procedures set forth by the administration, including the exclusion of the accused from some of the proceedings and denial to him of access to some of the evidence, it was held that there had been a violation of American standards of justice. Specifically "[b]ecause Hamdan has not been determined by a competent tribunal to be an offender triable under the law of war, 10 U.S.C. 821, and because in any event the procedures established for the Military Commission by the President's order are 'contrary to or inconsistent' with those applicable to courts-martial, 10 U.S.C. 836, Hamdan's petition . . ." was granted in part. Mr. Hamdan and the government sought special reviews by the Supreme Court. Both appeals were denied. The Secretary of Defense was enjoined from conducting further military commission proceedings against Mr. Hamdan. A hearing was scheduled before the Circuit Court of Appeals of Appeals for the District of Columbia in 2005.

The second case, Khlad v. Bush, also involved a petition for a writ of habeas corpus. It came before Judge Richard Leon who ruled on January 19, 2005 that this Guantanamo detainee had been correctly classified as an alien enemy combatant when captured in Afghanistan. Khlad urged that he was entitled to the protections respecting a fair trial set out in the Fifth Amendment to the United States Constitution, that he was a POW, and also entitled to the protections of numerous federal statutes and formal international agreements. Judge Leon dismissed the petition basing his decision on the holding of the United States Supreme Court in Rasul v. Bush (124 S. Ct. 2686, (June 28, 2004).) He held that a non-resident alien had no constitutional rights, that no existing federal statute rendered the detention unlawful, that no legally binding international agreement was applicable, and that international law was not controlling under the circumstances.

The third case, "In Re Guantanamo Detainee Cases,[25] also in the Federal District Court for the District of Columbia, was decided by Judge Joyce Hens Green on January 31, 2005. It included the case of Al Odah v. United States of America, who among numerous other detainees was seeking a writ of habeas corpus. Judge Green, also relying on Rasul v. Bush concluded that the litigants had established Fifth Amendment claims, and that they possessed enforceable constitutional rights. She concluded that "indefinite detention" violated due process of law, and that the petitioners possessed a valid claim under the POW Convention. Judge Green referred to the July 7, 2004 Memorandum issued by the Deputy Secretary of Defense to the Secretary of the Navy establishing Combatant Status Review Tribunals. It applied "only to foreign nationals held as enemy combatants in the control of the Department of Defense at the Guantanamo Bay Naval Base, Cuba."[26] She denied the government's motion to dismiss with respect to the claims arising from alleged violations of the Fifth Amendment's Due Process Clause and the Third Geneva Convention, but dismissed all other claims. Moreover, she concluded that the government incorrectly had been given the benefit of a presumption that a detainee was an alien enemy combatant. She joined in the view expressed by Judge Robertson that only after a ruling had been made by "a competent tribunal," could it be determined if a detainee were entitled to the protections contained in the POW Convention.

Both Judges Leon and Green referred to the fact that members of the judiciary should pay proper heed to the exercise of judicial restraint in reviewing executive branch decisions. This outlook related particularly to battlefield captures and the detention of non-resident aliens. A considerable amount of delicacy, it is often argued, applies to the application of the separation of powers principle when foreign policy and foreign military activities are present. The issue of judicial "deference" was an ongoing theme affecting the detainee cases.

Judge Robertson's decision was appealed to the Federal Circuit Court for the District of Columbia.[27] That court, in reversing the trial court, ruled on international law and constitutional issues. Under the latter heading attention was give to separation of powers, the role of Congress, the President's war powers, the validity and jurisdiction of military tribunals dealing with unlawful combatants, the duty of the President to enforce the constitution, treaties, and statutes of the United States, and the duty to insure that persons charged with crimes receive a fair trial in all United States courts including those identified in the Uniform Code of Military Justice,[28] while taking into account the "judicial guarantees recognized as indispensable by civilized peoples," a critical term of the POW Convention.

These three cases were reviewed by the Circuit Court for the District of Columbia in Dakdar Boumediene v. Bush, No. 05-5062, and Khaled A. F. Al Odah, No. 05-5063, on February 20, 2007. They challenged the constitutionality of the habeas corpus stripping provisions of the Military Commissions Act of October 17, 2006. Relying on its provisions the Court of

However, if the trial were before a military commission it was determined that Article 36(a) did not contain a provision affording this "procedural guarantee." The appeals court added that the Code "imposes only minimal restrictions . . ."on such procedures.

On November 7, 2005, Hamdan's petition for a writ of certiorari was granted with a hearing scheduled for March, 2006. The Supreme Court, voting 5 to 3, rendered its decision on June 29, 2006.[30] This case, similar to others relating to detainees, was a major contest between the President and Congress as to their respective powers and responsibilities. It, like the other detainee cases, presented the Supreme Court with all of the hazards likely to be encountered in entering the proverbial legal briar patch. It has also been described as the most important case reaching the Supreme Court in recent times. In a context of political dynamics the case has been described as having "a democracy-forcing" role to stimulate more congressional activity.

Presented for review were the "Authorization for Use of Military Force" adopted by Congress on September 18, 2001, the Presidential Order of November 13, 2001, the resultant DOD Military Commission Order Number 1 entitled "Procedures for Trials by Military Commissions of Certain Non-United States Citizens in the War Against Terrorism" of March 21, 2002, the provisions of Article 36(a) of the Uniform Code of Military Justice,[31] the text of Article 3(1)(d) of the common articles of the1949 Geneva Conventions, and key provisions of the federal Detainee Treatment Act (DTA) of December 30, 2005. Among these was whether its habeas corpus restriction applied to pending cases, including the case before it. The holding was that it did not.

Section 1005, entitled "Procedures for Status Review of Detainees Outside the United States" provided that "the Circuit Court of Appeals for the District of Columbia shall have exclusive jurisdiction to determine the validity of any final decision of a Combatant Status Review Tribunal that an alien is properly detained as an enemy combatant." The proceedings against Hamdan had been initiated prior to the enactment of the DTA. At the last moment the government, seeking to retain the jurisdiction of the military tribunal, moved for a dismissal of the case. The motion was denied and the Court proceeded to examine the issues on their merits. In the face of these provisions the majority of the Court determined that the Hamdan military commission lacked the power to proceed since "its structure and procedures violate both the Uniform Code of Military Justice and the Geneva Conventions of 1949." The Bush military commission was invalid.

Chief Justice Roberts, who had joined the majority in the Court of Appeals in its decision, recused himself. The majority held that the 2001 military commission was not a regularly constituted court meeting the Geneva Convention requirement of an "effective tribunal," since it did not have to conform to due process standards. The Court determined that it possessed jurisdiction to decide on the "military necessity" of the Presidential Order. Further, the Order was not an "expressly based" legislative enactment and failed to meet the requirements of common Article 3 of the Geneva Conventions, which as a part of the laws of war was incorporated by reference into the Uniform Code of Military Justice.[32] The government's contention that a conspiracy existed was dismissed on the ground that it was not covered in the concept of a "war crime." Rejected by the Court was the contention of the Bush administration that its disposition of the claims of the Guantanamo detainees was unreviewable in the federal courts.

The Court was also confronted by the newly enacted Detainee Treatment Act (DTA) of December 30, 2005.[33] It provided in Section 1005(e)(2)(A) "Procedures for Status Review of Detainees Outside the United States" that "the Circuit Court of Appeals for the District of Columbia Circuit shall have exclusive jurisdiction to determine the validity of any final decision of a Combat Status Review Tribunal that an alien is properly detained as an enemy combatant." The government, realizing that the foregoing language might not be applicable in the review, moved for a dismissal of the case, which was denied.

Justice Stevens delivered the opinion of the court. Joining him were Justices Kennedy, Souter, Ginsberg, and Breyer. Dissenting were Justices Scalia, Thomas, and Alito.

The majority examined the holding of the Court of Appeals that the Uniform Code imposed only minimum restrictions upon the form or functions of military commissions. This view was rejected. It was held that military commissions must meet the same due process requirements set forth in the Uniform Code. Basic to the majority opinion was the view that the procedures for the military commission violated both the Uniform Code of Military Justice and common Article three of the Geneva Conventions. Implicit in this holding was that a military commission, if it were obliged to conform to courts-martial procedures, would be lawful. The majority concluded that the Presidential Order had not met constitutional requirements, and that the Hamdan commission was invalid. The majority held that the efforts of Congress, reflected in Section 1005(e)[34] of the DTA, dealing with the" Judicial Review of Detention of Enemy Combatants," did not strip the Supreme Court of its power to deal with habeas corpus appeals on the part of the Guantanamo detainees whose cases were pending in trial courts prior to the effective date of the statute, December 30, 2005. Justice Stevens observed that Hamdan was not contesting any "final decision" of a Combatant Status Review Tribunal or of a military commission and that Hamdan's "action does not fall within the scope of subsection (e)(2) or (e)(3)." He also observed in footnote 14 of the case that there may have been habeas corpus cases that were pending in the lower courts at the time the DTA was enacted that might qualify as challenges to "final decisions within the meaning the subsection." The Supreme Court did not decide whether other federal courts retained jurisdiction to hear and decide the numerous detainee cases before them at the time of its decision.

The majority opinion compared the DTA with the Authorization to Use Military Force saying that they granted the President only "general" authority to convene military commissions "where justified under the Constitution and laws, including the laws of war." The opinion emphasized the role of Congress and that specific "authorization" by it was necessary for the President to establish military commissions. In a concurring opinion Justice Kennedy stated: "If Congress, after due consideration, deems it appropriate to change the controlling statutes [regarding military commissions], in conformance with the Constitution and other laws, it has the power and prerogatives to do so."

The majority examined the question whether Article 3(1)(d) of the 1949 Geneva Conventions was enforceable in the Court. It prohibited "[t]he passing of sentences and the carrying out of executions without previous judgment by a regularly constituted court affording all of the judicial guarantees which are recognized as indispensable by civilized peoples." They concluded that it was judicially enforceable and that Hamdan was protected by it. This was based on the finding that Hamdan, under commission rules and regulations, was not entitled to be present at commission hearings and that he should have been made privy to the evidence against him. It was also concluded that he had not been charged with crimes which under the laws and customs of war could be tried by a military commission.[35] The Court also took the view that even if a detainee did not possess the status of a prisoner of war, that each detainee must be treated in accordance with the Convention's Common Article 3. It prohibited, among other things, "outrages upon personal dignity, in particular humiliating and degrading treatment." This, too, was judicially enforceable.

In a concurring opinion Justice Breyer, joined by Justices Kennedy, Souter, and Ginsburg, stated that Congress had not issued the President "a blank check" for the commissions designed to prosecute detainees. Moreover, Congress had denied the President the legislative "authority to create military commissions of the kind at issue here." In assessing the role of the Supreme Court Justice Breyer referred to "judicial insistence" that a President must consult with Congress when no emergency prevented it from using "democratic means" to determine "how best . . ." to respond to the problem.

Justice Kennedy also wrote a concurring opinion, in which he was joined by Justices Souter, Ginsburg, and Breyer. He viewed the Military Order No.

1 as exceeding the "limits that certain statutes, enacted by Congress, have placed on the President's authority to convene military courts." He emphasized that "domestic statutes control the case, i. e. 10 U.S.C. #821, requiring military commissions to comply with the "law of war." For the reasons stated the majority reversed the decision of the Court of Appeals and remanded the case to the Federal District Court for the District of Columbia.

Justice Scalia in his dissent, joined by Justices Thomas and Alito, focused on the jurisdiction-stripping provisions of the Detainee Treatment Act of December 30, 2005. In his view the statute prevented the identified courts from considering applications for writs of habeas corpus by Guantanamo Bay detainees. He held that the majority was in error in its conclusion that a case pending in the courts on December 31 was immune from Section 1005(1)(a) of the statute.

Justice Thomas, joined by Justices Scalia and Alito, focused on the practical problems that would confront a President in complying with the majority decision. He stated that it would "sorely hamper the President's ability to confront and defeat a new and deadly enemy." It would undermine his ability to "preven[t] future attacks . . ."

In responding to the deep-seated differences, ranging throughout the entire American legal and political community, he wrote that the majority opinion "openly flaunts our well-established duty to respect the Executive's judgment in matters of military operations and foreign affairs." This was based on the view of the majority, as he construed it, that the Supreme Court "is qualified to pass on the 'military necessity' of the Commander in Chief's decision to employ a particular form of force against our enemies . . ." He considered this to be "antithetical to our constitutional structure."

The issue of deference to, or respect for, a President's exercise of his military and foreign affairs powers, as particularly identified in this case, has a long and contentious history. At the heart of the matter is the fact that American practice has not been to accord total judicial deference to Presidential preferences in these particular matters, or at the other end of the extreme, to abandon wholly judicial surveillance. It is evident that the Court's weighing of facts and circumstances—both legal and political—in particular cases has guided its approach to the application and implementation of relevant statutes, treaties, and its view of customary international law. Factors crossing judicial minds are the nature of the threats to basic civil and political rights and liberties, practical assessments of the relevant facts and circumstances, prospects for alternative approaches—such as intervening legislation—enacted over Presidential veto, and future risks to the utility of the Court as it implements the separation of powers triad. In today's world Supreme Court justices cannot escape what I have called in other contexts the "elapse of time syndrome," namely the fact that advances in science and technology as they heavily impact on globalization, have provided both terrorists and non-terrorists, with highly immediate responses involving the use of devastating weapons. The terms "immediate and impending," so well known to students of international law in the context of national self-defense, have been bobtailed. Reasonable and proportionate responses to the threats of terrorists may not await the product of standard rational and collective decisional processes. Ultimately, as suggested above, the appraisal accorded to the threat of terrorists in particular situations will become the basis for decision.

The Court in the Hamdan case was not so explicit. Highly visible critics of that decision have stated that it "represents a radical new judicial approach to the interpretation of laws relating to foreign affairs . . ." adding that "[n]ot only did the Hamdan court fail to defer to the executive's reasonable interpretations of the relevant statutes, treaties, and customary international law of war relating to military commissions, but it did not even justify its failure to depart from longstanding formal doctrines requiring such deference."[36]

Proponents of the majority holding acknowledged that the Court had never adopted a rule of absolute judicial deference. And, when deference has been employed doubts have arisen as to the need for and the fairness of the outcome. In Acree v. The Republic of Iraq U. S. Air Force personnel had been tortured following their capture in 1991.[37] The Federal District Court awarded them very sizeable damages. When appeal was taken to the United States Court of Appeals for the District of Columbia the award was set aside. At the time of trial and during the appeal the United States government was engaged in restoring and stabilizing the government of Iraq, with attendant costs. In dismissing the case the appeals court stated that the trial court had "failed to weigh the importance of this case to the United States' foreign policy interests."

The large numbers of proponents of the Hamdan ruling were seriously concerned not only about the constitutional basis for the establishment of military commissions. Many also held the view that defendants, both U. S. citizens and aliens, whether physically present in the United States or under the custody and control of the United States at the Guantanamo Naval base, were entitled to the basic rights provided by a "competent tribunal" available to defendants in cases coming before Federal District Courts. A fundamental concern was the likelihood of a fair trial. There was very little confidence that the Bush administration with the DOD's highly publicized Abu Ghraib torture practices, and fears that similar measures had been employed at the Guantanamo Naval Base, and with the policies identified in the RUDs to CAT, would be able to meet the required fair trial standard. Moreover, there was a general concern over the abuse of governmental authority. These and other consideration led to wide-ranging public support for judicial intervention.

On October 17, 2006, President Bush signed the Military Commission Act imposing limitations on the availability of the writ of habeas corpus.[38] Hamdan's lawyers tried to get the Supreme Court to review the jurisdiction-stripping provision preventing the issuance of writs of habeas corpus to detainees. Also before the court was the question of access to the writ under the constitution. It was also urged that the statute violated separation of powers, the Bill of Attainder Clause, and Equal Protection guarantees.

The Supreme Court, prior to the enactment of the Military Commissions Act, remanded the Hamdan decision for implementation to the Federal District Court of the District of Columbia where it was assigned to Judge Robertson. This resulted in a set of cases designed to secure an understanding of the relationships between the Hamdan case and the MCA. Focusing on the new habeas corpus provisions of the MCA on December 13, 2006 Judge Robertson dismissed the case before him.

He held that the petitioner did not have a constitutional entitlement to the writ and that he could not obtain it statutorily since the new law, containing "jurisdiction-stripping" provisions, had blocked access to it. He also stated that the Suspension Clause of the Constitution did not "guarantee the right to petition for it to non-resident enemy aliens captured and detained outside of the United States." The foregoing was based on the finding that Mr. Hamdan had never entered the United States and accordingly did not enjoy the "implied protection" that accompanies presence on American soil. He cited the Rasul decision at page 471 that while the Naval Station at Guantanamo was under the control of the military forces of the United States that it remained under the "ultimate sovereignty of the Republic of Cuba." Further, since the detention facility was outside the sovereign realm that only "U.S. citizens in such locations may claim entitlement to a constitutionally guaranteed writ." He stated that while Mr. Hamdan's presence within the exclusive jurisdiction of the United States was lawful, it was involuntary and was not that kind of presence indicating any "substantial connection with our country" that would "justify the invocation of a constitutional right to habeas corpus."[39] It was also noted that Mr. Hamdan had not been assimilated into the United States to the point where he could claim the attributes of U. S. nationality.[40]

Judge Robertson, having relied on the jurisdiction-stripping language of the MCA, stated specifically that he had not dealt with Mr. Hamdan's other arguments, namely, that "it does not provide an adequate substitute for habeas review, because it violates the principle of the separation of powers by instructing the courts to ignore the Supreme Court's ruling that the Geneva

Conventions afford judicially enforceable protections to petitioner Hamdan, because it is an unlawful Bill of Attainder, and because it violates Equal Protection."[41]

E. Boumediene v. Bush, No. 05-5062 and No. 05-5063, 476 F 3d 981 (D.C. Cir 2007), Al Odah v. United States, No. 05-5064 et. seq. , (2005-2007); oral argument, U. S. Supreme Court, No. 06-1195, No. 06-1196, November 26, 2007

These cases, also stemming from Hamdan v. Rumsfeld, were then appealed on February 3, 2005 to the Court of Appeals for the District of Columbia under the titles of Boumediene v. Bush, No. 05-5062 and No. 05-5063 and Al Odah v. United States of America, No.05-5064, et. seq. Arguments were presented to the Circuit Court on September 8, 2005. The case was not decided until February 20, 2007.[42] During this period the Detainee Treatment Act had become law on December 30, 2005, and the Military Commissions Act on October 17, 2006.[43]

In ruling that the three decisions of the District Court were to be vacated and the appeals dismissed for lack of jurisdiction the Court of Appeals asked: "Do federal courts have jurisdiction over petitions for writs of habeas corpus filed by aliens captured abroad and detained as enemy combatants at an overseas military base leased from a foreign government . . ." namely at the Guantanamo Bay Naval Station? The petitioners alleged violations of the Constitution, treaties, statutes, regulations, the common law, and the law of nations. In reaching its decision the court referred to Section 7 (a), subsection (b) of the Military Commissions Act stating that it applied to "all cases without exception pending on or after the date of the enactment of this Act which relate to any aspect of the detention, transfer, treatment, trial, or conditions of detention of an alien detained by the United States since September 11, 2001." These terms were held to be applicable to the habeas corpus petitions of the detainees. It was clear from the holding that federal courts had no jurisdiction over habeas corpus petitions filed by alien enemies abroad and detained as enemy combatants in a military base outside the sovereign territory of the United States. However, the court's ruling, in this case, dealt only with Guantanamo detainees.

The court also ruled that the statute was not an unconstitutional suspension of the writ of habeas corpus saying that the clause only protected the writ "as it existed in 1789" when Congress gave to the federal courts the right to issue the writ. It was noted that Congress had changed the terms for the grant on many times since 1789. It was also pointed out that aliens do not have a "common law or constitutionally protected right to the writ . . . when captured abroad and detained outside the United States or in territory over which the United States exercises exclusive jurisdiction or control." Further, precedents did not exist calling for the conferral of rights "on aliens without property or presence in the United States."

In a dissent Justice Rogers challenged the right of Congress to enact jurisdiction-stripping provisions relating to the writ of habeas corpus. In her view the enactment violated the Suspension Clause of the Constitution since there had not been a rebellion or an invasion of the United States. It was her position that the Clause, being general, and not referring to those persons intended to be protected by it, should be construed as applicable to both U. S. citizens and alien detainees. Further, the Constitution itself gave direct but limited protection to all persons held in U. S. custody without the need for legislative intervention. Only where the peace and security of the United States became jeopardized could there be a valid suspension. This required an assessment of whether the national emergency, reflected in the war against terrorism, declared by the Bush administration was substantial enough to support the MCA provisions. In her view it was not.

She saw the detainees in a "catch-22" situation. They could not appeal from a decision of a Military Commission. The government had been slow in establishing them, although one of the reasons for their creation had been the speeding up of a judicial process for bringing suspected Al Qaeda members to trial. In the interim no charges had been made and no appeals were possible.

Counsel for the detainees having reexamined the facts surrounding their cases decided to focus on the procedures available to their clients in Combatant Status Review Tribunals coupled with the extended periods of detention at the Guantanamo Naval Base. It was decided that obtaining affidavits from military officers stationed at the Base and familiar with the proceedings before the Tribunals might demonstrate fundamental unfairness. They were successful in obtaining affidavits that in some instances the hearing officers had been pressured to rule in favor of keeping the detainees in prison as enemy combatants. Attention was also called to the harsh conditions facing the prisoners, including the fact that Mr. Al Odah had been held for about six years with no charges having been filed against him.

The appeal for a hearing before the U. S. Supreme Court was turned down on April 2, 2007. However, on June 29, 2007, a majority of the members of the court in a very rare decision set aside its April holding on the ground that if it were found that an "unlawful confinement" was occurring, this might result in a ruling by a Federal trial court allowing the detainees to plead their innocence. In the April decision Justices Souter, Ginsburg, and Breyer had voted to consider the matter, while Justices Stevens and Kennedy favored the application of "traditional rules governing our decision of constitutional questions," and the practice of requiring "the exhaustion of available remedies as a precondition to accepting jurisdiction over applications for the writ of habeas corpus." This meant that the applicants would have to go through the appeals process of the Combatant Status Review Tribunals. They noted, however, that the doctrine did not "require the exhaustion of inadequate remedies." To this was added that if the petitioners were later to offer proof that the government "has unreasonably delayed proceedings under the Detainee Treatment Act of 2005, Title X, 119 Stat. 2739, or some other and ongoing inquiry, alternate means exist for us to consider our jurisdiction over the allegations made by petitioners before the Court of Appeals. See 28 U.S.C. ##1651(a), 2241. Were the Government to take additional steps to prejudice the position of petitioners in seeking review in this Court, 'courts of competent jurisdiction,' including the Court, 'should act promptly to ensure that the office and purposes of the writ of habeas corpus are not compromised.' Padilla v. Hanft, 547 U. S. 1062, 1064."

The June 29, 2007, vote appears to have resulted from an affidavit filed by a military officer citing alleged deficiencies in the procedures employed in cases before Combatant Status Review Tribunals. The new order allowed the Supreme Court to review the Court of Appeals holding of February 20, 2007 that the jurisdiction stripping of habeas corpus jurisdiction was valid. This was consistent with the Solicitor General's supplemental brief urging that the MCA did not violate the suspension clause because the petitioners had no constitutional right and because both the MCA and the DTA provided an unprecedented level of judicial review for the claims of the enemy aliens held at Guantanamo. This allowed the matter to come before the Supreme Court by way of a writ of certiorari in the term beginning on October 1, 2007. In granting the writ of certiorari attention was drawn to two cases pending in 2007 in the Court of Appeals for the District of Columbia, Bismulla v. Gates, No. 06-1197, and Parhat v. Gates, No. 06-1397.They, like the two cases under consideration raised the issue of the availability of the writ of habeas corpus to alien enemy unlawful combatants situated outside the United States.

The United States also holds detainees at a military prison in Bagram, Afghanistan. In a case filed in the Federal District Court for the District of Columbia in September 2006, Fadi Al Maqaleh, a Yemeni national, sought his release based on a writ of habeas corpus filed on his behalf by the International Justice Network. In a ruling on July 18, 2007, the trial court held that it had jurisdiction in the matter. It indicated that the decision was based on the June 29, 2007, decision regarding the issuance of a writ of certiorari by the Supreme Court in the Boumediene and Al Odah cases.

On November 26, 2007 the Supreme Court in the Boumediene case (No. 06-1195) and in the Al Odah case (No. 06-1196) heard oral arguments by the parties. The session covered one and one-half hours. Important issues faced the court. Among them was whether the Military Commissions Act validly stripped federal courts of jurisdiction over habeas corpus petitions filed by foreign citizens imprisoned indefinitely at the Guantanamo Naval Station. Did the habeas corpus petitions, in this situation involving these periods of incarceration demonstrate unlawful confinement requiring the grant of the habeas corpus writ, or at least a hearing on the merits? Was the Naval Station constructively a part of the United States? Was the procedure calling for the use of a Combatant Status Review Tribunal, with appeals to the Circuit Court of the District of Columbia, an adequate and effective substitute for the constitutional right to habeas corpus?

During the oral argument the following issues were specifically identified by counsel for the detainees: (1) Had the government during the extended periods of detention given reasonable notice to the detainees of the factual grounds or a fair opportunity to dispute those grounds before a neutral decision maker? (2) Under the holdings of the lower courts was there a prospect that the detainees would ever have that opportunity? (3) Were the detainees innocent of all wrongdoing and did the CSRT process provide for a reliable inquiry as to the Executive Department's asserted authority for detaining these individuals, and would the CSRT process constitute an adequate substitute for a traditional judicial review? What was the relevance of the six years that the detainees had been held in custody? What was the worth of the argument that the review provided for in the Detainee Treatment Act constituted an adequate substitute for the issuance of a writ of habeas corpus, in light of the Government's position that the DTA provision allowing for review of CSRT decisions was a substantial liberalization of statutes and historical common law outlooks on the issuance of the writ? What could be made of the suitability and the completeness of review granted to the Circuit Court of the District of Columbia by the DTA in appeals to it from the CSRTs? Posed to the Supreme Court was whether the provisions governing CSRT procedures were sufficient to assure a fair trial for a detainee, and whether under existing procedural rules there could be a satisfactory disposition by the Circuit Court of matters coming to it from the CSRTs.

The Solicitor-General in response to questioning by the members of the Court urged that the DTA was an adequate substitute for a writ of habeas corpus. In support he stated that a ruling by the District Court of Appeal, an Article III court, would include an order requiring the release of a detainee, that under the statute a detainee possessed rights and accession to administrative and judicial review, that a detainee could make preponderance of the evidence claims, submit documentary evidence, to receive notice of charges as well as statutory and constitutional claims, in a case before the Court of Appeals of the Federal District, if and when there was an appeal from a

Combatant Status Review Tribunal. A detainee was entitled to be represented by "counsel," although that person would not possess the full latitude of powers possessed by traditional counsel in non-detainee cases. The issuance of the writ was denied to other Federal courts located around the country. Notice was taken that the terms of legislation adopted by Congress had been modified over the years, with the Solicitor-General asserting that the DTA statute granted broader and more extensive rights that had existed in 1789 and in 1941. The Solicitor-General also raised the question whether the case was ripe for consideration by the Supreme Court, with several justices stating that the appellant's claim might have been better considered by the Federal Circuit Court, and then an appeal might have been addressed by a party to the Supreme Court.

The holding and the reasoning produced by this case will impact on international law and on America's treatment of a person who can not meet the conditions for being a POW and who has been designated an unlawful alien enemy combatant. Many countries have a legitimate interest in forestalling terrorist activities and in the disposition of them when captured. Many factors, including the reviving of the full habeas corpus writ in the United States, undoubtedly will have to be considered. One, that this study has brought to public awareness is the trend toward the "militarization" of governmental rights and processes, based on the uncertain boundaries of a president's war powers under the Constitution and the basic civil and political rights and duties belonging to American citizens. Those citizens privileged to exercise high powers, as they conform their conduct to the principle of separation of powers, have enormous responsibilities. Only through an understanding of their roles, inculcated by an alert and informed electorate, will the country work its way through critical times.

F. Hamdan (Khadr) v. Gates, April 30, 2007, No. 07-1156 (2007)

Mr. Hamdan and Mr. Omar Khadr, a Canadian national, also detained at the Guantanamo Naval Station, in a case entitled Khadr v. Gates, appealed to the United States Supreme Court seeking an order that their proposed war crimes trials before military commissions should be delayed.[44] Both asked the court to allow them to continue with their habeas corpus challenge to the commission process. On April 30, 2007 the court refused to accept the appeals over the dissents of Justices Souter, Ginsburg, and Breyer. Justices Stevens and Kennedy said the detainees must exhaust judicial remedies available to them before turning to the high court. This meant that the detainees had to look to the appeals process of CSRTs for a resolution of their situations. This was followed by a ruling on May 30, 2007 by the Court of Appeals of the District of

Columbia that it possessed no authority to prevent forthcoming prosecutions in military commissions. It held that it did not have the power to delay a commission trial until it could determine whether a detainee had been validly classified as an "enemy combatant."

In their petitions counsel for the two detainees asked the Supreme Court to rule on the constitutionality of the October 17, 2006 Military Commissions Act including the right to file habeas corpus challenges in U. S. federal courts. In opposition the U. S. Solicitor General urged that the legislation had struck a balance between the legal protections enjoyed by the accused, the availability of judicial review, and the power of the executive to wage a war against terrorists. In the Khadr case the Supreme Court held that the Military Commissions Act had removed the jurisdiction of the federal courts to take any action involving war crimes, at least until after a trial was over and a verdict of guilty had been reached. This followed the terms of 10 U.S.C. subsection 950j(b) of the statute dealing with the sole basis for review of military commission procedures and actions, which stated that "Except as otherwise provided in this chapter and notwithstanding any other provision of law (including section 2241 of title 28 [the habeas corpus statute] or any other habeas corpus provision), [which had been referred to by Justices Stevens and Kennedy in their April 2, 2007 statement in the Boumediene v. Bush certiorari petition] no court, justice or judge shall have jurisdiction to hear or consider any claim or cause of action whatsoever, including any action pending on or filed after the date of the enactment of the [MCA], relating to the prosecution, trial, or judgment of a military commission under this chapter, including challenges to the lawfulness of procedures of military commissions. . . ." Section 2241 was also amended in Section 7 of the MCA by adding subsection (e)(1) confirming that "No court, justice, or judge shall have jurisdiction to hear or consider an application for a writ of habeas corpus filed by or on behalf of an alien detained by the United States who has been determined by the United States to have been properly detained as an enemy combatant or is awaiting such determination." The MCA in subsection (e)(2) extended the foregoing limitation to hearing or considering "any other action against the United States or its agents relating to any aspect of the detention, transfer or treatment, trial or conditions of confinement of an alien who is or was detained by the United States and has been determined by the United States to have been properly detained as an enemy combatant or is awaiting such determination" except as otherwise provided in paragraphs (2) and (3) of section 1005(e) of the Detainee Treatment Act of 2005 (10 U.S.C. 801 note).

Following the Supreme Court's ruling in the Khadr v. Gates case (No. 07-1156) Mr. Khadr asked the Court of Appeals to decide whether he had been properly classified by his Combatant Status Review Tribunal as an enemy combatant basing his appeal on non-compliance with the provisions of the MCA. This request was denied. This holding meant that the status of the Guantanamo detainees had to be resolved first by military commissions to be followed by appeals to be taken to the Court of Appeals for the District of Columbia.

G. Hamdan v. Gates, Khadr v. Gates, No. 06-1169 (April 30, 2007)

On April 30, 2007, the Supreme Court, in a case with a new defendant (Robert Gates, Secretary of Defense, case number 06-1169) voted 4 to 3 not to grant a writ of certiorari.[45] This holding was consistent with that in case number 07-1156. This meant that a prosecution in a new 2006 Military Commission could take place. On May 10, 2007, new charges were filed. These included acts of conspiracy with Osama Bin Laden and other Al Qaeda leaders to engage in hostile acts against the United States. These were the 1998 bombings of U. S. embassies in Tanzania and Kenya, the 2000 attack on the destroyer Cole in a Yemeni harbor, and the 9/11 attacks resulting in the deaths of about 3,000 persons. Arraignment was scheduled for early in June, 2007. So, at long last, or so it seemed, Hamdan was to receive a hearing before a specially configured court, a Military Commission, based on Federal legislation, composed of military judges. The trial was required to begin within 120 days of when the charges were filed with the Commission. In December 2007, Hamdan, who had been held since 2002 at the Guantanamo Naval Base, received a hearing before a Military Commission. Hamdan contended that he had not supported Al Qaeda, although for four years he had driven vehicles for Osama bin Laden. Testimony was received that he had picked up and delivered surface to air missiles. A witness for Mr. Hamdan stated that Hamdan had transported a box of dates. Disbelieving the latter, Mr. Hamdan was convicted of conspiracy and material support to terrorist acts. Sanctions include up to life in prison. Awaiting trial were a number of other detainees who have contended that they were Taliban soldiers. If this were proven, they would have to be held as POWs, unless it also could be proven that they also served the Al Qaeda forces.

H. Al-Marri v. Wright, Commander, Consolidated Naval Brig (June 11, 2007), Court of Appeals No. 06-7427 (2007)

Mr. Al-Marri, an alien resident in the United States, was taken into custody by military authorities, following a Presidential Order, in June 2003. He was held without charges except for being an enemy combatant. The facts causing his detention were set forth in the Rapp Memorandum prepared by the Director of the Joint Inspection Task Force for Combating Terrorism. Mr. Al-Marri petitioned the Federal District Court in Charleston, South Carolina for a writ of habeas corpus.[46] It was denied and the case was dismissed in August 2006.

On appeal to the Court of Appeals for the Fourth Circuit in a two to one decision it was held that the appellant was entitled to the issuance of a writ of habeas corpus. In arriving at that decision the court took into account inadequacies of the Rapp memorandum, namely, it did not assert that the detainee "(1) is a citizen or affiliate of the armed forces, of any nation at war with the United States; (2) was seized on or near a battlefield on which the armed forces of the United States or its allies were engaged in combat; (3) was even in Afghanistan during the armed conflict between the United States and the Taliban there; or (4) directly participated in any hostilities against the United States or allied armed forces.

Approaching the legal aspects of the cases the appeals court accepted the applicability of Section 7(b) of the MCA to "all cases without exception pending on or after the date of the enactment of this Act . . ." dealing with the issuance of a writ of habeas corpus. The court of appeals accepted the applicability of Hamdi v. Rumsfeld (542 U. S. 507, 525 (2004) when it held that "an alien captured and detained within the United States has a right to be protected by the Constitution's Suspension Clause." Additional constitutional protections were afforded by the Due Process provisions of the 5th Amendment, which was treated as the basis for the grant of the habeas corpus writ.

The majority concluded that the MCA did not apply to the accused. He was in the United States. The statute applied to Guantanamo Bay detainees including the right of access to Combat Status Review Tribunals.

The case was remanded to the trial court with instructions to issue a writ of habeas corpus directing the Secretary of Defense to release Mr. Al Marri from military custody within a reasonable time. The appeals court stated that the "government can transfer al-Marri to civilian authorities to face criminal charges, initiate deportation proceedings against him, hold him as a material witness in connection with grand jury proceedings, or detain him for a limited time pursuant to the Patriot Act. But, military detention of al-Marri must cease." On the government's request an en banc rehearing was granted for August 22, 2007.[47]

I. Boumediene v. Bush, Al Odah v. United States, Opinion (June 12, 2008), 453 U. S.—(2008)

1. Introduction

On June 12, 2008, the Supreme Court in a 5-4 holding ruled on issues presented by alien enemy combatant detainees imprisoned at the U. S. Naval

Station, Guantanamo, Cuba. One set of litigants was grouped under the title Boumediene v. Bush; another included the Al Odah detainees, bringing before the court 58 petitioners.

The majority opinion was written by Justice Kennedy. He was joined by Justices Stevens, Souter, Ginsburg and Breyer. A second opinion was that of Justice Souter, who was joined by Justices Ginsburg and Breyer. A dissenting opinion was penned by Chief Justice Roberts. Joining him were Justices Scalia, Thomas, and Alito. Justice Scalia wrote a separate dissenting opinion. He was joined by Justices Roberts, Thomas and Alito.[48]

All justices were in agreement as to the major issue presented to them. Justice Kennedy, noting that petitioners had presented a question not resolved in earlier detainee cases, which he identified as "whether they have the constitutional privilege of habeas corpus, a privilege not to be withdrawn except in conformance with the Suspension Clause, Art. I, #9, cl.2." (Kennedy Slip Opinion, p. 1) Later he rephrased the issue: "whether foreign nationals, apprehended and detained in distant countries during a time of serious threats to our Nation's security, may assert the privilege of the writ and seek its protection." (p. 15). Chief Justice Roberts accepted that formulation while asserting that the majority's "misguided" and "fruitless" holding had struck down as inadequate the "most generous set of procedural protections ever afforded aliens detained by this country as enemy combatants." (Roberts, Slip Opinion, p.1.)

Justice Scalia phrased the issue: Should the Supreme Court "confer a constitutional right to habeas corpus on alien enemies detained abroad by our military forces in the course of an ongoing war." (Scalia, Slip Opinion, p. 1.) Justice Souter before identifying the issue as seen to him called attention to the Court's ruling in Rasul v. Bush (2004) and its immobilization in the Military Commissions Act (MCA) in 2006. He emphasized that the statute with its elimination of statutory habeas corpus jurisdiction over those claims had produced the result that "now there must be constitutionally based jurisdiction or none at all." (Souter, Slip Opinion, p. 1.) The Boumediene decision meant that there was a "constitutional habeas corpus jurisdiction over aliens imprisoned by the military outside an area of de jure national sovereignty." (Ibid.) Before arriving at that conclusion the members of the court had to consider whether the procedures to be employed in reviewing the status of a detainee were adequate and effective substitutes for habeas corpus. At issue was Section 7 of the MCA which contained alternate procedures for the writ of habeas corpus. Justice Kennedy identified this as the "threshold matter" in this litigation, since among other things, the statute denied to the federal courts the right to hear habeas corpus actions pending at the time of the enactment. He stated that it was clear that the MCA did deny jurisdiction, so that if the statute were constitutional it would require the dismissal of the petitioners' cases. (Kennedy, p. 5) As will be seen the court inquired into this situation with great care before determining that the statutory provisions could not be a substitute for the writ. The majority decision was a narrow one. They made it clear that it had not addressed "whether the President has authority to detain these petitioners nor do we hold that the writ must issue." (Kennedy, p. 2.) Justice Kennedy stated: "it bears repeating that that our opinion does not address the content of the law that governs petitioners' detention. This is a matter yet to be determined." (Kennedy, p. 69). In short, the constitutional privilege was still alive; the alternate procedures set forth the 2005 Detainee Treatment Act (DTA) intended to be an adequate and effective substitute for habeas corpus did not serve that purpose and # 7 of the MCA operated as an unconstitutional suspension of the writ. With the remand of these cases to Federal District Courts, and with prospects of appeals, much work over an extended time span can be anticipated.

2. The Kennedy Opinion

In arriving at the majority holding Justice Kennedy considered the history of the writ of habeas corpus as it had evolved in the common law of England. Its territorial application had not been uniform in England or in distant areas where the Crown exercised authority but did not possess unrestricted sovereignty. He also examined the substantive content of English precedents and decided they did not provide a sufficiently definitive or reliable basis for American use and were inapplicable although he recited at length the basic values contained in the British experience. Justice Kenney also traced the historic acceptance of the writ in American constitutional history calling attention to the fact that the Founding Father's had included the writ in Article I, thereby according to the privilege a preferred condition, since the Constitution did not contain a Bill of Rights.

Much of the Kennedy opinion dealt with the Detainee Treatment Act containing, with respect to Guantanamo detainees, critical jurisdiction stripping provisions whereby the detainees did not have access to the writ in Federal District Courts. He focused on defects contained in the new regime and compared the legislative provisions with Due Process requirements. His view of the DTA was identified in his comparison of it with the Columbia Court Reform and Criminal Procedure Act of 1970 saying that "the purpose and effect of the statute was to expedite consideration of the prisoner's claims, not to delay or frustrate it" and that the statute was intended to "strengthen, rather than dilute, the writ's protection." (Kennedy, Slip Opinion, pp. 45–46.) Thus, the DTA and the MCA "were intended to circumscribe habeas review." (Id. at. 47.) No savings clauses were set forth in either the DTA or the MCA.

Several aspects of this case have attracted much attention. One has been the fact that some of the detainees had been in custody for up to six years during which they had not received the benefit of judicial oversight or the privilege of habeas corpus or an adequate substitute. Because of these circumstances Justice Kennedy pointed out that there had been no showing that the "executive faces such onerous burdens that it cannot respond to habeas corpus actions. To require these detainees to complete DTA review before proceeding with their habeas corpus actions would be to require additional months, if not years, of delay. The first DTA review applications were filed over a year ago, but no decisions on the merits have been issued. While some delay in fashioning new procedures is unavoidable, the costs of delay can no longer be borne by those who are held in custody. The detainees in these cases are entitled to a prompt habeas corpus hearing." (Id. at, 66.)

The military in endeavoring to identify whether detainees should be prosecuted or released had established Administrative Review Boards, Combatant Status Review Tribunals, and Military Commissions. It was to these bodies that the majority had referred in assessing the Due Process aspects of long periods of incarceration. As was noted in Chapter Eleven the Department of Defense had established these procedures on the belief that the writ of habeas corpus did not apply at the Naval Station. It was true, however, that the establishment of such bodies with rules governing their procedures had taken much time. When instituted it was the claim of the military, particularly regarding the use of Military Commissions, that the detainees had been slow in seeking access to them. Taking a different point of view was Justice Souter who stated that the outlook of the dissenters had a "hollow ring" when they suggested that the "Court is somehow precipitating the judiciary into reviewing claims that the military (subject to appeal to the Court of Appeals for the District of Columbia Circuit) could handle within some reasonable period of time." (Souter, Slip Opinion, p. 2.)

Turning to the detainees' contentions that the CSRT process was so laden with infirmities and deficiencies, with the most relevant being "the constraints upon the detainee's ability to rebut the factual basis for the Government's assertion that that he is an enemy combatant" (Kennedy, p. 54.) that it would not be possible to obtain a fair hearing before a neutral decision maker. More specifically, the majority noted at the CSRT level the "detainee has limited means to find or present evidence to challenge the Government's case against him. He does not have the assistance of counsel and may not be aware of the most critical allegations that the Government relied upon to order his detention." (Ibid., 54–55.) Moreover, while a detainee may confront witnesses who testify in CSRT hearings, they are subject "(in effect to) no limits on the admission of hearsay evidence—the only requirement is that the tribunal deem the evidence 'reliable and helpful,'" resulting in a situation in which "the detainees' opportunity to question witnesses is likely to be more theoretical than real."(Id. at 55.)

Agreeing with petitioners the majority noted that even if the parties in this process acted with diligence and in good faith, "there is considerable risk of error in the tribunal's finding of fact." (Id. at 66.) The lack of finality in such proceedings according to petitioners violated rights to a speedy and public trial, violated due process rights, and because if the very absence of a decision had wrongfully precluded and denied the right to a trial. Further defects were identified. Even if habeas corpus or a constitutional substitute were to be an effective and proper remedy the tribunal conducting the habeas corpus proceeding "must have the means to correct errors that occurred during the CSRT proceedings." (Id., 57). Further, that tribunal must have "some authority to admit and consider relevant exculpatory evidence that was not introduced during the earlier proceeding. . . . Here that opportunity is constitutionally required." (Ibid.) Moreover, where there had been an appropriate invocation of the judicial officer's authority to make a determination in light of the relevant law and facts, that officer must have adequate authority "to formulate and issue appropriate orders for relief, including, if necessary, an order directing the prisoner's release." (Id., at 58).

The next step was to determine whether the terms of the DTA granted the Court of Appeals for the District of Columbia the jurisdiction to apply the foregoing standards. At this point in the majority opinion there was a pause. The majority asked whether the DTA allowed the Court of Appeals to conduct a proceeding meeting the identified standards. The majority wanted to know if they were bound by the canon of constitutional avoidance or whether traditional modes of statutory interpretation were allowed. Note was taken of holdings that the canon came into play "only when, after the application if ordinary textual analysis, the statute is found to be susceptible of more than one construction; and the canon functions as a means of choosing between them." That was not the case here. The court added "We cannot ignore the text and purpose of a statute in order to save it." (Id., p. 58).

Following a review of the applicable provisions of the DTA when compared with the foregoing criteria, it was decided that the "DTA review proceeding falls short of being a constitutionally adequate substitute . . ." with the majority noting specifically that a "detainee still would have no opportunity to present evidence discovered after the CSRT proceedings concluded." (Id., at 60–61). Thus, the majority held that "Petitioners have met their burden of establishing that the DTA review process, is, on its face, an inadequate substitute for habeas corpus." (Id., at 63–64). Thus, it was decided that MCA # 7 "effects an unconstitutional suspension of the writ." (Id., at 64.)

The majority then considered the question whether there were any prudential barriers to habeas corpus review under the existing circumstances. If such
barriers were present the Court could temporarily abstain or require the exhaustion if alternate remedies. In the instant case, however, these alternatives
were deemed inapplicable, because so many years had elapsed between the
dates of detention and the judicial oversight that were demanded by habeas
corpus or an adequate substitute. The majority, nonetheless, indicated an
awareness of the need for a prudential outlook. They stated "Except in cases
of undue delay federal courts should refrain from entertaining an enemy combatant's habeas corpus petition at least until after the Department, acting via
the CSRT, has had a chance to review his status." (Id. at pp. 66–67.)

The majority also acknowledged that "proper deference must be accorded
to the political branches" when they sought to establish procedural and substantive standards relating to detention and the prevention of acts of terrorism. (Id. at 68). At the same time the majority stated that "Security subsists,
too, in fidelity to freedom's first principles. Chief among these are freedom
from arbitrary and unlawful restraint and the personal liberty that is secured
by adherence to the separation of powers." (Id. at p.69) For, within that structure "few exercises of judicial power are as legitimate or as necessary as the
responsibility to hear challenges to the authority of the Executive to imprison
a person." (Ibid.) He had stated earlier in the majority opinion that the separation of powers principle was based on the need to make "[g]overnment ac-
countable but also to secure individual liberty." (Id. at 12). The principle
"protects persons as well as citizens."(Ibid.)

Although the members of the court had viewed the relevant statutes from
substantially different perspectives they found themselves in even greater disagreement with regard to Supreme Court decisions. Their manifestly great efforts to fit the facts, relevant statutes, constitutional provisions, practical realities, and the on-going well-being of the country into a common outlook failed.
Although the members of the Court were in disagreement as to the meaning to
be given to particular cases, such as Johnson v. Eisentrager, 339 U. S. 763
(1950), and to the terms of the Lease of Lands for Coaling and Naval Stations
Agreement of February 23, 1903 (T.S. No.418) and the Treaty Defining Relations with Cuba, May 29, 1934, (48 Stat. 1683, T. S. No. 866) it was clear that
the majority had rejected the view that Cuba exercised a sufficient amount of
sovereignty over the Naval Station so as to exclude the Court's exercise of jurisdiction to rule on the issuance of habeas corpus writs sought by petitioners
held by U.S. military forces at the Naval Station. This decision, in effect, made
all of the prior holdings of the Supreme Court on the subject academic. The
fact was that the majority had not been able to arrive at a clear and consistent
statement regarding the holdings in these cases, although they stated that a

common thread ran through them, namely "the idea that questions of extraterritoriality turn on objective factors and practical concerns not formalism." (Id., at p. 34.) In the same breath the majority observed that its disparate precedents displayed a "functional approach to questions of extraterritoriality" at odds with the government's "formalistic, sovereignty-based test . . ." and functionalism was the preferred approach. (Ibid.).) This allowed the majority to negate the government's position that the U. S. lacked sovereignty in a legal and technical sense. Substance was to prevail over form.

The majority's appraisal then turned immediately to the observation that the Government's formal sovereignty-based test raised troubling separation of powers concerns as well. The majority expressed the fear that if the United States were to surrender formal sovereignty over any unincorporated territory to a third party, "while at the same time entering into a lease that grants total control over the territory back to the United States, it would be possible for the political branches to govern without legal constraints." (Id., at 35.) The majority addressed this prospect by saying that the Court would not allow the political branches to "switch the Constitution on or off at will . . ." (Ibid.) The majority rejected a regime "in which Congress and the President, not this Court, say 'what the law is.'" (Id., at 36.)

The majority then tied together the separation of powers principle and the habeas corpus privilege. They observed: "These concerns have particular bearing upon the Suspension Clause question in the cases now before us, for the writ of habeas corpus is itself an indispensable mechanism for monitoring the separation of powers. The test for determining the scope of this provision must not be subject to manipulation by those whose power it is designed to restrain." (Ibid.)

Continuing with its analysis of the reach of the Suspension Clause the majority returned to the opinions in the Eisentrager and the other extraterritoriality cases which they had reviewed. They concluded that from these cases could be distilled three relevant factors applicable to the reach of the Clause, e. g., "(1) the citizenship and status of the detainee and the adequacy of the process through which the status determination was made; (2) the nature of the sites where apprehension and then detention took place; and (3) the practical obstacles inherent in resolving the petitioner's entitlement to the writ." Reference was made to the fact that in the above extraterritoriality cases the prisoners had been afforded broader procedural protections than those applicable in the CSRT hearings with the need for habeas corpus review for the CSRT hearings. (Id., at 37). The majority noted that the Government had not presented any credible arguments that the mission at the Naval Station "would be compromised if habeas corpus had jurisdiction to hear the detainees' claims." (Id., at 39.) They concluded that if the privilege were to be denied to these petitioners it would be necessary for Congress to act "in accordance with the requirements of the Suspension Clause." (Id., at 41.)

The majority at the close of its wide-ranging opinion reviewed its operative mandate. The opinion stated: "Our decision today holds only that the petitioners before us are entitled to seek the writ; that the DTA review procedures are an inadequate substitute for habeas corpus; and that the petitioners in these cases need not exhaust the review procedures of the Court of Appeals before proceeding with their habeas corpus actions in the District Court. The only law we identify as unconstitutional is MCA # 7 . . . Accordingly, both the DTA and CSRT process remain intact. Our holding with regard to exhaustion should not be read to imply that a habeas court should intervene the moment an enemy combatant steps foot in a territory where the writ runs. The Executive is entitled to a reasonable period of time to determine a detainee's status before a court entertains the detainee's habeas corpus petition at least until after the Department, acting via the CSRT, has had a chance to review his status." (Id., at 66–67.) Some will applaud what they view as a practical way to deal with detainees. Others, favoring greater latitude for the military in the management of combat operations will consider that the Court has imposed its fiat on the separation of powers principle. Supporters of the Court will reply as Justice Kennedy has reminded us, it is the Court's responsibility to proclaim "what the law is."

3. The Roberts Dissenting Opinion

The dissenting opinion of Chief Justice Roberts by its very nature constituted an attack on the assumed facts, general assumptions, and logic of the majority. It called into question their assessment and interpretation of relevant cases and statutes, particularly their views on the DTA. He provided examples of the practical operational effect of the majority opinion, ridiculed the majority's proposed process with its foreseen infirmities and defects, and concluded that the process set forth in the DTA would have afforded more substantial and more immediate benefits to non-citizen detainees than a future process worked out in the Federal District Courts which followed the proposals enunciated by the majority. He took the position that the rights of U. S. citizen detainees should not be fewer than those of non-citizen detainees. In his words: "For my part, I will assume that any due process rights petitioners may possess are no greater than those of American citizens detained as enemy combatants." (Slip Opinion, p. 15).

Highlighted in the Roberts' dissent was the view that the majority had misread pertinent statutes, that there had been a rejection of the statutory procedures contained in the DTA without "bothering to say what due process rights the detainees possess, without explaining how the statute fails to vindicate those rights, and before a single petitioner has even attempted to avail himself or the law's operation, "(Id., at 1). that there had been disregard for precedent and tradition, that the majority had embarked on abstract and hypothetical concerns, that their opinion had produced a series of impractical and unrealistic processes and procedures, that the majority's outlook was "misguided" and "fruitless," (Id. at 3.) and that despite the guidance and assurances put forward by the majority they had left unanswered identifiable problems so that in the absence of specific rulings the distinct possibility remained that the majority's habeas remedy "will, when all is said and done, end up looking a great deal like the DTA review it rejects." (Id. at 26).

Chief Justice Roberts was attentive to the principle of separation of powers, to due process concerns, to reliance on logical implications relating to the meaning of a statute in order to "avoid constitutional infirmity," (Id., at 23), e. g., the need to "ascertain whether a construction of the statute is fairly possibly by which the [constitutional] question may be avoided . . ." (Id., at 24), to a premature acceptance by the Supreme Court of litigation, i.e., where there had not been a suitable exhaustion of administrative remedies (in this case a declination by the Supreme Court to intervene) "until the D. C. Circuit had addressed the nature and validity of the congressionally mandated proceedings in a given detainee's case," (Id. at 3.), to the availability of the privilege of habeas corpus to the petitioners, to the needs of the American armed forces as they were obliged to deal with security and intelligence-gathering activities, to earlier Supreme Court decisions (specifically to the plurality opinion in Hamdi v. Rumsfeld (2004).

While urging that the majority had not taken a "real world" approach, Chief Justice Roberts claimed that the DTA set forth "the most generous set of procedural protections ever afforded aliens detained by this country as enemy combatants." (Id., at 1.) The separation of powers principle was uppermost in the thinking of the dissenting justices. Much reliance was accorded to the statutory system, including the DTA, constructed by the political branches of the government. It was considered that existing statutes adequately protected all of the constitutional rights to which enemy aliens captured abroad and detained as unlawful combatants might lay claim. Hence, the dissenting justices opposed the majority opinion on the ground that it had shifted sensitive foreign policy and security decision-making from the elected branches of the government to the Federal Judiciary. (Id., at 3). On the basis of this premise the Chief Justice concluded that the majority decision was not "really about the detainees at all, but about the control of federal policy regarding enemy combatants." (Id., at p. 2). The minority justices considered this to be an impermissible inroad into the domain of the political branches.

In examining the role of the Supreme Court within the context of the separation of powers principle he called attention to the view that a statute was presumed to be constitutional. He did not refer to the view that in military and foreign policy matters the federal courts have often expressed deference to Executive views. In his opinion, as in all of the other opinions in this case, there was no mention of "the war against terrorism," although, as in the other opinions, references were made to combatants, enemy combatants, alien enemy combatants, detainees, prisoners of war, terrorism, including acts of terrorism, terrorists, threats by terrorists, and on-going armed conflict.

Chief Justice Roberts agreed that the writ of habeas corpus was intended to protect the fundamental right from suspension unless the public safety required it in the event of rebellion or invasion. The Constitution does not limit this to "persons" or "citizens." It carried with it the right to have access to Federal Courts to test the legality of executive detention. It was his view that "the critical threshold question in these cases, prior to any inquiry about the writ's scope, is whether the system the political branches designed protects whatever rights the detainees may possess." (Id., at 2).

The dissenters acknowledged that in a CSRT proceeding that a detainee would not have all of the rights available in an Article III Court such as access to classified information, although he was entitled to receive an unclassified summary of the evidence in advance of a hearing. It was to be in the detainee's native language. He was able to introduce relevant documentary evidence. However, he was not entitled to counsel. This function was to be replaced by the appointment of a Personal Representative, who was to assist the detainee before the Tribunal, whose function was not to determine innocence or guilt but to determine if the detainee should be classified as an alien enemy combatant. It was urged that non-availability of counsel was counterbalanced by the right to confront witnesses and to call witnesses who were reasonably available. It was noted that a detainee's Personal Representative had access to classified information and was permitted to summarize it for a detainee. The representative could also assist a detainee in the preparation of his case and aid the detainee in presenting evidence to a tribunal. When a case reached the Court of Appeals detainees were to have full access to appellate counsel "and the right to challenge the factual and legal bases of their detentions." (Id., at 19). This position was summarized in the statement that under the DTA a detainee had larger opportunities and more extended processes "in fact, than that afforded prisoners of war or any other alleged enemy combatants in history." (Ibid.) It was concluded that a detainee had an adequate opportunity to know and to contest the grounds for detention and that this was all that was required to meet due process standards.

The dissenters acknowledged that the CSRT procedure allowed for the admission of certain forms of hearsay evidence. Their response was that the Hamdi case expressly approved this use of hearsay by habeas courts. That court had ruled that hearsay evidence "may need to be accepted as the most reliable available evidence from the Government." (Id., at 17). The DTA had imposed limitations on its use. The minority urged that when a review of the detainee's case occurred a ruling could be obtained whether the indicated hearsay violated due process.

The dissenters were frustrated with the majority's holding regarding the applicability of the DTA saying "[r]emarkably, this Court does not require petitioners to exhaust their remedies under the statute; it does not wait to see whether those remedies will prove sufficient to protect petitioners' rights. Instead, it not only denies the D. C. Circuit the opportunity to assess the statutes remedies, it refuses to do so itself: the majority expressly declines to decide whether the CSRT procedures, coupled with Article III review, satisfy the process." (Id., at 4).

The Roberts' opinion emphasized that the majority, because of their misreading of the statute, had failed to understand how the DTA was capable of working, that the majority's concerns were in fact addressed and resolved in the DTA, especially the major problem advanced in the majority holding, namely, that the detainees were not able to introduce at the appeal stage exculpatory evidence discovered after the conclusion of their CSRT proceedings. (Id., at 20).

In addition the majority had established a criterion which had to be met in order to allow for an adequate substitute for habeas corpus. It required the "power to order the conditional release of an individual unlawfully detained." (Majority opinion at p. 59; Roberts' dissent at p. 23). The dissent cited a 2005 Supreme Court decision reading: "The writ's history makes clear that it traditionally has been accepted as the specific instrument to obtain release from [unlawful] confinement." (Id., at 24). The dissenters urged that the DTA could be read similarly. Support for this conclusion was found in the power of the Court of Appeals, the head of Administrative Review Boards, and the CSRTs to order release.

Additionally the minority considered that #10005(e)(2) of the DTA should be read to confer on the Court of Appeals "the authority to order release in appropriate circumstances." Id., at 24. The majority's opposing view was taken to mean that "any interpretation of the statute that would make it an adequate substitute for habeas must be rejected, because Congress could not possibly have intended to enact an adequate substitute for habeas. The Court could have saved itself a lot of trouble if it had simply announced this Catch-22 approach at the beginning rather than the end of its opinion." (Id., at 25)

Based on the proposition that the DTA process would allow a CSRT or an Article III court to base a ruling on facts, the dissent asserted that the majority had invented a "sort of reverse facial challenge . . ." which had been applied "with gusto. If there is any scenario in which the statute might be constitutionally infirm, the law must be struck down." (Id., a t 23 .)

Chief Justice Roberts approached the majority's concern by stating "This court does not require petitioners to exhaust their remedies under the statute; it does not wait to see whether those remedies will prove sufficient to protect petitioners' rights. Instead, it not only denies the D. C. Circuit the opportunity to assess the statute's remedies, it refuses to do so itself: the majority expressly declines to decide whether the CSRT procedures, could with Article III review, satisfy due process." (Id., at 4.)

The Roberts' opinion called attention to the majority's view that in "the ordinary course" the Court would not decide the DTA's constitutionality at this stage, but that it had abandoned that "ordinary course" because of the "gravity" of the constitutional issues presented and the prospect of additional delay. His response was that "It is, however, precisely when the issues presented are grave that adherence to the ordinary course is most important. A principle applied only when it is unimportant is not much of a principle at all, and charges of judicial activism are most effectively rebutted when courts can fairly argue they are following normal practices." (Id., at 6–7).

Chief Justice Roberts also levied a highly practical indictment against the majority's manifest concern with delay. In his view the majority opinion extended the prospects for delay by erecting one set of delays upon the first set. In his view "There is no reason to suppose that review according to procedures the Federal Judiciary will design, case by case, will proceed any faster than the DTA process petitioners disdained." (Id., at 7) Further, since "nobody knows how these new layers of 'habeas' review will operate, or what new procedures they will require, their contours will undoubtedly be subject to fresh bouts of litigation. If the majority were truly concerned about delay, it would have required petitioners to use the DTA process that has been available to them for 2½ years, with its Article III review in the D. C. Circuit." (Ibid).

The minority justices found that the majority opinion had created more problems than helpful results leaving unanswered procedural standards and jurisdictional markers. In their view no guidance was put forward that elaborated how exactly the majority's remedies would differ from the procedural protections available to detainees under the DTA. They asked: "What, for example, will become of the CSRT process?" (Id., at 25). "What makes the majority think witnesses will become magically available when the review procedure is label 'habeas'"? (Ibid) "Or will subpoenas issued by American habeas courts run to Basra?" (Id., p. 26) "Will detainees be able to call active-duty military officers as witnesses? If not, why not?" (Ibid.)

The minority identified the rights to be accorded in the DTA to detainees. They were: (1) "The right to hear the bases of charges against them, including a summary of classified evidence," (2) "The ability to challenge the bases of their detention before military tribunals modeled after Geneva Convention procedures,"(3) "the right before CSRT, to testify, introduce evidence, call witnesses, question those the Government calls, and secure release, if and when appropriate," (4) "the right to the aid of a personal representative in arranging and presenting their cases before a CSRT," and (5) "before the D. C. Circuit, the right to employ counsel, challenge the factual record, contest the lower tribunal's legal determinations ensure compliance with the Constitution and laws, and secure release, if any errors below establish their entitlement to such relief." (Id., at 26–27). They concluded that the DTA satisfied the majority's criteria for assessing adequacy.

In order to bring into bold relief such lessons as may have been learned from the hostile activities of alleged terrorists and the combined efforts of the Executive, Congress and the Court to cope in a timely manner with past, and predictably future, threats to the security of America, the minority justices, after naming five interested groups and institutions: the detainees, Congress, the Great Writ, the rule of law, and the American people asked: "So who has won?" (Id., at 27) Regrettably, the response was: No one.

Chief Justice Roberts provided this grave assessment: "Not the detainees. The Court's analysis leaves them with only the prospect of further litigation to determine the content of their new habeas corpus right, followed by further litigation to resolve their particular cases, followed by further litigation before the D. C. Circuit—where they could have started had they invoked the DTA procedure. Not Congress, whose attempt to 'determine—through democratic means—how best' to balance the security of the American people with the detainees' liberty interests, see Hamdan v. Rumsfeld, 548 U.S. 557, 636 (2006) (Breyer, J., concurring), has been unceremoniously brushed aside. Not the Great Writ, whose majesty is hardly enhanced by its extension to a jurisdictionally quirky outpost, with no tangible results to anyone. Not to the rule of law, unless by that is meant the rule of lawyers, who will now arguably have a greater role than military and intelligence officials in shaping policy for alien enemy combatants. And certainly not the American people, who today lose a bit more control over the conduct of this Nation's foreign policy to unelected politically unaccountable judges." (Id., at 27–28).

If all were losers, the question might still be asked, could there have been any winners?

4. The Scalia Dissenting Opinion

Justice Scalia's dissent began with the view that the Court's intervention was ultra vires. If the majority had adopted that option as it approached the case the DTA would have been implemented by rulings emanating from the Federal Court of Appeals of the District of Columbia. This would have resulted in minimizing the stress placed on the separation of powers system by the majority opinion. When the Scalia view was rejected by the majority he attacked "the legal errors contained in the opinion of the Court." (Scalia, slip opinion, p. 2.) These errors were of a different nature. The graver was the majority's misunderstanding of the Court's role in balancing the separation of powers principle resulting in an overreaching Supreme Court and to judicial supremacy. The second related to the majority's holdings on the combined efforts of the two political branches as reflected in the MCA and the DTA statutes. Also within this second category were judicial views of prior Supreme Court cases and historical views of the geographical reach of the writ of habeas corpus.

Justice Scalia's views were captured in the first paragraph of his dissent: "[t]oday, for the first time in our Nation's history, the Court confers a constitutional right to habeas corpus on alien enemies detained abroad by our military forces in the course of an ongoing war. The Chief Justice's dissent, which I join, shows that the procedures prescribed by Congress in the Detainee Treatment Act provide the essential protections that habeas corpus guarantees; there has been no suspension of the writ; and no basis exists for judicial intervention beyond what the Act allows. My problem with today's opinion is more fundamental still: The writ of habeas corpus does not, and never has, run in favor of aliens abroad: the Suspension Clause thus has no application, and the Court's intervention in this military matter is entirely ultra vires." (Id., at 1.)

With the rejection of this view Justice Scalia mounted an attack on the majority opinion. He challenged their assumptions, their understanding of basic constitutional principles and the meaning to be accorded to them plus the adverse impact the opinion would have on the wellbeing and security of the United States. He was particularly critical of the prospect that alien enemy detainees at Guantanamo might be given greater constitutional rights than those guaranteed to U. S. citizens. Following an extended discussion of the historic aspects of the geographical reach of the habeas corpus writ he held that the distinction between citizens and aliens followed "from the undoubted proposition that the Constitution does not create, nor do general principles of law create, any juridical relation between our country and some undefined, limitless class of noncitizens who are beyond our territory."(Id., at p. 25. Citing Verdo-Urquidez, 404 U. S. 269–270.")

Particularly distasteful to him was the creation by the Supreme Court of the concept of functional sovereignty (as opposed to de jure, with its treaty base) and its application to the U. S. Naval station at Guantanamo. His view stemmed from the holding of the Supreme Court in the Eisentrager case which he construed as holding that the "Constitution does not ensure habeas for aliens held by the United States in areas over which our Government is not sovereign." (Id., at 10). This view was addressed by the majority at considerable length leading Justice Scalia to observe that by "blatantly distorting Eisentrager, the Court avoids the difficulty of explaining why it should be overruled." (Id., at 17.) Further, although the functional test had evaded the "precedential landmine" (Id., p. 18.) of Eisentrager it was "so inherently subjective that it clears a wide path for the Court to traverse in the years to come." (Ibid.)

Justice Scalia placed much emphasis on the separation of powers system. One example was the response of the political branches to the Supreme Court's 2006 holding in Hamdan v. Rumsfeld, where the Court had held that the DTA had not prevented detainees from petitioning district courts for a writ of habeas corpus. The response of the political branches was the adoption of the MCA which "emphatically reassert[ed] " (Id., at 5.) that they "did not want these prisoners filing habeas corpus petitions." (Ibid.) He added "It is therefore clear that Congress and the Executive—both political branches— have determined that limiting the role of civilian courts in adjudicating whether prisoners captured abroad are properly detained is important to success in the war that some 190,000 of our men and women are fighting." (Id., at 5-6).

In concluding that the separation principle had been disregarded by the majority, Justice Scalia said: "The Court today decrees that no good reason to accept the judgment of the other two branches is 'apparent.' [Citation omitted]. 'The Government,' [the Court] declares, 'presents no credible arguments that the military mission at Guantanamo could be compromised if habeas corpus courts had jurisdiction to hear the detainees' claims.' [Citation omitted]. What competence does the Court have to second-guess the judgment of Congress and the President on such a point? None whatever. But the Court blunders in nonetheless. Henceforth, as today's opinion makes unnervingly clear, how to handle enemy prisoners in this war will ultimately lie with the branch that knows least about the national security concerns that the subject entails." (Id., p. 6.)

He suggested that in order to understand the full range of the separation of powers principle each would have to be examined one at a time since only then would the full shape of the principles emerge. He concluded that if the scope of the writ were designed to restrain the actions of the Executive that "the understood limits upon that scope were (as the Court seems not to grasp) just as much 'designed to restrain' the incursions of the Third Branch." (Id., at pp. 8–9). He concluded that "manipulation" of the territorial reach of the writ by either the courts or by the executive branch constituted a threat to the separation of powers. But, even so, the President possessed the final authority over such crucial wartime determinations regarding the "status and continued confinement" of these detainees. (Id., at p. 9). At this point he also asserted that the principle "must be interpreted to mean what they were understood to mean when the people ratified them." (Id. at p. 8).

He concluded his dissent in these words: "Today the Court warps our Constitution in a way that goes beyond the narrow issue of the reach of the Suspension Clause, invoking judicially brainstormed separation-of-powers principles to establish a manipulable 'functional' test for the extraterritorial reach of habeas corpus (and, no doubt, for the extraterritorial reach of other constitutional protections as well). It blatantly misdescribes important precedents, most conspicuously Justice Jackson's opinion for the Court in Johnson v. Eisentrager. It breaks a chain of precedent as old as the common law that prohibits judicial inquiry into detentions of aliens abroad absent statutory authorization. And, most tragically, it sets our military commanders the impossible task of proving to a civilian court under whatever standards the Court devises in the future, that evidence supports the confinement if each and every prisoner." (Id., at 25). He concluded that the ruling of the Court "will make the war harder on us. It will most certainly cause more Americans to be killed." (Slip opinion, p. 2.)

5. An Appraisal

Between 2004 and 2008 the Supreme Court decided five cases involving the rights of alleged terrorists all of which, except for the case of Jose Padilla, dealt with the rights of alien enemy combatants held at the Guantanamo Naval Station in Cuba. Depending on the composition of the Court dissenters generally included Chief Justice Rehnquist, Chief Justice Roberts, and Justices Scalia, Thomas, and Alito. Forming majorities were Justices Stevens, Kennedy, Souter, Ginsburg, and Breyer. Justice Kennedy occupied an important swing position voting with the conservative minority in the Padilla case and the liberal majority in the Boumediene case.

Speaking for the majority in the Boumediene case Justice Kennedy stressed the rights of Guantanamo detainees to several constitutional protections. The first was the Article I guarantee of the privilege of habeas corpus, a constitutional rather than a statutory protection, one that the political branches may not "switch on or off at will." The second was the right under the Due Process amendment to have a "meaningful opportunity to be heard" relating to their engagement in terrorist activities. Undoubtedly such holdings will lead to efforts by the Guantanamo Bay detainees to obtain additional protections contained in the Constitution. Counsel will also, almost certainly, seek to seek to obtain such protections for non-citizen clients situated within the "functional territorial sovereignty" of the United States.

The majority also cast doubt on the precedential value of a long list of Supreme Court cases dealing with enemy aliens, declared unconstitutional Section 7 of the MCA as it sought to provide a valid alternative guarantee to the habeas corpus privilege, and if predictions of the dissenting justices in the Boumediene were correct, will measurably extend the time during which detainees will be held in custody. Much time, it was argued, will be consumed in preparations for trial, the trial, appeals, review, and working out places and conditions of detention for the more dangerous detainees. The majority noted that its judgment applied only to the 58 petitioners before the court, and referred to the need for forums and procedures applicable to the remaining detainees.

As a result of 9/11 the White House embarked on a vast array of military measures aimed at the terrorists which were based on the "war powers" of the president. It was undoubtedly true that the Executive Department somewhat shifted the boundaries of the three branches of the government, with the prior separation of powers balance being weighted more in favor of the Executive Department. This posed concerns over the correct balancing of the powers of the respective branches and raised questions dealing with the traditional civil and political rights and liberties long enjoyed in a free society. These concerns became more evident as battleground combat conditions were disclosed by the media and as the use of torture in detentions and interrogations was routinely reported. Sight was not lost of the fact that there were strong cultural and religious differences between the terrorists and their victims. The selection of weapons and military tactics by the terrorists and their style of warfare produced the condition of asymmetrical war, which required a considerable amount of reorientation on the part of the West. As casualties and fatalities mounted people began to wonder if there was any end to it. Concerned observers began to ask if there were not better approaches for dealing with the detainees than were being practiced.

One assessment has been that of Benjamin Wittes[49] who has urged that Congress create an "administrative detention scheme" allowing for "indefinite incarceration" to be supervised by a special civilian court for detainees, but subject to the imperative of "fundamental fairness and due process." It would accord fewer rights than those normally available to criminal defendants in Article III courts. This thesis has been described by Curtis A.

Bradley[50] as an effort to "move the debate beyond formal arguments about what is and what is not allowed under existing law toward consideration of a new legal regime that would provide the government with needed flexibility while protecting individual liberties." Joining the dialogue was Kenneth Roth who has phrased the issue as "whether the United States' criminal justice system can handle terrorism cases or whether due process should be sacrificed in the name of security."[51] In his view the employment of preventive detention "would effectively move Guantanamo onshore and make its detention regime a regular part of the U. S. government's arsenal. The temptation would be enormous to exploit the proceedings' secrecy and lax standards of evidence in order to pursue people with only tenuous connections to terrorist activity. Adopting such a system would transform the United States from one of the world's most progressive nations when it comes to protecting the rights of criminal suspects to one of the least."[52]

While such suggestions reflect concerns over whether Article III courts or Military Commissions can supply "practical justice," and whether something worse may be in store, the fact remains that counsel both for detainees and the Department of Defense are engaged in an on-going contest to obtain the advantages available or potentially available to each by a preferred process.

Following the decisions of the Supreme Court in the five detainee cases a critic can examine the wisdom of the Bush administration's decision in 2001 to use its "war powers" to create a class of persons described as unlawful alien enemy combatants. That the Guantanamo detainees did not fit into the Geneva definition of a prisoner of war and the need for a scheme of classification was sufficiently evident. In the 2004 decision of the Supreme Court in Hamdi v. Rumsfeld there had been an opportunity to define the legal components of an unlawful enemy combatant and to determine how long a Guantanamo prisoner could be detained. This void was filled with the adoption of the Military Commissions Act on October 17, 2006. At the time President Bush in 2001 decided to use his "war powers" to establish the executive-based military commission, it was by no means clear that this action would be invalidated by the Supreme Court. In retrospect the Bush administration would have been much wiser, particularly when Congress was heavily influenced by the enormity of the 9/11 disaster, to have sought legislation providing for a military commission and other procedures designed to inhibit the actions of terrorists. Yet, the Bush decision was not an entirely wasted effort, since the infrastructures of the early commission were used when the Administrative Review Boards, Combatant Status Review Tribunals, and the new Military Commissions were being constituted. Their provisions would be tested later in terms of constitutionality.

The Boumediene decision was unquestionably influenced by the long time detention of the petitioners without access to counsel. The justices held differing opinions as how to bring their cases to closure as promptly as possible following remand to the trial courts. Account had to be taken of the need to establish trial dates to consider the habeas corpus petitions, hearings, opinions, appeals, and all of the other aspects of the grist of the legal mill. The consolidation of petitions would serve to expedite matters. The minority justices in the case considered that with the Military Commissions coming into operation that the most expeditious process for the detainees was to make use of the Commissions with appeals to the Court of Appeals of the District of Columbia.

Justice Kennedy was aware that delays might be occasioned in both situations. He observed that if there were a petition before a habeas corpus court that the judge would have to be persuaded that the Executive Department had engaged in "undue delay" before granting the petition. Further, the DOD was to have the right to "review the status" of a detainee whose case was before a CSRT before a writ were issued. A habeas corpus court might have to make "accommodations" favorable to the government but without "impermissibly diluting the protection of the writ." But, even in this preferred status Justice Kennedy, following an expression of confidence in the expertise and competence of District Court judges, stated that in an application by a detainee for the writ that the process need not "duplicate" the legal procedures more generally applied by a Federal District court "in all respects."

An unknown variable would be the length of delay caused in the appeals process in each of the two situations. Perhaps some guidance can be obtained through the review of the problems faced by international criminal tribunals as they have endeavored to match the presence of distant witnesses and accession to factual materials available from distant locations.

The practice of torture and other cruel, inhuman, or degrading treatment or punishment in contravention of the 1984 CAT by the armed forces at Guantanamo may have influenced the outcome in the Boumediene case. Highly publicized reports plus very extended periods of imprisonment for many of the detainees during which harsh measures most certainly took place added to the credibility of prisoner complaints. Such activities fitted the patterns of conduct known to have taken place by DOD personnel and CIA officials in Afghanistan and Iraq. Numerous governmental reports subsequently confirmed the early concerns of the judiciary.

The Boumediene case with its adoption of the "functional equivalent" of territorial sovereignty to an offshore area will undoubtedly be employed by counsel seeking the application of other constitutional guarantees to the claims of detainees, and even, perhaps to persons who have few normal relationships with the United States but who have arguable grievances attributable to the United States or its legal persons. In the former category was the claim presented on behalf of Salim Ahmed Hamdan in July, 2008, to the Military Commission exercising jurisdiction in his case. It was argued that he would be deprived of the Equal Protection of the Laws if he were to be tried before a Military Commission characterized as an untested judicial system.[53] The argument was based on the proposition that such an untested system would ultimately be declared unconstitutional and therefore that the Military Commission option should not be allowed to proceed. This argument was rejected by both a Federal District Court judge and the president of the Military Commission. If these rulings are upheld the constitutional protections to be accorded to Al Qaeda defendants will not be augmented.

The constitutional "moving sidewalk" is healthy and present and future justices, although they may object to some of its characteristics and the freight being transported, can be counted on to make continuing and effective use of it.

6. Parhat v. Gates, D. C. Cir., June 20, 2008, No. 06-1397

This was the first case to reach the Court of Appeals for the District of Columbia from a Combatant Status Review Tribunal established under the DTA of 2005. Guantanamo Bay detainees consisting of Uighur Moslems of Chinese nationality had been classified as alien enemy combatants. They had been captured in Afghanistan following their flight from China where they had been persecuted because of their religion. They contended that they were no threat to the United States. In the proceedings before the CSRT the government argued that they had been trained in the use of small arms at a camp operated by the East Turkistan Islam Movement (ETIM), which had been supported by the Taliban and Al Qaeda and had become terrorists supporting anti-American activities.

In the proceedings before the CSRT the government, after first identifying them "as attractive candidates for release," determined that sufficient grounds existed for detention. Following that decision these individuals became the first to ask for a review by the Court of Appeals. The Court of Appeals then examined the provisions of the DTA relating to the evidence that had to be presented to the CSRT in order support a finding. The Appeals Court found that the tribunals decision had not been supported "by a preponderance of the evidence," and that the government's evidence had been based on unverified claims contained in Department of State and DOD documents. The Court of Appeals rejected the government's effort to protect from public disclosure the non-classified information presented to it. It also determined that the names the government officials involved in the findings should be made public. A question arose relating to the weight of rebuttable presumptions provided for in the statute. While the government was entitled to the benefits of such presumptions, the court held that it had not been able to assess the reliability of the government's evidence, including a review of the government's secret evidence, and consequently held that the presumption was not available. The court, while agreeing that the government could make use of hearsay evidence, declared that its introduction would be subject to the Court's review of its reliability. The Court also rejected the government's view that the legislation permitted the condition of an "essentially unreviewable executive discretion."

It was held that the government's case was not consistent with the standards and procedures established by the DOD. As a result the government was directed to release these detainees, or transfer them to a hospitable government, or to convene a new CSRT that would apply the legal requirements identified in the opinion.

The Court noticed, as had been pointed out in the Boumediene case of June 12, 2008, that an alternative procedure was available, namely a petition for a writ of habeas corpus to a Federal District Court.

2. Criminal Prosecutions in Foreign Courts

On October 26, 2007, while former Secretary of Defense Rumsfeld was in France, three foreign Human-Rights organizations and the American Center for Constitutional Rights (CCR) filed criminal charges alleging that he had ordered and sponsored torture while in office. The case was initiated in the Tribunal de Grande Instance in Paris. The CAT Convention of 1984 to which both the United States and France are parties, as well as his presence in France, were citied as grounds for French jurisdiction. The French court was provided with the affidavit of U. S. Army Brigadier General Janis Karpinski, the former commandant of the Abu Ghraib prison in Iraq, identifying the defendant's responsibility for the abuse of detainees.

Cases had been filed in Germany in 2004 and in 2006 against Secretary of Defense Rumsfeld. The first case was dismissed in February 2005 as a result of official U. S. pressures. The second case, brought by the CCR and the International Federation for Human Rights, on behalf of 12 Iraqi citizens who had been subjected to torture at Abu Ghraib, was dismissed in April 2007, although Germany subscribes to the universal theory of jurisdiction. An appeal was lodged.

Two other cases were filed against the Secretary of Defense. One was in Argentina in 2005; the second Sweden in 2007. Each charged the Secretary of Defense with criminal conduct. The reasons underlying such charges, as well as before privately organized international tribunals often consisting of legal scholars, and also persons possessing particular professional competences in the social sciences, religious studies, and philosophy, have been varied. In some instances there was a genuine belief on the part of the persons instituting the suits that convictions would result and penalties would be assessed. In other cases the purpose is to use the judicial process to publicize both factual and legal criteria. The long-term expectation is that either through convictions or the attendant publicity that in the future highly placed political figures will avoid conduct identified as torture.

3. CONCLUSION

The decision of the Bush administration that terrorist detainees, who were not within the boundaries of the United States, were to be treated as unlawful enemy combatants and were not entitled to the legal benefits belonging to Prisoners of War, produced the litigation that has been described above. A central aspect of that litigation has been based on the availability to such detainees of the guarantees of the Constitution, principally the right to a writ of habeas corpus as identified in the Suspension Clause and in ensuing legislation. The case of Boumediene v. Bush and the companion case of Al Odah v.United States are landmark decisions and will become an insightful source for understanding the dynamics associated with the separation of powers principle as it relates to war, "war powers," and to the use of armed force.

NOTES

1. 321 F. 3d 1136 (D.D.C. 2002).
2. 321 F. 3d 1144 (C.A.D.C, 2003).
3. Proof of the wisdom of this outlook has been demonstrated in 2006 and 2007 by the growth in numbers and the high commitments of Al Qaeda members. B. Riedel, Al Qaeda Strikes Back, 86 Foreign Affairs , No. 3, p.24 (May/June 2007).
4. S. I. Vladeck, A Small Problem of Precedents: 18 U.S.C. #4001(9) and the Detention of U. S. Citizen "Enemy Combatants", 112 Yale L. J. p. 961, No. 4 (January 2003).
5. Los Angeles Times, A30, December 3, 2003.
6. Los Angeles Times, A16, December 4, 2003.
7. Patriot Act, Pub. L. 107-40, #2(a), 115 Stat. 224 (2001).
8. Directive, President Bush to Secretary of Defense Rumsfeld, June 9, 2002. www://findlaw.com.

9 352 F. 3d. 695.

10. 343 U. S. 579, 637–638 (1952).

11. 542 U. S. 426 (2004).

12. 415 F. 3d 33 (D. C. Cir. 2005).

13. 423 F. 3d 386 (4th Cir 2005).

14. 71 U. S. (Wall.) 2 (1866).

15. No. 06-633, 547 U. S.—(2006).

16. No. 05-6396.

17. Id., at pp. 10–13.

18. Christian Science Monitor, August 31, 2006, p. 4.

19. Los Angeles Times, February 27, 2007, p. A10.

20. Los Angeles Times, February 23, 2007, p. A16.

21. Ibid.

22. Los Angeles Times, p. A-11, May 9, 2007.

23. Christian Science Monitor, p. 10, November 16, 2006.

24. 344 F. Supp. 2d 152 (DDC 2004) November 8, 2004. Memorandum Opinion, July 15, 44 ILM, No. 5, p. 1276 (September 2005).

25. 355 F. Supp. 2d 443 (D.D.C. 2005).

26. This subject is dealt with in detail below in section E.

27. 415 F. 3d 33 (D. C. Cir 2005).

28. 64 Stat.115.

29. 542 U.S. 466 (2004).

30. 126 S. Ct. 2749 (2006).

31. 64 Stat. 115.

32. J. P. Cerone, Status of Detainees in Non-International Armed Conflict and Their Protection in the Course of Criminal Proceedings: The Case of Hamdan v. Rumsfeld, 10 ASIL Insights, No. 7, p. 1, July 14, 2006.

33. Pub. L. 109-148, 119 Stat. 2680.

34. Ibid.

35. 10 U.S.C. # 821.

36. J. Ku and J. Yoo, Hamdan v. Rumsfeld: The Functional Case for Foreign Affairs Deference to the Executive Branch, 23 Constitutional Commentary (2006). The authors argued that the holding would "further disrupt the traditional system of political cooperation between Congress and the President in the conduct of wars," "would raise the transaction costs for policy making in wartime," and that the "executive branch has strong institutional advantages over courts in the interpretation of laws relating to the conduct of war."http://papers.ssrn.com/sol3/papers.cfm?abstract_id =945454. N. K. Katyal, Counsel of Record in Hamdan v. Rumsfeld has observed that the case was "a rare Supreme Court rebuke to the President during armed conflict." Hamdan v. Rumsfeld: The Legal Academy Goes to Practice, 120 Har. L. Rev. 66 (2006). However, members of the Senate, namely, Jon Kyl and Lindsey Graham filed amicus briefs supporting the powers of the President. For a constructive recommendation, see B. C. Baldrate, The Supreme Court's Role in Defining the Jurisdiction of Military Tribunals: A Study, Critique & Proposal for Hamdan v. Rumsfeld, 186 Mil. L. Rev. 1 (Winter 2005).

37. 370 Fed. 3d 41 D.C. (2004). Reliance was placed on Cicippio-Puleo v. Islamic Republic of Iran, 353 Fed. 3d 1024 (D. C. Cir 2004). President Bush at the end of 2007 threatened not to sign the Department of Defense Authorization bill since it include a provision that would revive the right of these plaintiffs to obtain judicial relief. The plaintiffs indicated that they did not expect Iraq to pay the judicially determined damages, but they believed that with such legislation the Executive Department would have to negotiate with Iraq in order to protect their interests. The President, evidently, considered such legislation to be a Congressional effort to control his foreign relations powers.

38. Pub. L. 109-366, 120 Stat. 2600. See Chapter 7.2. for an extended treatment.

39. Hamdan v. Rumsfeld. Citing, United States v. Verdugo-Urquidez, 294 U.S. 259, 271 (1990). He added: "My ruling does not address whether and to what extent enemy aliens may invoke other constitutional rights; I find only that the Suspension Clause does not guarantee the right to petition for habeas corpus to non-resident enemy aliens captured and detained outside the United States." p. 21, fn. 15.

40. Ibid., p. 22, fn. 16. Judge Robertson was careful to point out that his ruling was based on the divestment of habeas corpus jurisdiction and that he had not dealt with the other arguments that the "MCA is unconstitutional—because it does not provide an adequate substitute for habeas review, because it violates the principle of separation of powers by instructing the courts to ignore the Supreme Court's ruling that the Geneva Conventions afford judicially enforceable protections . . . , because it is an unlawful Bill of Attainder, and because it violates Equal Protection."

41. Ibid.

42. 476 F 3d 981 (D.C. Cir. 2007). On January 19, 2005 a Federal District Court of the District of Columbia had ruled in the cases of Boumediene v. Bush, No.04cv1166 and Khalid v. Bush, No. 04cv1141 on the "novel issue of whether there is any viable legal theory under which a federal court could issue a writ of habeas corpus challenging the legality of the detention of non-resident aliens captured abroad and detained outside the territorial sovereignty of the United States, pursuant to lawful military orders, during a Congressionally authorized conflict." 335 F. Supp. 2d 311, 314 (D.D.C. 2005). Finding no "viable theory" under which the writs could be issued, the Court also found that "with respect to [Petitioners'] allegations that the conditions of their custody might violate existing United States law, such alleged conduct, even if it had occurred . . . does not support the issuance of the writ because, though deplorable if true, it does not render the custody itself unlawful." Id. at 324. Accordingly a Final Judgment dismissing the habeas corpus petitions was entered on February 18, 2005.

43. Numerous amicus briefs were filed during that period. One, dated November 1, 2006, filed by seven former federal judges urged the court to consider such matters as: allowing the life long detention of a detainee when credible evidence indicated he had been tortured, that the statutory scheme was an inadequate surrogate for the writ of habeas corpus, that evidence gathered through torture was "inherently unreliable," and permitting detentions based on such evidence tainted the judicial process. In their view the "common law of the Constitution" should be taken into account in determining if the MCA and the DTA had suspended the writ of habeas corpus.

44. Hamdan/Khadr v. Gates, 06-1169.

45. Two cases were under review: Hamdan v. Gates and Khadr v. Bush (06-1169). The charge against Khadr was killing an Army Green Beret with a hand grenade. Justices Kennedy, Scalia, Thomas, and Alito voted against the hearing; Justice Souter, Ginsburg, and Breyer wished to hear the matter. The petitioners' procedures were unusual in three respects: two separate cases were combined in a single petition for certiorari, and in Hamdan's case there had not been a final decision from a court of appeals. This meant that he was seeking the writ prior to judgment, a highly unusual procedure. Third, they sought an expedited hearing prior to the June recess of the Court.

46. 2.04-cv002257.Hff.

47. Al-Marri v. Wright, Court of Appeals, 4th Circuit, No.06-7427 (2007) p. 53.

48. An early appraisal of the Boumediene case written by Andrew Kent, is Supreme Court Holds that Noncitizens Detained at Guantanamo Have a Constitutional Right to Habeas Corpus Review by Federal Civilian Courts, 12 ASIL Insight, No., 1, p. 1, June 20, 2008.

49. B. WITTES, LAW AND THE LONG WAR, THE FUTURE OF JUSTICE IN THE AGE OF TERROR (2008).

50. Terror and the Law, The Limits of Judicial Reasoning in the Post-9/11 World, 87 Foreign Affairs No. 4, July/August (2008), p. 133.

51. Kenneth Roth, After Guantanamo, The Case Against Preventive Detention, 87 Foreign Affairs, No.3, May/June (2008), p. 9.

52. Id., at 12. Mr. Roth is Executive Director of Human Rights Watch.

53. Los Angeles Times, A14, July 18, 2008. The motion was denied by the Federal District Court judge and by the president of the Commission. It was the contention of Hamdan's lawyers that it didn't make sense "to conduct a trial under rules that are likely to be found unconstitutional later on. Proceeding with this trial now will only draw out a legal process that has taken far too long already and further discredit[s] a system that has been a disgrace from the start." Ibid.

Chapter Ten

The Decisions of Military Commissions, June 4, 2007, and Subsequent Proceedings

1. THE DECISIONS OF JUNE 4, 2007.

All of this in the Military Commission cases of Mr.Omar Ahmed Khadr[1] and Mr. Salim Ahmed Hamdan[2] came to a sudden and grinding halt on June 4, 2007. Opinions rendered on that date by Colonel Peter E. Brownback III, Military Judge in the Khadr case and Captain Keith J. Allred, Military Judge in the Hamdan case, both of whom had been detailed by the Department of Defense to serve on Military Commissions, held that the Commissions did not have jurisdiction to proceed. The judges based this holding on their finding that the Combatant Status Review Tribunals that had been created prior to the enactment of the MCA on October 17, 2006 had failed to make the required technical determinations regarding the legal status of the detainees required to vest jurisdiction in the Commissions. The Tribunals, had classified detainees as "enemy combatants" and had defined them as "an individual who was part of or supporting Taliban of Al Qaeda forces, or associated forces that are engaged in hostilities against the United States or its coalition partners. This includes any person who has committed a belligerent act or has directly supported hostilities in aid of enemy armed forces." The instructions were based on the DOD Order of July 7, 2004 that established the CSRTs. The June 4, Military Commission 2007 Orders held that intervening legislation, namely the MCA, required a finding by the CSRTs that the detained person was "an unlawful enemy combatant . . ." and that "until such time as a CSRT (or other competent tribunal) makes a finding that a person is an unlawful enemy combatant, the provisions of the MCA do not come into play and such person may not be charged, charges may not be referred to a military commission for trial, and the military commission has no jurisdiction to try him."[3] The failure to recite the precise language of the statute was deemed to prevent the Commission from exercising jurisdiction.[4]

The 2006 MCA in section 948d(a) granted jurisdiction to a Military Commission to try identified offenses "when committed by an alien unlawful enemy combatant." It added in Section 948d(b) that such commissions "shall not have jurisdiction over lawful enemy combatants." These provisions contemplated that two steps would be pursued. First, there was to be an administrative decision by the CSRT establishing the status of a person for purposes of the MCA. That status would be either of a lawful enemy combatant or of an unlawful enemy combatant. Second, when the status hearing resulted in a finding that a person was an unlawful enemy combatant the provisions of the MCA became relevant regarding the imposition of applicable penalties. The initial finding would have to be more than that the detainee was an "enemy combatant;" it had to indicate that the person was an "unlawful enemy combatant." The failure of the CSRT to make this distinction, prevented, pursuant to the rulings of Colonel Brownback and Captain Allred, the Military Commissions from proceeding to the second stage for lack of jurisdiction. Both judges held that the dismissals were without prejudice to new governmental initiatives.

Following these decisions the prosecution in the Khadr case moved for reconsideration. On June 29, 2007 Judge Brownback ruled that the prosecution had not produced any new facts or that the law had been changed and upheld the earlier ruling.[5] At issue was the jurisdiction of the Commission and whether under the existing laws and regulations whether jurisdiction was to be established initially in the Combatant Status Review Tribunal proceedings, or if this could be presented initially to the Commission subject to the determination to be made there. Colonel Brownback held that the condition of jurisdiction had to be determined prior to a reference of a matter to a Commission. In noting that the prosecution is "the proponent for jurisdiction over an individual . . . the prosecution was alerted well ahead of time that it was going to be required to state in open court that there was a CSRT determination that the accused was an alien unlawful enemy combatant. Such a determination was not presented."[6] Only if that fact had been initially determined would the Commission then possess the power to adjudicate the matter.

However, to this was added by Colonel Brownback: "In paragraphs 6d thru 6r of its motion the government appears to assert that the Military Judge was unaware of his authority to determine his jurisdiction in the case. In subparagraph 6i, the government directs the Military Judge's attention to R.M.C. [Rules for Military Commission] 201(b)(3)-'A military commission always has jurisdiction to determine whether it has jurisdiction.' This entire line of argument is confusing given the ruling complained about by the prosecution in this case. The Military Judge determined that he had jurisdiction to decide jurisdiction. He then decided the Military Commission did not have jurisdiction. The written order is entitled 'Order on Jurisdiction' (AE 015)."[7]

Colonel Brownback then held that the following factors required the establishment of the initial jurisdiction by the CSRT before the Commission could proceed. The Commission's authority was subject to the Supreme Court's ruling in Hamdan v. Rumsfeld that common Article 3 of the Geneva Conventions applied to the trial of detainees by Military Commissions. And that the article required that such trials be conducted by "a regularly constituted court, affording all the judicial guarantees which are recognized as indispensable by civilized peoples." While acknowledging that most courts do not insist on proof of jurisdiction before starting the trial of an accused, "Military Commissions are distinct and different from any other court in the United States."[8] Further, "[a]lthough there is no express statutory directive that the government must establish jurisdiction before it is allowed to proceed with a Military Commission, there are clear and unambiguous indicia that Congress intended that such initial jurisdiction be established before the mechanism set up by the M.C.A. was used in the case of a given person."

Additional reliance was based on the fundamental distinction between "lawful" and "unlawful" enemy combatants. Colonel Brownback noted that "lawful" enemy combatants can "never be tried by a Military Commission . . . [and that such persons] should be excluded by a proper CSRT at the front end of the process, and should never be subjected to the Military Commission system or process."[9] Further support was found in the 2004 holdings of the Supreme Court in both the Rasul v. Bush and Hamdi v. Rumsfeld cases and the DTA of 2005 calling or the creation of CSRTs and Administrative Review Boards. Additional support was derived from the Hamdan case and the enactment of the M.C.A. which in "dispositive" language required the acceptance of a CSRT determination. He concluded that it was the function lf the CSRT to "separate the 'unlawful enemy combatant' detainees from the 'enemy combatant detainees, and that only those detainees designated as unlawful enemy combatants by a CSRT or other competent tribunal be handled by the Military Commission process established by the M.C.A."[10]

Colonel Brownback concluded his procedural review of the Khadr case: "Given that the use of military courts to try civilians is not favored, Congress could not have intended the logical, if unintended, result of the government's argument and position in this case: the military can seize whomever it wants, charge them, refer them to trial by Military Commission, and only then, after the Commission has been called to order, will the initial question of jurisdiction in accordance with the M.C.A. be resolved."[11]

Turning to a review of his earlier substantive holding Colonel Brownback concluded that the Commission had been presented only with a charge sheet alleging that Mr. Khadr was "an enemy combatant," as determined by the CSRT and since the term "unlawful enemy combatant" had not been used, and since the only other relevant fact was the President's Memorandum of February, 2002, that "initial jurisdiction to try the accused had not been established."[12]

Captain Allred stated in the case before him that the MCA "offers another route to a finding of jurisdiction: a finding by a CSRT 'before, on, or after' the enactment of the MCA, that an accused is an alien unlawful enemy combatant. The October 2004 CSRT finding was before the enactment of the MCA, but it found only that the accused was an enemy combatant"[13] These holdings would require reopening the two cases, and others where the government wished to prosecute persons deemed to be alien unlawful enemy combatants. Guidance would be available in the terms of Article 3 of the 1949 POW Geneva Convention, which clearly identifies the conditions which have to be met in order to qualify as lawful enemy combatants. Those aliens who were captured while engaging in hostile military activities, but who did not meet the Article 3 requirements, would be deemed to be alien unlawful enemy combatants. POWs have been described as privileged combatants with their normal battlefield conduct excluded from prosecutions. Persons failing to meet POW status do not achieve the status of privileged or lawful combatants, and when aliens, and when engaged in hostile military activities, do meet the status of unlawful enemy combatants.

The efforts to dispose of these matters are reminiscent of the observation that everything takes place when it occurs, unless a little later. Or, as Yogi Berra historically observed" It isn't over until its over."

Governments operate in the same manner, at least in the United States. Congress enacts a bill, the President signs and proclaims a new statute, and following transactions relying on the law, the Supreme Court throws a switch and says that the transaction was flawed. That was what happened when the Military Commission judges ruled that they had no jurisdiction in the 2007 cases because the executive branch had not complied with the MCA—that the currency of "enemy combatants" did not meet the debt to be paid in the currency of "unlawful enemy combatants."

If a way can be found to designate the Guantanamo Bay detainees as "unlawful enemy combatants," in situations where that classification can be justified, the Military Commissions would possess the required jurisdiction. The existing, highly detailed, conditions governing the procedures and findings of Combat Status Reviews Tribunals and the decisions of Military Commissions, should ensure that, if they are followed, future determinations by the Military Commission would meet the requirements of a fair and impartial trial. Thus, to remedy the problem of jurisdiction, a new Presidential or DOD Order might call for a new review in each case, to determine if the existing evidence would support a finding of "unlawful enemy combatant" status. This, however, has been subject to dispute with the argument having been made that whatever changes might be required respecting CSTR procedures and hearings would have to receive Congressional approval. A response to such an approach has called attention to the fact that at the second or trial stage of Military Commission proceedings the MCA allows Commission members to accept or reject the factual findings of the CSRTs.

The two decisions have rekindled earlier criticism of the Combatant Status Review Tribunals process by defense lawyers, Human Rights activists, and administration opponents. It has also been suggested that alien enemy combatants charged with violations of American criminal laws dealing with illegal terrorist activities should be prosecuted in civilian courts. The burdens imposed on early and speedy trials by access to such courts constitute a substantial concern. Nonetheless, this has not prevented proposals to close the detention facility at the U. S. Naval Station at Guantanamo. Among those in July, 2007, who favored such action were Secretary of Defense Gates, former Secretary of State Powell, and many of the candidates campaigning in 2007 for the office of President. It has been suggested that failure of individuals to meet the Article 3 Geneva Convention conditions while engaging in military operations is not necessarily a crime under the laws of war. Also there has been a certain amount of confusion over the unqualified expression "combatants." If lawful combatants, and meeting Geneva POW requirements, it would not be a crime for them to engage in hostilities against American troops. But, terrorists are not parties to the Geneva Convention, and are not able to establish any grounds under it against prosecutions under national laws. And, if they were unlawful combatants, even when not taking into account allegations that they are terrorists, they could not claim Geneva protections and would be subject to existing U.S. and international law.

The New York Times editorial of June 6, 2007, entitled "Gitmo: A National Disgrace," taking its cue from the first two holdings in the Military Commission cases, described the "special detention system [as being] so fundamentally corrupt that the only solution is to tear it down and start again." The CSRTs were described as being "in fact, kangaroo courts that give the inmates no chance to defend themselves, allow evidence that was obtained through torture and can be repeated until one produces the answer the Pentagon wants." Congress was called upon to "restore the right of inmates of Guantanamo Bay to challenge their detentions." It "should repeal the Military Commission Act and start anew on a just system for determining whether prisoners are unlawful combatants," and should "shut down" the Naval Base. In summary, the editorial asserted that "The camp was created on a myth—

that the American judicial system could not handle prisoners of 'the war against terror.' It was built on a lie—that the hundreds of detainees at Gitmo are all dangerous terrorists. And it was organized around a fiction—that Mr. Bush had the power to create this rogue system in the first place."[14] The words have a populist ring. The problem, while taking the indicated sentiments into account, is whether the desired goals would be more likely to be achieved by modifying and perfecting the existing model than by starting completely anew so that a workable system could be delivered within a reasonable time frame. The recent history of the art of accommodation in the Congress has demonstrated that there could not be any quick and easy fixes.

The June 4, 2007 Commission decisions are governed by Section 950g. of the Military Commissions Act. It provides that the Court of Appeals for the District of Columbia "shall have exclusive jurisdiction to determine the final judgment rendered by a military commission (as approved by the convening authority) under this chapter." However, there first must be either a waiver or exhaustion of "all other appeals" under the chapter. Further, in the two cases the Commissioners kept the door open for governmental responses. Until such action takes place it is doubtful that the "finality" required by the statue had occurred.

2. OPINION OF U. S MILITARY COMMISSION REVIEW COURT, CMCR 07-001, SEPTEMBER 24, 2007

Happily in these two cases it was not necessary to reinvent the wheel or to pursue overly imaginative legal proposals. The authors of the 2006 MCA statute made provision for a Court of Military Commission Review. Section 950 (f)(d) limited its jurisdiction to "only with respect to matters of law." On July 4, 2007, the prosecutors filed an appeal with the Court. On September 24, 2007, the Court overruled the decision of the trial judge in the Khadr case and reinstated terrorism charges against him. In doing so the tribunal indicated that the distinction between "enemy combatant" and "unlawful enemy combatant" was essentially semantic and concluded that the military tribunal system had the authority to try Khadr. In reaching that conclusion the tribunal indicated that it had not been established whether Khadr was in fact an illegal enemy combatant and that this was to be determined by the judge in the commission proceedings. The government asked the appeal's panel to review the holdings of the trial judges. The Court concluded that the trial judges possessed the required jurisdiction to decide whether the accused were "unlawful enemy combatants."[15] This resulted in restating the charges originally made. While it was agreed that the trial judges initially had, in some respects, properly viewed the terms of the statute, ultimately they had failed to recognize that a trial judge was obliged to be the first to determine if the court could decide the issue of jurisdiction. In focusing on the accused as "enemy combatants" the trial judges failed to employ "less exacting standards" than those contained in the statute. The Court also offered several observations relating to the role of trial court judges. These will render it easier to proceed against a detainee when the next case arises relating to such unlawful enemy combatants. A Commission had the power to receive evidence of the activity of an accused so as to allow it to determine the status of a combatant. The extent of an involvement in terrorism could be weighed.

3. THE DECISION OF DECEMBER 5, 2007

In the December 5, 2007 case, which involved Salim Ahmed Hamdan, a Military Commission was asked to revise its early classification. It was argued that he was a civilian in a support role as Osama bin Ladens's driver, and that he should have been classified as a POW and not an unlawful enemy combatant. In this case Mr. Hamdan had been able to obtain legal counsel. Counsel for Mr. Hamdan tried unsuccessfully to bring other detainees before the Commission as witnesses for the purpose of substantiating the contention. His counsel was successful in securing the testimony of detainees that Mr. Hamdan was subject to more stringent detention conditions than they were. The ruling that other high level detainees could not testify, including civilian witnesses from Yemen, was based principally on the inadequacy of security facilities at Guantanamo rather than on the belief that they did not have meaningful testimony to offer to the Commission. As in the first two cases the Commission faulted the Combatant Status Review Tribunal for not making a sufficient inquiry into the nature of Hamdan's combatant conduct. The presiding judge at the Commission hearing ruled that there was ample doubt as to the Commission's jurisdiction to let the defense argue the status issue.

It is doubtful if the issues presented in these truly historic cases have been completely resolved. Future litigation is likely to result relating to the DTA and the MCA and to the powers of the President during a period of armed conflict contesting orders and decrees issued by him. The Supreme Court may still be asked to resolve whether terrorists can qualify as prisoners of war, on what legal grounds an appellant can challenge his detention, and the appropriate American tribunal to render a valid decision.

From a practical point of view the government may decide to release to a country willing to accept them of those inconsequential detainees without trial while reserving for trial those deemed to be the principal leaders of terrorist movements. Such prosecutions would be in courts, military or civilian, affording required constitutional due process guarantees. Relevant to these questions are the provisions of the DTA and the MCA. This requires an assessment of their terms, the political and legal considerations underlying them, and the outlooks of influential opinion makers. Not to be overlooked is the unresolved problem of the amount of judicial "deference" to be accorded to decisions made by the executive department.

The respect to be accorded to decisions of military commissions has resulted in appraisals of how their work is conducted. Section 949a of the statute, entitled "Rules," refers to pretrial, trial, and post-trial procedures, "including elements and modes of proof," which may be prescribed by the Secretary of Defense. He is required by the statute, in so far as this is considered "practical or consistent with military and intelligence activities," to be guided by "the principles of law and the rules of evidence in trial by general courts-martial." Section 949b then enumerates several of traditional procedural guarantees embraced in federal statutes for cases tried in American constitutional courts. Highlighted are rules relating to the admissibility of evidence.

The appraisals also extend to powers of the Convening Authority. Section 948h. prescribes that the Secretary of Defense "or by "any officer or official of the United States designated by the Secretary for that purpose" may convene a military commission.

To ensure the independence of such commissions and its members Section 949b states that no convening authority "may censure, reprimand, or admonish the military commission . . . with respect to the findings or sentence adjudged by the military commission, or with respect to any other exercises of its or his functions in the conduct of the proceedings." The Secretary of Defense appointed Major General John Altenburg to this position.

Following a trial before a military commission its finding and sentence are to be reported to the Convening Authority for review pursuant to Sections 950b., 950c., and 950d. of the statute. The question has arisen whether in 2007 military commissions were operating in compliance with the provisions of the statute, and more particularly whether high level political appointees through their actions had restricted the impartiality of the convening authority and had presented questions as to the legitimacy of the commission structure.[16]

4. THE FILING OF FORMAL CHARGES AGAINST SIX DETAINEES ON FEBRUARY 11, 2008

On February 11, 2008 the Department of Defense announced that it was serving charges against six Guantanamo detainees. The Convening Authority for the proposed prosecutions was Susan J. Crawford, a DOD official, who had been appointed to that post on February 7, 2008. Brigadier General Thomas H. Hartman, USAF, occupied the office of legal advisor to the Convening Authority.

Questions were immediately asked why it had taken the DOD so long in bringing charges against the accused. Military personnel accounted for the delay by stating that it had been necessary to obtain sworn statements in order to determine if probable cause existed prior to referring the matter to trial. It was also indicated that that the gathering of information had taken place over an extended period in many remote foreign areas, and that the proposed evidence had to be compared with existing statutes before effective proceedings could be instituted. Particular care, it was urged, was justified since a Commission could in appropriate cases, render a death sentence.

During the period prior to February 11, 2008 the DOD had been able to issue important legal documents intended to facilitate prosecutions. These included a Military Commission Manual dated January 1, 2007, which contained procedural rules for Military Commissions, and a recitation of crimes containing the elements of the identified crimes. Additional documentation included a Regulation dated April 27, 2007 designed to implement the Military Commission Act and the functions of a Commission, a Trial Judiciary Rule of Court dated November 2, 2007, which contained eight rules of procedure covering 36 pages, and a United States Court of Justice Review dated June 27, 2007, setting forth records of case actions which had occurred prior to that date.

Named for prosecution were Khalid Shaikh Mohammed, Walid bib Attash, also known as Kallad, Ramzi Binalshibh, Ali Abdul Aziz Ali, also known as Ammar Baluchi, Mustafa Ahmed Hawsawi, and Mohammed Qahtani. All were identified as "alien enemy unlawful combatants" within "the context of and associated with armed conflict." All were charged with violations of 10 U. S. Code Section 950v and the subparagraphs identified blow.

Charge 1 was based on conspiracy, with special reference to subparagraph 28. Charge 2 was based on attacking civilians. Charge 3 was attacking civilian objects. Charge 4 was intentionally causing severe bodily injury. Charge 5 was murder in violation of the laws of war. Charge 6 was destruction of property and violations of the laws of war. Charge seven was hijacking or hazarding of vessels or aircraft. Charge eight was terrorism. Charge nine was providing material support for terrorism. Some 169 events were identified as falling within the scope of prosecution.

To assist in the regularization of prosecutions a formal charge sheet was established for each detainee. It contained the name of the accused, his aliases, his identification number, the specific charge or charges, the name of the accuser, namely the criminal investigation task force, specific name of individual accusers, the date of the accusation, the date of the notice to be given to the accused by the assigned Military Commission, the date the Convening Authority had received the charges, the designation of the Convening Authority, and the date of the service of the charges.

The DOD in preparing for the prosecution of the Guantanamo detainees before a Military Commission attempted to fashion its procedures and substantive law on the provisions of the Uniform Code of Military Justice. The expectation was that this would allow for fair and speedy trials. The several DOD publications of 2007 eliminated the use of secret evidence, evidence gathered via torture of a detainee, with evidence obtained under controversial forms of coercion to be determined by the Convening Authority, which was also empowered to determine in which cases a death penalty might be imposed. Appeals from a decision of a Military Commission would be taken to the Court of Appeals for the District of Columbia, with ultimate review by the U. S. Supreme Court.

A Military Commission would be able to impose a death sentence if all of the members of the Commission were in agreement. Defendants under the UCMJ-based procedures would enjoy the right to remain silent, the right to be represented by counsel, the right to call witnesses and to be present when evidence against them was being presented. They were entitled to offer favorable evidence. On the other hand, hearsay evidence would be admissible if the presiding judge were to consider it trustworthy. Self-incrimination was not precluded. These and other relevant issues may reach the U. S. Supreme Court. In the process there is every reason to believe that the detainee will have received, especially through amicus briefs, the most careful and astute thinking of the American legal profession.

Highlighting the defense of Khald Shaikh Mohammed will be the disclosure that the CIA in 2002 and in 2003 had employed waterboarding on him to obtain intelligence information.[17]

It is doubtful if the issues presented or which remain to be pursued in these truly historic cases have been completely resolved. Future litigation is likely to result relating to the DTA and the MCA and to the powers of the President during a period of armed conflict when challenges are raised as to the legality of executive orders and decrees. The Supreme Court may still be asked to rule on whether terrorists have received sufficient protection under the laws and procedures governing the jurisdiction of Military Commissions. So long as terrorism constitutes a dangerous aspect of today's world it is doubtful that foreign terrorists operating from foreign bases will be allowed to benefit from all constitutional protections.

5. THE HAMDAN DECISION OF AUGUST 6, 2008

Following many delays a Military Commission reached a verdict in the case of Osama bin Laden's driver on August 6, 2008. A jury of six military officers found Salim Hamdan guilty of providing material support to a terror group. On the more serious charge that he had been a willing participant with Al Qaeda in a terror conspiracy the jury rendered a verdict of not guilty. He was sentenced to five and one-half years in prison with the court rejecting the government's view that a life imprisonment would be appropriate. The president of the Commission had to the power to reduce the sentence based on the length of his imprisonment, with counsel for the defense urging that a shorter sentence was appropriate because of the solitary confinement of the defendant for almost a year. Following the verdict speculation arose if the government would release Mr. Hamdan, and, if so, when. Not withstanding the verdict he was considered still to be an alien enemy combatant and, as such, subject to imprisonment as long as hostilities with terrorists continued. Since prisoners of war could be held until hostilities had been concluded it was wondered if terrorists were to be accorded more favorable treatment.

The Hamdan case provided needed experience in the functioning's of the Military Commission system. Attention was drawn to the proposed prosecution of Khalid Shaikh Mohammed and his confederates for their roles, as alleged, in plotting of the 9/11 attacks or of leading Al Qaeda. Such a trial, described as a "high value" prosecution would present a set of facts considerably more incriminating than those in the Hamdan case.

NOTES

1. For background on Mr. Khadr see Chapter 8, # 6, where reference is made to the charges against him for murder, attempted murder, conspiracy, material support for terrorism, and espionage. Among the charges was killing an American soldier with a hand grenade in Afghanistan in 2002. Hamdan/Khadr, No. 07-1156 (2007).

2. For Mr. Hamdan see Chapter 8, # 7, where his involvement with Osama bin Laden and Al Qaeda is described. 126 S. Ct. 2749 (June 29, 2006).

3. Brownback Order on Jurisdiction, p. 1 (June 4, 2007).

4. Ibid.

5. Disposition of Prosecution Motion for Reconsideration P001, p. 1 (June 29, 2007).

6. Supra, note 3, p. 2.

7. Ibid., p. 3.

8. Ibid.

9. Id at p. 7.

10. Id. at p. 8.

11. Ibid.

12. Id., at pp. 9–10.

13. Decision and Order-Motion to Dismiss for Lack of Jurisdiction, June 4, 2007, p. 3. He noted that the CSRT "was not charged with determining, and therefore did not determine that the accused is an 'alien unlawful enemy combatant.'" p. 1.

14. A more scholarly appraisal of a better way to address the problems of detainees can be found in P. Zelikow, Legal Policy for a Twilight War, University of Houston School of Law, April 26, 2007. University of Houston Journal of International Law, Fall, 2007. Mr. Zelikow was Executive Director of The 9/11 Commission.

15. The Court found that "the military judge had the power and authority under subsection (i) of # 948a(1)(A) of the M.C.A. to hear evidence concerning, and to ultimately decide, Mr. Khadr's 'unlawful enemy combatant' status . . ." It also declared that it "need not address whether or not a military commission is 'another competent tribunal' under subsection (ii) to make that decision." Opinion of the Court, CMCR 07-001, September 24, 2007, p. 25. In a third case , that of Salim Ahmed Hamdan, also before a Military Commission it was decided on December 20, 2007 that he was an unlawful enemy combatant and that the Commission possessed the jurisdiction to prosecute him. See Chapter 8, 1.D and 1.G.

16. M. D. Davis, AWOL Military Justice, Los Angeles Times, A15, December 10, 2007. Until October 4, 2007, when he resigned, Colonel Davis was chief prosecutor for the Office of Military Commissions for the Guantanamo Bay detainees. He was concerned that this convening authority following its selection of the charges to be made could not be impartial in reviewing judicial outcomes, that a high level of transparency in the trials was missing, and that he was fearful that his instructions to trial counsel not to offer any evidence "derived by waterboarding . . . [which] "the administration has sanctioned" might not be sustained.

17. During that period non-charged detainees Abu Zubahdah and Abu Al Rahim al Nashirihad also had been waterboarded. The Bush administration has taken the position that such measures were legal at that time. In 2006 the CIA was banned from such behavior. In 2008 reasonable doubt existed whether the CIA had complied with the banning order.

Chapter Eleven

Department of Defense Procedures for Investigation and Release of Detainees

The Department of Defense prior to and following the decision in 2006 of the Supreme Court in Hamdan v. Rumsfeld published a large number of directives designed to provide clearly stated procedures enabling military authorities to classify the Guantanamo Naval Base detainees. The procedures were based on the Bush policy that had been established for terrorists in 2001 that alien enemy combatants could not qualify as POWs under the 1949 Geneva Conventions and that they were to be subject to military courts and military law rather than civilian courts and civilian law. The goal was to determine which detainees should be retained in custody and which would be subject to release. Three procedures were identified, with the first two being administrative in nature, while the third was judicial. They were Administrative Review Boards, Combatant Status Review Tribunals, and Military Commissions.

1. ADMINISTRATIVE REVIEW BOARDS (ARB) AND PROCEDURES

In February, 2004, the Department of Defense announced the procedures, with implementing instructions, to be employed by the Administrative Review Boards that were investigating the grounds for holding the Guantanamo detainees.

When the DOD on July 7, 2004, one week after the Supreme Court decision in Rasul v. Bush, issued the Combatant Status Review Tribunal Order, it was careful to state that "this tribunal does not replace the administrative review procedure announced earlier this year."

On May 11, 2004 the DOD and the DOJ announced the "Final Administrative Review Procedures."[1] The Boards were described as administrative rather than prosecutorial. They were charged with finding facts rather than imposing criminal sanctions. They were to be the first step in determining if detainees possessed important intelligence information, whether they were security risks, or were sufficiently harmless so that they might qualify for release. As non-adversarial proceedings, which the government asserted were not legally required, the government did not issue instructions based on U. S. constitutional rights or trial court procedures. Nonetheless, the procedures were to assure that all relevant facts be discovered and weighed.

Every detainee had the right to appear before the Board where he could make an oral or submit a written statement explaining why he was no longer a threat to the United States or its allies, and to provide information to support his release. Prior to the hearing he was entitled to receive a governmental statement indicating why or why not he should be continued in detention. He was to have the assistance of a military officer in organizing and preparing a response. The reviewing officers were to be aided in their findings by a presentation by a second military officer who was expected to identify the grounds for continuing detention or for release. The Board was to receive communications from members of the detainee's family, from the government of the country of which he was a national, and from counsel representing him in the habeas corpus proceedings. Relevant U. S. government departments, such as State, Defense, Homeland Security, and the CIA were to be provided with a notice of the hearing so that they might provide supplemental information. The detainee was to have the assistance of an interpreter and a translator who would meet with the detainee and the assisting U. S. military representative. The Board was to consist of three military persons. Following its finding of facts the Board was to recommend to the presidentially appointed Designated Civilian Official (DCO) whether there should or should not be a release. If it were determined that a release should not take place the detainee was to be reviewed again within 12 months. An earlier review could occur if substantial grounds were present. The DOD reported that the first of the Board hearings had taken place on December 14, 2004.

In a report dated February 9, 2006, the DOD stated that the DCO had reviewed 463 recommendations of the Boards. This resulted in 14 releases, 120 transfers, with 329 remaining in detention. On December 23, 2006, the Board made its second report. It disclosed that 330 detainees had been reviewed with decisions having been completed for 211. Of these 46 were determined to be eligible for transfer, while the remaining 165 were to remain in custody. Excluded from the review process were detainees awaiting hearings by Military Commissions. These were the persons that were affected by the holding in Rasul v. Bush. A new Military Commission was established in the Detainee Treatment Act of December 30, 2005.[2] Persons whose status was being considered by the old Commission were transferred to the new Commission.

2. COMBATANT STATUS REVIEW TRIBUNALS (CSRT)

On June 28, 2004, the Supreme Court in Rasul v. Bush, 542 U.S. 466 (2004) and Hamdi v. Rumsfeld, 542 U. S. 507 (2004) ruled that the Guantanamo detainees were entitled to access to the federal courts through a writ of habeas corpus to challenge the grounds for their detention. Seeking to retain military jurisdiction over the persons classified as alien enemy combatants the Deputy Secretary of Defense on July 7, 2004, the Deputy Secretary of Defense issued a Memorandum to the Secretary of the Navy entitled "Order Establishing Combatant Status Review Tribunal."[3] The affected detainees were referred to as "enemy combatants." The Order was based on the proposition that a CSRT met the mandate of Article 5 of the 1949 Geneva POW Convention for the establishment of a competent tribunal rather than having to identify or convene a separate Article 5 tribunal to verify a detainee's POW status.

Unlike an Article 5 tribunal, the CSRT guarantees the detainee additional rights, such as the right to a Personal Representative to assist in reviewing information and preparing the detainee's case, presenting information, and questioning witnesses at CSRT hearings. The rules entitled the detainee to receive an unclassified summary of the evidence in advance of the hearing in the detainee's native language, and to introduce relevant documentary evidence. The rules also required the Recorder to search government files for, and provide to the Tribunal, any "evidence to suggest that the detainee should not be designated as an enemy combatant." The detainee's Personal Representative also had access to the government files and could search for and provide relevant evidence that would support a detainee's position.

In connection with such procedures it has been asserted that "Article 5 tribunals and CSRTs exist for different purposes and are charged with making different adjudications: whereas Article 5 tribunals exist to determine POW status, the CSRTs were created to classify enemy combatants."[4]

The Order contained definitions, including that of an "enemy combatant," identified the composition of the Tribunal, and dealt with such matters as the role of a Personal Representative, procedural details including the rights of detainees, and the disposition of those detainees that were found not to be alien enemy combatants. It contained an important provision relating to the availability of a writ of habeas corpus. At the time a CSRT was convened a prisoner was advised that his status review was not a substitute for his habeas rights and that he had the right to "seek a writ of habeas corpus in the courts of the United States."

A comparison with the rules applicable to the ARBs established on May 18, 2004, illustrates the differences. The July Memorandum contained a definition of an "enemy combatant," namely "any individual who was part of or supporting Taliban or Al Qaeda forces, or associated forces that are engaged in hostilities against the United States or its coalition partners. This includes any person who has committed a belligerent act or has directly supported hostilities in aid of enemy armed forces."[5] Each detainee has the opportunity to contest this designation. The Memorandum stated that all such persons had been found to be enemy combatants as a result of "multiple levels of review by officers of the Department of Defense."

The Order dealt in detail with procedural rules. It required that all detainees be given immediate notice of its terms. It called attention to their right to contest the finding of enemy combatant status. They were afforded an opportunity to consult with and be assisted by a Personal Representative serving in the military forces. The representative was to participate in Tribunal hearings. The Personal Representative was given the right to "review any reasonably available information in the possession of the Department of Defense relating to the reasons leading to the classification." This information could be shared with detainees, except for classified information. Detainees were to be notified of the "right to seek a writ of habeas corpus in the courts of the United States."

A detainee was to be provided with the facts developed by the government in his case prior to a hearing. He was given the right to be present in the proceedings except where classified information was under review. He could call witnesses, question witnesses called by the Tribunal, testify or otherwise address the tribunal, not be compelled to testify, and to attend the open portions of the proceedings. An interpreter was to be present during proceedings. Witnesses were subject to examination. The detainee could testify or remain silent. The Tribunal was not bound by the rules of evidence "such as would apply in a court of law." It was free to consider any information it deemed "relevant and helpful to a resolution of the issue before it." Further, at the "discretion of the Tribunal . . . it may consider hearsay evidence, taking into account the reliability of such evidence in the circumstances." Decisions are based on a preponderance of the evidence. They require a majority vote. Members are under oath to execute their duties impartially. The voting procedures were established. A record of the hearing was to be maintained. If it were determined that a detainee was not an enemy combatant the Secretary of Defense was to be notified. He, in coordination with the Secretary of State, was to arrange for the transfer of the detainee to the detainee's country of nationality, or other disposition consistent with the "domestic and international obligations and foreign policy of the United States."

The Order described the Tribunal's function to be one of "management." The process was "not intended to, and does not, create any right, benefit, substantive or procedural, enforceable at law, in equity, or otherwise by any party against the United States, its department, agencies, instrumentalities or entities, its officers, employees or agents, or any other person." Reminiscent of the "signing statements" attached by presidents to legislation which they considered as imposing constraints on their constitutional power, the Order stated that "it shall not be construed to limit, impair, or otherwise affect the constitutional authority of the President as Commander-in-Chief or any authority granted by statute to the President or the Secretary of Defense."

The July 7, 2004, Memorandum was subsequently revised by the Deputy Secretary of Defense on July 14, 2006. The work of the CSRTs provided for in the 2004 Memorandum, having been completed in March, 2005, the need arose for procedures for the detainees who remained in custody or who were captured later. Issued to high level military commanders it was entitled "Implementation of Combatant Status Review Tribunal Procedures for Enemy Combatants Detained at the U. S. Naval Base, Guantanamo Bay, Cuba." The new Memorandum, which referred to many of the procedures contained in US Army Regulation 190-8, fleshed out the terms of the earlier one. It established the position of Director, Combatant Status Review Tribunals. He was given wide-ranging management responsibilities. After dealing with the composition, including a Recorder, and counsel consisting of Personal Representatives to assist enemy combatants, and judge advocate officers to serve as Legal Advisors, and other supporting personnel, the Memorandum detailed the procedural rights of detainees and the functions of the personal representatives assigned to assist detainees in the non-adversarial proceedings. The Memorandum spelled out the procedures for handling classified material, to determine the mental competence of detainees, role of witnesses, taking of oaths, options open to detainees to testify, rules governing tribunal procedures, availability of evidence, burden of proof, conduct of hearings, post-hearing procedures, and administrative provisions designed to facilitate the operation of the Tribunals. The Order did not contain an outright prohibition on secret hearings. The practice of open hearings ended in March, 2007, when 14 Guantanamo Bay detainees, suspected of leadership roles in Al Qaeda, were obliged to participate in secret hearings. Those who have opposed in camera proceedings have urged that when hearings occur behind closed doors there is a reasonable suspicion that they are not fair. Secretary of Defense Robert Gates, on the other hand, has supported closed sessions because "a good deal of the discussion associated with their evaluation is going to [involve] classified information."[6] There was no provision for an appeal to be taken within the structure of the Tribunal. However, the Director, CSRT, after reviewing a decision was authorized to return the record to a Tribunal for further proceedings. If he approved the decision that a detainee was not to be classified any longer as an enemy combatant, he would advise the Secretary of the Navy. The latter then would inform the DOD Office of Detainee Affairs, the Secretary of States, and other relevant governmental agencies. The Secretary of State is charged with arranging for the transfer of the detainee to his country of nationality or otherwise finding a way to deliver the detainee to a foreign governmental entity.

So that the information collected and used in a proceeding and the details of each proceeding would follow the same format a highly detailed and standardized reporting system was established.[7] Attached as enclosures to the July 14, 2006 Memorandum were, among others, a notice to detainees regarding the CSRT process, a sample detainee election form, and a sample nominee questionnaire for approval of tribunal members, Recorders, and Personal Representatives. A form was provided for appointment letters to be signed by the CSRT Director as the convening authority. One enclosure consisted of a CSRT hearing guide. Another enclosure was to be used for reports on the part of the convening authority. A final directive provided that requirements of the DTA were to be observed by a CSRT. Little opportunity was allowed for inconsistencies. In addition to the cabinet officers mentioned above, copies of the Memorandum were to be provided to the Assistant to the President for National Security Affairs, Counsel to the President, Director, FBI, and the Director, Office of Administrative Review of the Detention of Enemy Combatants.

The DOD has released extensive reports of the findings and conclusions of CSRTs. Several scholarly analyses of detainee CSRT hearings have been published by Mark Denbeaux and Joshua Denbeaux. One dealing with the proceedings of the government's CSRTs, based exclusively on DOD documents, describing 102 hearings, concluded that "[the] process that was promised was modest at best. The process that was actually provided was far less than the written procedures appear to require."[8] Conclusions included the failure of the government to produce any witnesses in any hearing, nondelivery of documentary evidence to a detainee prior to a hearing in 96% of the cases; while each detainee was always presented with a summary of classified evidence, it was deemed by the tribunal as "conclusory" and not persuasive; that the only basis for detention provided detainees was the summary of the evidence dealing with the reasons for his being considered an enemy combatant; that the Government's classified evidence was always presumed to be reliable and valid; that all requests by detainees to inspect the classified evidence were denied; that all requests by detainees for witnesses not already held at Guantanamo were denied; and that there was a pattern of repeated reviews before different tribunals until a finding was reached that the person under review was an enemy combatant. The analysis listed 15 findings. Based on them the authors described the hearings as "shams."[9]

As indicated the Boards and the Tribunal provided a "screening process" so that a determination could be made for referrals to Military Commissions. There were findings leading to a release or transfer of a limited number of detainees. Following the Supreme Court ruling in Rasul v. Bush a new Military Commission was established in the Detainee Treatment Act of December 30, 2005.

NOTES

1. http://www.defenselink.mil.releases/2004/nr200040518-0806.html.

2. Pub. L. 109-359.

3. The CSRT order was issued as a response to the Supreme Court's June, 2004, decision in Hamdi v. Rumsfeld (542 U. S. 507, 509) that Hamdi, as a citizen of the United States, and held in the United States, "as an enemy combatant [must] be given a meaningful opportunity to contest the factual basis for that detention before a neutral decision maker."

4. J. Blocher, Combatant Status Review Tribunals: Flawed Answers to the Wrong Question, 116 Yale L. J. 667, 674 (2006). He concluded that the CSRTs "did not fulfill Article 5's mandate. As a result, they did not and could not strip detainees of their presumptive POW status." See: G. Corn, E. T. Jensen, S. Watts, Understanding the Distinct Function of the Combat Status Review Tribunals: A Response to Blocher, 116 Yale L. J. Pocket Part 327 (2007).

5. It has been noted that this definition did "not conform to the legal framework of the [1949 Geneva] Convention." It was concluded that the Convention "provide[d] the appropriate legal rules for the courts to apply." L. D. Sloss, Availability of U. S. Courts to Detainees at Guantanamo Bay Naval Base, 98 AJIL, No. 4, p. 793 (October, 2004).

6. Los Angeles Times, A14, March 3, 2007.

7. DOD, Documents Concerning Combatant Status Review Tribunal (CSRT) Procedures for Enemy Combatants Detained at Guantanamo Bay Naval Base, Cuba, http://www.dod.mil/pubs/foi/detainees.

8. M.Denbeaux and J. Denbeaux, No-Hearings CSRT: The Modern Habeas Corpus?, http://law.shu.edu/news/final.no hearing hearings report.pdf., Nov. 17, 2006, p. 4.

9. Los Angeles Times, A33, November 17, 2006.

Chapter Twelve

The New Army Field Manual 2-22.3 September 6, 2006

1. INTRODUCTION

The Army began to rewrite FM-34-52 in 2004 following the Abu Ghraib prison scandal. Seeking to avoid a repetition of this debacle the Department of Defense called for the preparation of formal policies and procedures. One important step was taken in 2004 with the issuance of a directive to the Joint Chiefs of Staff to prepare applicable rules and regulations. A document entitled "Joint Doctrine for Detainee Operations" was issued on March 23, 2005.[1] It was based on the premise that the war against terrorism was a continuing struggle. The statement referred to terrorists as "members of Al Qaeda, Taliban, or other international terrorist organizations against whom the United States is engaged in armed conflict."[2] Also included were individuals and entities who may become subject to detainment under the "laws or customs of war."

The Joint Chiefs of Staff publication retained the important distinction between the recently devised expression "enemy combatants," and the long-accepted term "prisoners of war." The former, according to the Publication, who did not fall within the definitions contained in the POW Convention were "still entitled to be treated humanely, subject to military necessity, consistent with the principles of the Geneva Convention, and without adverse discrimination based on race, color, religion, gender, birth, wealth, or any similar criteria and afforded adequate food, drinking water, shelter, clothing and medical treatment [and] allowed the free exercise of religion, consistent with the requirements of such detention."[3] Anticipating concerns over the use of "military necessity" in the joint publication it stated "There is no military exception to this humane treatment mandate . . . [and added] neither the stress of combat operations, the need for actionable information, nor the provocations by captured/detained personnel justify deviation from this obligation." To avoid the blurring of functions at a prison facility the publication stated that military police should exercise custody and control over detainees and not to fix the conditions for interrogation as had occurred in Iraq and at Guantanamo.

The joint publication recommended functional improvements including the designation of a Chief of Detainee Operations to serve under operational commanders. These individuals would exercise command responsibilities and would be charged with the operation of detention facilities. This person would be particularly alert to the possibility of inhumane conditions, investigate allegations of mistreatment, and coordinate with the International Committee of the Red Cross on subjects of mutual concern.

The statement called for identification numbers to be assigned to all persons subject to military custody or control thereby eliminating "ghost detainees." Critics who opposed the classification of persons as "enemy combatants" contended that detainees be classified only as prisoners of war.

On November 5, 2005, a new Department of Defense Directive was issued regulating the conduct of interrogations conducted by the U. S. armed forces. Referring to DOD "policy" it stated that "All captured or detained personnel shall be treated humanely, in accordance with applicable law, and applicable directives, including DOD Directive 2310.01 [under revision], instructions or other issuances. Acts of physical or mental torture are prohibited."

The Directive contained provisions on the reporting of incidents, general principles for interrogation operations, medical issues, detention, and operational issues. Under the last heading was included the provision that non-DOD personnel who conducted intelligence gathering interrogations had to agree to comply with the DOD Directive. Dogs were not to be used during interrogations "nor to harass, intimidate, threat, or coerce a detainee for interrogation purposes." The 2005 Policy Directive was modified on September 5, 2006 to read: "All detainees shall be treated humanely and in accordance with U. S. laws, the law of war, and applicable U. S. policy." Added was a provision that the treatment of detainees was to conform, as a minimum, to the requirements of Common Article 3 of the Geneva Conventions as interpreted by U. S. law. Reference was made to the rights of prisoners of war. Administrative measures regarding detainees included the assignment of registration numbers. The International Committee of the Red Cross was to be allowed to offer its service "during an armed conflict, however characterized, to which the United States is a party."

On September 6, 2006, the Department of Defense issued a new Field Manual 2-23.3 entitled "Human Intelligence Collector Operations." [HUMINIT] It set forth specific requirements to be followed in interrogating enemy combatants. Section 5-75 specifically prohibited identified interrogation techniques and offered guidance for assessing other techniques. The following methods were prohibited: requiring a detainee to be naked, placing hoods over their heads, engaging in beatings, electrical shocks, burns, or other forms of physical pain, "waterboarding" [quotation marks were employed in the original source], using working dogs, hyperthermia or heat injury, conducting mock executions, depriving detainees of necessary food, water, and medical care." Additional prohibitions were listed. In the event of doubt whether a procedure was prohibited, the questioner was obliged to ask: "If the proposed technique were used by the enemy against one of your fellow soldiers, would you believe that the soldier has been abused?" And, "Could your conduct in carrying out the proposed technique violate a law or regulation? Keep in mind that even if you personally would not consider your action to constitute abuse, the law may be more restrictive."

The Field Manual in Section 5.6 described a "detainee as any person captured or otherwise detained by an armed force." Section 5.27 stated that American HUMINT collectors must remember that regardless of the legal status of the detainee that they must be treated in a manner consistent with the Geneva Conventions.

The Field Manual was buttressed by a number of highly specific Appendices. One of the most important was Appendix M entitled "Restricted Interrogation Technique-Separation." Covering 9 pages of detailed instructions, including a chart entitled "Separation Approval Process," it dealt with the removal of a detainee from the general detainee population, held separately, and accorded different forms of interrogation.

Since such procedures might be highly sensitive the Appendix identified in detail the conditions under which this status could be established. To avoid misapplication of the directive, it contained an additional chart for an "Interrogation Plan for Use of Restricted Separation Technique," which contained highly specific limitations on such projects, including the requirement of three separate approvals before it could be implemented. Section M-2 made it clear that there would have to be compliance "with the basic standards of humane treatment or punishment, as defined in the Detainee Treatment Act of 2005 and addressed in GPW Article (Common Article III)."[4] In characterizing the Appendix it was stated that it was not "a stand-alone doctrinal product and must be used in conjunction with the main portion of this manual."

The Army was aware that non-DOD agencies were engaged in conducting interrogations in Army facilities. In section 5-55 of Field Manual 2-22.3 provision for this contingency was made, subject to the prior approval of very high level military commanders, for the presence of trained and certified Army interrogators who were to be present as observers during the non-Army interrogations, and to the requirement that the non-DOD agencies must comply with the same standards for the conduct of interrogation operations and treatment of detainees as do Army personnel, with the requirement that in the event of violations of Army interrogation standards the fact would be reported immediately to appropriate commanders with the instant suspension of "access of non-DOD personnel to the facility." The Army was also aware that foreign government interrogators might seek permission to engage in like activities. Under section 5-56 such persons were required to comply with the same conditions stipulated in section 5-55.

Under the heading "Legal, Regulatory, and Policy Principles and Guidelines" an effort was made to provide balance for the commitment by the military forces to FM 2-22.3 It stipulated that "Authority for conducting interrogations of personnel detained by military forces rests primarily upon the traditional concept that the commander may use all available resources and lawful means to accomplish the mission and to protect and secure the unit."[5]

The document is a well-considered and a well-crafted compendium of rules and regulations. Had it been effective at the time of Abu Ghraib the outcome there might have quite different. The detail of the Field Manual will require a good bit of formal instruction on its topics for affected persons. As a part of the evolving regulatory detail its impact has also been felt at the Guantanamo Naval Station.

The standards contained in Field Manual 2-23.3 were applicable to all United States military services, to all DOD personnel, including private contract interrogators while on DOD facilities. It was not applicable to the Central Intelligence Agency.

While the Army was revising FM-34-52, and before the issuance of Field Manual 2-23.3, Congress adopted the Detainee Treatment Act of 2005, with effective date of December 30, 2005. It applied pursuant to the terms of Section 1002(a) to persons "in the custody or under the effective control of the Department of Defense or under detention in a Department of Defense facility." Persons so held were not to be "subject to any treatment or technique of interrogation not authorized by and listed in the United States Army Field Manual on Intelligence Operation" e. g., Field Manual 2-23.3. Section 1003(a) set forth the prohibited conduct. It stated that "No individual in the custody or physical control of the United States government, regardless of nationality or physical location, shall be subject to cruel, inhuman, or degrading treatment or punishment." The statute did not refer to torture nor did it refer to waterboarding. Torture is governed by the CAT, the American RUDs, and either actually or prospectively, and in a variety of situations, by a variety of statutes as set forth in Chapter Three. These legal sources did not refer to waterboarding by the United States.

2. NOMINATION OF MICHAEL B. MUKASEY TO BE ATTORNEY GENERAL OF THE UNITED STATES

With the nomination of Mr. Mukasey the Senate Committee on the Judiciary in October, 2007 began hearings to determine his suitability for this high office. This led to important questions on his understanding of the law relating to torture and the lesser included offenses referred to above, and, in particular, whether "waterboarding" was a crime. During the hearings, continued in November, he stated that "waterboarding" was clearly repugnant but he declined to say that it constituted "torture." He took the position that the question was hypothetical and should not be answered. Apparently this was based in part on his assumption that in responding to one hypothetical this would open the door to a series of other hypotheticals and that as Attorney General he would be obliged to deal (as had been the case when he was a Federal District Court judge) with actual situations rather than imaginary ones. Some of the Committee members and a number of international lawyers, teaching or practicing in the United States, also called for a direct response. They indicated that a failure to address the question should be considered as a sufficient reason for not approving his confirmation.

The positions of the Mukasey critics proved troublesome to many since the critics seemingly had arrived at conclusions of what constituted waterboarding even though the Department of Army Field Manual had referred to "waterboarding" without providing either a description or a definition. It was designated an Army rule; it made no pretense to be a general statute. It was the only governmental reference to the subject. This cast doubts on whether the critics were in possession of an adequate factual definition or description of waterboarding since nothing of this kind had been provided. Secondly, the combination of an inadequate definition or description resulted in uncertainty as to what it was, in their view that might properly be considered to be illegal. This being the case there was a failure both as to the evidence of what constituted the act and what was to serve as a proof of illegality. A described act coupled with intent is required to establish the elements of the crime of waterboarding. No treaty or statute met these requirements. The basic question remained: What was the evidence?

The Army Field Manual in assessing the status of personnel having interrogation assignments raised doubts respecting possible procedures. One related to the question of whether if "the proposed approach technique were used by the enemy against one of your fellow soldiers, would you believe the soldier had been abused?"[6] The second asked "Could your conduct in carrying out the proposed technique violate a law or regulation?"[7] The official response to both of the tests was that if either could be responded to in the affirmative that the contemplated action should not be undertaken. Further evidence of the lack of understanding of the term was found in the requirement that if a HUMINT collector had any doubts then the collector should seek immediate guidance within the chain of command and consult with the unit's legal officer to obtain a legal review of the proposed approach or technique. Pending the rendering of such advice the collector was obliged to stop the interrogation immediately while awaiting legal advice from the chain of command.[8]

The following "Caution" was added, all of which emphasized the uncertainty of the concept of "waterboarding." "Although no single comprehensive source defines impermissible coercion certain acts are clearly prohibited. Certain prohibited physical coercion may be obvious, such as physically abusing the subject of the screening or interrogation. Other forms of impermissible coercion may be more subtle, and may include threats to turn the individual over to others to be abused; subjecting the individual to impermissible humiliating or degrading treatment; implying harm to the individual or to his property. Where there is doubt, you should consult your supervisor or servicing judge advocate."[9] The Army directive also seemed clear respecting a hypothetical case of "waterboarding." Until such an event were likely to occur and the requisite inquiries and rulings were handed down there was no way to determine the legality of the proposed conduct. On the other hand, there is no doubt that the activities identified with "waterboarding" constitute an assault on the person of the detainee, with such activities being prohibited by numerous Federal statutes.[10]

The concerns of those opposing the Mukasey appointment, better grounded in the issues of civil and political rights and liberties, were confronted by a number of practical considerations. He had served with distinction as a Federal District Court judge, where he had tried a substantial number of security cases. Experts deemed that challenging a potential appointee with hypothetical questions would be an unfair "litmus test" as to personal matters, as well as being unduly time-consuming and counter-productive if hypothetical questions were extended to other topics that had been employed in the context of torture or cruel, inhuman or degrading courses of conduct, a feeling on the part of influential Senators that a replacement nominee might not be as well qualified, while at the same time recognizing a trait of independence in Judge Mukasey, and the recognition that a headless Department of Justice, at a time when many legal problems were crying for disposition, was not in the general interest of the United States. Thus, the inability of his critics to make a case against him and these practical considerations resulted in October, 2007, with his approval by the Senate and the confirmation of his appointment.

NOTES

1. Joint Publication 3–63, Final Coordination. http://hrw.org/campaigns/torture/jpointdoctrine00705.pdf.

2. Ibid., p.1–12.

3. Id., at 1–11.

4. FM 2-22.3, Appendix M, p. 347 (M-1) (2006).

5. Ibid., p. 93, 5-17.

6. FM 2.22-3, 5 76. 5-22 (2006).

7. Ibid.

8. FM 2.22-3, 5-77, 5-22 (2006).

9. Ibid.

10. E. J. Wallach, Drop by Drop: Forgetting the History of Water Torture in U. S. Courts, 45 Colum. J. Transnat'l L. 468 (2007).

Chapter Thirteen

The Presidential Directive of July 20, 2007 on CIA Detentions and Interrogations-New Revelations and the Continuing Conflict between the White House and Congress

The Department of Justice, based on wide-ranging disclosures of probable violations by the CIA of CAT and the 1949 Geneva POW Convention in Afghanistan, Iraq, and in widely placed other countries, and influenced by a report of the Senate Intelligence Committee questioning whether the CIA needed special rules allowing for torture in detainee cases, began to analyze the problem. On July 20, 2007 President Bush issued a Directive. It bore the title "Interpretation of the Geneva Conventions Common Article 3 as Applied to a Program of Detention and Interrogation Operated by the Central Intelligence Agency."[1] It was grounded on the authority vested in him as President and Commander in Chief of the Armed Forces by the Constitution and existing laws, including the Authorization for Use of the Military Force (Public Law 107-40), the MCA of 2006 (Public Law 109-366), and the terms of section 301 of title 3, U. S. Code (general authority to delegate functions). The Directive contained five sections.

Section 1. contained general "determinations." In it the President confirmed the February 7, 2002 decision that for the United States "members of Al Qaeda, the Taliban, and associated forces are unlawful enemy combatants who are not entitled to the protections that the Third Geneva Convention provides to prisoners of war." He added that the MCA defined "certain provisions of Common Article 3 for U. S. law, and it reaffirms and reinforces the authority of the President to interpret the meaning and application of the Geneva Conventions."

Section 2. dealt with definitions. It included references to the 1949 Geneva Conventions, including Article 3 of the POW Convention, with its references to "cruel treatment and torture," and "outrages upon personal dignity, in particular, humiliating and degrading treatment." Section 2.(c) defined "Cruel,

inhuman, or degrading treatment or punishment" as meaning "the cruel, unusual, and inhumane treatment or punishment prohibited by the Fifth, Eighth,
and Fourteen Amendments to the Constitution of the United States." The
2007 formula followed the terms of the Senate's reservation I(1) to the CAT
treaty which subsequently became parts of Federal statutes.

Section 3. was entitled "Compliance of a Central Intelligence Agency Detention and Interrogation Program with Common Article 3." In Section 3.(a)
the President stated that his order "interprets the meaning and application of
the text of Common Article 3 with respect to certain detentions and interrogations, and shall be treated as authoritative for all purposes as a matter of
United States law, including satisfaction of the international obligations of the
United States." Left to be determined was the meaning of "certain detentions
and interrogations." The Order continued: "I hereby determine that Common
Article 3 shall apply to a program of detention and interrogation operated by
the Central Intelligence Agency as set forth in this section." Section 3.(b) confirmed that "a program of detention and interrogation approved by the Director of the Central Intelligence Agency fully complies with . . ." U. S. obligations under Common Article 3. This authority of the Director was subject to
four provisions imposing conditions on CIA implementation of the directive.

The first condition, dealing with "conditions of confinement and interrogation practices of the program [approved by the Director] do not include:
(A) torture, as defined in section 2340 of title 18, United States Code [The
Criminal Torture Act of 1994, amended 2006]; (B) any of the acts prohibited
by section 2441(d) of title 18, United States Code [The War Crimes Act of
1996], including murder, torture, cruel or inhuman treatment, mutilation or
maiming, intentionally causing serious bodily injury, rape, sexual assault or
abuse, taking of hostages, or performing biological experiments." These prohibitions have their statutory source in the War Crimes Act of 2006, Section
6 "Implementation of Treaty Obligations," at paragraphs (d) (1)(A) through
(I). The statute identifies the critical elements of each of the crimes." These
prohibitions also are contained in The Manual for Military Commissions of
January 18, 2007, with "performing biological experiments" being replaced
by "intentionally mistreating a dead body." The Manual also repeats for easy
reference the texts, elements, and statutory definitions of such crimes as torture and cruel or inhuman treatment and texts, elements, and maximum punishments on such subjects as terrorism, providing material support for terrorism, wrongfully aiding the enemy, spying, and conspiracy. It remains to be
seen if the CIA will promulgate an operative Manual similar to that issued by
the DOD dealing with the same or additional subjects and details.

Although the other prohibitions listed in the Manual with regard to the conduct of military personnel do not appear in the Executive Order, there are

other important prohibitions on the conduct of CIA personnel. Those included in (C) are "other acts of violence serious enough to be considered comparable to murder, torture, mutilation, and cruel or inhuman treatment, as defined in section 2441(d) of title 18, United States Code, (D) any other acts of cruel, inhuman or degrading treatment or punishment prohibited by the Military Commissions Act (subsection 6(c) of Public Law 109/366) and the Detainee Treatment Act of 2005 (section 1003 of Public Law 109/148 and Section 1403 of Public Law 109/163); (E) willful and outrageous acts of personal abuse done for the purpose of humiliating or degrading the individual in a manner so serious that any reasonable person, considering the circumstances, would deem the acts to be beyond the bounds of human decency, such as sexual or sexually indecent acts undertaken for the purpose of humiliation, forcing the individual to perform sexual acts or to pose sexually, threatening the individual with sexual mutilation, or using the individual as a human shield; or (F) acts intended to denigrate the religion, religions practices, or religious objects of the individual."

These provisions depict the fundamental problem in endeavoring to find the right choice of terms to identify unacceptable governmental behavior flowing from such words as "torture," "cruel or inhuman or degrading" treatment or conduct, or "willful and outrageous acts of personal abuse" extending beyond the "bounds of human decency."

Vague, at the outset, as they may appear to be, it is necessary to consider that there has been no void in many statutory efforts, augmented by many governmental directives, including references to very important provisions of the U.S. Constitution, so as to make them sufficiently meaningful for legal consequences to be assigned to them. Of vast significance is the fact that all of the foregoing prescriptions are prohibitory in nature.

While it is true that the Presidential Directive did not enumerate, since references had been made to original sources, all of the prohibitions relating to torture and its companion crimes identified in the Geneva Conventions, in CAT, in applicable federal statutes, in Executive Department Memos, in Presidential Orders and Directives, in DOD manuals, rules and regulations, and in judicial opinions where the issue of torture had been considered, the Directive imposed important and extensive prohibitions. Critics of the Directive have viewed it as providing the CIA with "enhanced interrogation methods" meaning that the specific prohibitions contained in the Directive were limited and incomplete with the CIA being able to engage in other questionable methods and actions extending " beyond the bounds of human decency . . . " On July 22, 2007, the National Intelligence Director denied the applicability of the term "enhanced," and without disclosing the approved methods of interrogation stated: "It is not torture, and there would be no permanent damage to that citizen."

Such acts, however, even if described as "harsh," under existing legal constraints, can not go so far as to constitute torture and acts of cruel, inhumane, or degrading treatment or punishment.

In assessing the problem it is necessary to remember that evidence produced by torture has become highly suspect, with the general belief that the utility of such activity is highly questionable. Rules have also been promulgated requiring the exclusion of such evidence in judicial and administrative hearings, subject to judicial determinations.

Contributing to the uncertainty respecting interrogation techniques was the provision in the Directive requiring the issuance of a separate classified document identifying lawful methods. They will have to be tested in legal, including judicial proceedings, following their employment. The meaning and the effect of the challenged interrogation procedures may be limited in light of the extended prohibitions identified above and the guidance derived from presidential statements that the United States does not engage in torture. Because of the DOD's efforts to separate the military forces from CIA interrogation practices, such activity will be centered in CIA facilities, either in the United States or abroad. This poses the possibility that claims of indefinite detentions of CIA detainees will produce litigation.

The directive also stated in Section 3.(b)(ii) that a person, who was an "alien detainee" was subject to "the conditions of confinement and interrogation practices" if that person were determined by the Director of the CIA "(A) to be a member or part of or supporting al Qaeda, the Taliban, or associated organizations;" and "(B) likely to be in possession of information that: (1) could assist in detecting, mitigating, or preventing terrorist attacks, such as attacks within the United States or against its Armed Forces or other personnel, citizens, or facilities, or against allies or other countries cooperating in the war on terror with the United States, or their armed forces or other personnel, citizens, or facilities, or; (2) could assist in locating the senior leadership of al Qaeda, the Taliban, or associated forces." Such interrogation practices, as determined by the Director, would also depend "upon professional advice, to be safe for use with each detainee with whom they are used."

The "likely to be in possession of information" provision set forth in Section 3. (b)(ii)(B) pertained to the "could assist" prospect of finding specific facts and identifying certain persons, such as those supporting terrorist organizations "or associated forces." These terms are not defined. This seems to open the door to the CIA's taking custody or control of persons based on very little reliable evidence.

It was also provided in Section 3(b)(iv) that detainees in the program were to receive the "basic necessities of life, including adequate food and water, shelter from the elements, necessary clothing, protection from extremes of heat and cold, and essential medical care." The reference to these amenities serves as a reminder of the policy not to treat detainees as prisoners of war.

The implementation of the foregoing provisions will raise a number of practical problems. The issue of classification, as reflected in the DOD's experience with Military Administrative Boards, Combat Status Review Tribunals, and Military Commissions, has demonstrated the need for an extensive body of experts engaged in planning and in operational activities with a heavy time-consuming potential. Each of the terms may lead to extended inquiries, such as the word "member" of an identified organization. In the prosecution of Jose Padilla in a Federal District Court in 2007 the government relied on a document, challenged by Mr. Padilla, purporting to be a written application for membership in Al Qaeda. The document was discovered almost accidentally in Afghanistan. Since prohibited interrogation methods are extensive this may mean that the CIA may only prove "membership" by voluntary statements or other credible evidence and testimony.

The President authorized the Director " of the CIA to issue written policies governing the "program" including guidelines for CIA personnel, who are to be charged with the implementation of the critical aspects of the foregoing, to ensure "(c) (i) safe and professional operations of the program; (ii) the development of an approved plan of interrogation tailored for each detainee in the program to be interrogated, consistent with subsection 3(b)(iv) of this order; (iii) appropriate training for interrogators and all personnel operating the program; (iv) effective monitoring of the program, including with respect to medical matters, to ensure the safety of those in the program; and (v) compliance with applicable law and this order."

Section 4. was entitled Assignment of Function. It reads: "With respect to the program addressed in this order, the function of the President under Section 6(3)(3) of the Military Commissions Act of 2006 is assigned to the Director of National Intelligence."

Section 5. concluded with two "General Provisions." First, "subject to subsection (b) of this section, this order is not intended to, and does not, create any right or benefit, substantive or procedural, enforceable at law or in equity, against the United States, its departments, agencies, or other entities, its officers or employees, or any other person." Second, "Nothing in this order shall be construed to prevent or to limit reliance upon this order in a civil, criminal, or administrative proceeding, or otherwise, by the Central Intelligence Agency or by any individual acting on behalf of the Central Intelligence Agency in connection with the program addressed in this order."

Unlike the terms "alien unlawful enemy combatant," "unlawful enemy combatant," and "lawful enemy combatant" defined and employed in the 2006 MCA, the Executive Order refers to "an alien detainee." Since the President in issuing the Executive Order relied, in part, on the 2006 MCA, this appears to mean that he recognized the existence of "enemy combatants" as identified and defined in the statute. For the Executive Order to be meaningful it would be necessary to have a clear-cut definition of the category of persons identified in it as "alien detainees." Undoubtedly questions will be raised whether the descriptive terms found in Section 3.(b)(ii)(A)and (B) have achieved the specificity required to support the required "conditions of confinement and interrogation practices . . ." as determined by the Director of the CIA.

Affecting the implementation of the Directive will be the criticism directed at it as allowing for "enhanced interrogation techniques," with their World War II history.[2] Jane Mayer has studied the situation and has written that the Executive Order "promis[ed] that the C.I.A. would adjust its methods in order to meet the Geneva Standards. At the same time, the Bush order pointedly did not disavow the use of 'enhanced interrogation techniques' that would likely be found illegal if used by officials inside the United States. The executive order means that the agency can once again hold foreign terror suspects indefinitely and without charges, in black sites, without notifying their families or local authorities, or offering access to legal counsel."[3]

The Directive has received and will continue to receive much adverse criticism. On August 13, 2007, the House of Delegates of the American Bar Association vigorously criticized the Directive. Based on the belief that the Directive allowed the CIA to engage in sensory and sleep deprivation and "waterboarding" of detainees, it voted to ask President Bush to override the Directive so that these methods would be specifically prohibited. Present and future concerns will be manifested until a closer and tighter executive rein is imposed on the methods lawfully available to the CIA. Methods, which have not been openly announced, being generally perceived as being practiced in secret, will produce speculation, with the conclusion being that they do not meet lawful standards.

Critics have asked the government to identify the acts and methods that are acceptable. This raises the age old question of inclusion and exclusion. Does it mean by prohibiting a wide range of methods that all of the other or remaining unnamed methods are acceptable? This approach has not been well received by international lawyers working on a definition of genocide or on a definition of international terrorism. Allegations have been made that such enumerative definitions are both practically or logically impossible, although the CAT employed an enumerative process—resulting in the adoption by the

United States of its own RUDs. The same problems exist in trying to make a definitive list of prohibited conduct.

However, the prohibitions in Federal statutes and rules and regulations for military personnel are very considerable. Despite the long delay in their promulgation they now appear to have created an operational threshold for prohibited conduct. In the light of such prohibitions it is possible to argue that the C.I.A., subject to such prohibitions, would be subject to enormous criticism if it embarked on or engaged in newly identified abusive procedures. It has been urged that the C.I.A. personnel, even if restricted by its Director, would not engage in wrongful acts or personal abuse prohibited by the Armed Forces. That, of course, is a possibility. However, lessons learned by the Armed Forces may serve as a constant reminder of what society at large expects of the C.I.A.

The problem with interrogational methods is that more frequently than not they do not result in prosecutions of detainees. Their purpose is to identify, either from the detainee or suspected detainees, the presence, behavior, and plans of non-detained terrorist leaders. Where prosecutions are the object there is the concern that coercive methods will produce unreliable results. Since the CIA is not concerned with prosecutions, there is an invitation to consider coercive measures of personal abuse.

On September 10, 2007, CIA Director Michael V. Hayden replied to critics of the CIA's detention practices and identified their perceived misconceptions. He emphasized his belief that terrorists continued to be a very substantial threat to the United States and that this was recognized generally as supportive of "a willingness of the broader political culture to be comfortable with the things we believe are both lawful and necessary to fight this war."[4] His perspective was similar to that of J. Michael McConnell, Director of National Intelligence, who in August, 2007, had called on Congress to give his agency expanded electronic surveillance powers.

The CIA Director endeavored to set the record straight as to CIA overseas operations. He observed that extraterritorial renditions had been limited to fewer than 100 instances, that findings of CIA abuses by the European Union were "wild speculation," that air transportation of detainees, which had been stated in the press as being 1,245 was a "mere fraction of that," with the other flights engaged in carrying equipment, or documents to be shared with allies and senior CIA officials in the field, or for the transportation of officials to conferences with foreign counterparts. He stated that prior to engaging in extraterritorial renditions that transfers were not made until assurances had been received from the country of destination that the matter would "be handled in a way that is consistent with international law."[5]

In his speech he defended the use of overseas prisons and interrogation methods which the Department of Defense had prohibited to the Army in its rules and regulations and in the revised Army Field Manual 2.23-3, dated September 5, 2006. Mr. Hayden stated that the CIA had not been consulted by the DOD in its identification of prohibitions and volunteered that "no one ever claimed the Army Field Manual exhausted the lawful tools America could have to protect itself."[6] He also noted there was a vast difference between the training received by military interrogators and those of the CIA, with the former often being junior and not highly trained personnel, while those of the CIA had an average age of 43 and who had received hundreds of hours of specialized training. Despite general concerns over the reliability of coercive interrogations he stated that they remained a highly valuable procedure accounting for more than 70% of the human intelligence cited in a recent National Intelligence Estimate on terrorism trends. In his view it was "less rather than more likely that individuals would be tortured."[7]

He spoke at length concerning the extensive practice of the press to publish "leaks" of intelligence secrets, noting that this could be likened to revelations of ship or troop movements, which had resulted in the imprisonment of a CIA source and had prompted counterterrorism sources to withdraw their cooperation. His remarks supported the Presidential Directive of July, 20, 2007 and constituted an affirmation of the CIA's functions and procedures.

The CIA practices produced scathing editorial commentary. At the close of 2007 the following appeared in the New York Times: "Out of panic and ideology President Bush squandered America's position of moral and political leadership, swept aside international institutions and treaties, sullied America's global image and trampled on the constitutional principles that have supported our democracy through the most terrifying and challenging times . These policies led to world anger and isolation and have not made us any safer."[8] A call was made for integrity, commitment to principle, and to decency.

Aside from the technical aspects of the Directive it will have to be measured against the policy recommendations contained in the "Iraq Study Group Report: The Way Forward—A New Approach."[9]

1. KHALED EL MASRI V. TENET, 437 F. SUPP. 2D 530 (E.D. VA 2006)

The terms of the Directive, proposals of the Study Group, and the numerous statements of President Bush that the United States does not engage in torture were confronted in the case of Khaled el Masri v. Tenet, CIA director.[10]

Khaled el Mari, a Lebanese born German national, was taken into custody by CIA agents in 2003 in Macedonia, flown to Afghanistan where he was extensively tortured by the CIA. He was believed to be Khalid el Masri, who as a member of the Hamburg Al Qaeda cell had participated actively in planning for 9/11 attacks on New York City and Washington, D. C. When it became evident to the CIA that it had mistakenly identified the detainee with a person having a similar name (el Mari) el Masri was flown to Albania and released.

Returning to Germany he instituted a civil action against the CIA Director alleging unlawful abduction, unlawful arbitrary detention, and torture by agents of the United States. His complaint identified in detail the times and places in which a variety of torture practices had been employed. He sought ordinary, punitive, and exemplary damages.

The government asked the trial court to dismiss the action on the grounds that it was necessary to "protect classified intelligence resources." The trial judge accepted the validity of that claim and dismissed the action.

The case was appealed to the United States Court of Appeals for the Fourth Circuit,[11] which rendered its opinion on October 2, 2007. It adopted the view that there was a continuing need to protect "classified intelligence resources," although the details of the case had received international publicity and were well known to all parties to the action. Speaking for the ACLU, which had been instrumental in instituting the suit, a representative stated that "By denying justice to an innocent victim of this country's anti-terrorism policies, the court has provided the government with complete immunity for its shameful human rights and due process violations."[12]

The Court of Appeals acknowledged that the acts complained of fell "within the body of acts that violate" definitions of torture that had been "confirmed in international agreements" and that the alleged conduct fell within the "body of acts deemed actionable" in Sosa v. Alvarez Machain.[13] It was held that the facts were actionable under the Federal Tort Claims Act of 1789. Nonetheless, the case was dismissed because of the need to protect classified intelligence resources. In supporting that proposition the Court of Appeals relied on cases in which federal courts had given deference to presidential determinations in matters involving national security and presidential military authority.[14] On appeal to the United States Supreme Court the appeal was rejected in a one line statement. It is expected that the Supreme Court will have to address the extent of the "state secrecy" doctrine in cases pending in the American judicial system involving Guantanamo detainees as well as in situations where there have been warrantless wiretappings of U. S. citizens.

The case of Khaled el Masri resulted in a request by the German government to the United States to turn over 13 CIA agents who had been involved in the case in Germany. The request was denied.

All of the foregoing was placed in considerable jeopardy on December 10, 2007 when Mr. John Kirikou, an official of the CIA, in an interview with NBC's Today program stated in the questioning of Abu Zubaydah, an Al Qaeda operative linked to the activities of terrorists on 9/11, that the 2002 interrogations had employed highly controversial techniques. Included were sleep deprivation, unnatural physical positions, and waterboarding. Tapes had been made of these events. The tapes were subsequently destroyed by the CIA. This was in the face of the assumption that whomever was in possession of the tapes would have known or reasonably could believe that such tapes would be called for by members of Congress charged with investigating such actions.

It is believed that the tapes were destroyed late in 2005 after the 9/11 Commission had made an unsuccessful effort to view the tapes and at a time when substantial efforts were being made to adopt and issue new rules designed to prevent torture. In early December, 2007, the present Director of the CIA stated that the tapes had been destroyed during the tenure of a prior Director, because they were "not relevant to any internal, legislative or judicial inquiries,"[15] and, if made public, could identify the CIA employees making them vulnerable to retaliation by militants. Revelations in the tapes might also have been useful to the government in the prosecutions of Zacarias Moussaoui and Jose Padilla, and in the civil action brought on behalf of Mr. Padilla in the case of LeBron v. Rumsfeld The last has not been heard in the Moussaoui case. Late in February, 2008, counsel filed an action in a Federal District Court in the District of Columbia urging that Mr. Moussaoui, because of the imposition of secrecy at the time of trial, had been prevented from presenting an adequate defense.

2. THE INTELLIGENCE AUTHORIZATION BILL FOR FY 2008

Members of Congress, particularly members of the Intelligence Committees, were incensed by the indicated conduct by the CIA, the fact that the conduct had been taped, that they had been refused access to the tapes on the ground that they did not exist, that the CIA had failed to conform to its promise not to destroy them, and the announcement that they had been destroyed. Members of the Intelligence Committees have indicated the need to make suitable inquiries.

On December 13, 2007, following the furor occasioned by the then recent CIA disclosures, the House of Representatives turned to the adoption of the FY Intelligence Authorization Act of 2008. Affecting legislative outlooks was the belief that the tapes demonstrated how recalcitrant prisoners were forced to talk, including the use of the "waterboarding" technique. On December 13, 2007, the House of Representatives in Bill 2082 (House Report 110-478) gave its approval by an announced vote of 222 to 199 to the measure that would require the CIA to conform to the prescriptions applicable in the Armed Forces involving detentions and interrogations of unlawful enemy aliens. Section 327 contained two parts with the first imposing limitations on treatments or techniques employed during interrogations. The second defined the term "instrumentality" as employed in the limitation provision. Paragraph (a) of the section reads: "No individual in the custody or under the effective control of an element of the intelligence community or instrumentality thereof, regardless of nationality or physical location, shall be subject to any treatment or technique of interrogation not authorized by the United States Army Field Manual on Human Intelligence Collector Operations." "Instrumentality with respect to an element of the intelligence community" was defined in paragraph (b) to include "a contractor or subcontractor at any tier of the element of the intelligence community." The identified Army Field Manual listed "waterboarding" as one of the impermissible techniques. On February 13, 2008, the Senate adopted the equivalent measure by a vote of 51–45.

Supporters of the legislation noted that in the general language of the 1949 Geneva Conventions no specific reference had been made to "waterboarding," either by way of description or definition, and that a crime under the United States Constitution calls for the formal enactment of a criminal statute. This was also based on the assumption that even if the Geneva Conventions could be construed to prohibit "waterboarding" that the Conventions were not "self-executing." They were also aware that the Army Field Manual did not apply to the CIA, and also that the Department of Defense may have adopted the Manual on the basis of a Presidential Order, unsupported by federal legislation, and perhaps might in the future be found to be without force much as had been the case of the Military Commission announced by the President in his Executive Order of September 25, 2001.

Commentators who disapproved of "waterboarding" were critical of the Bill. They considered that the treaty prohibitions against cruel, inhuman, and degrading conduct could be, and, should properly be construed as including "waterboarding," and that it was already a crime notwithstanding the terms of the proposed Bill. This meant that with the enactment of the Bill into law there would have been no prior statutory prohibition of "waterboarding" and that the pre-statutory CIA offenders would go free. Commentators also speculated that President Bush would attach a "signing statement" to whatever measure was finally adopted, even though they viewed such statements as unenforceable in American courts.

Also questioning the policy ramifications of the proposed statute were presidential supporters who considered that if the CIA were limited to Armed Force restrictions that the CIA would not be able to cope effectively with those who engage in acts of terrorism. Persons supporting traditional procedures held that such conduct was a threat to democratic principles and must be prevented. Moreover, coerced confessions were deemed unreliable. One response was that such conduct was not designed to secure confessions but rather to discover critically needed information. No one claimed that practices of torture by American officials could advance an image supportive of the rule of law. There was speculation that the President would veto the measure on the ground that the legislation would prevent the United States from conducting lawful interrogations of senior Al Qaeda terrorists to obtain intelligence needed to protect Americans from attack.

The vote taken in the Senate on the proposed statute had been preceded by a statement made on February 5, 2008 by the Director of the CIA. It consisted of an acknowledgement that the CIA had employed waterboarding techniques three times between 2002 and 2003. The victims included Khalid Shaikh Mohammed, who was named as a defendant in a Military Commission case on February 11, 2008, Abdu Zubahah, and Abu el Rahim al Nashiri. The first two had engaged in the 9/11 attacks. The third had participated in the bombing of the United States destroyer in Yemen in 2000.

The February 5, 2008 disclosure was confirmed in a White House press briefing on February 6, 2008. The Press Secretary, Mr. Tony Fratto, called attention to the Presidential Executive Order of July 20, 2007, noting that "torture is illegal," that the government must observe "the rule of law," that waterboarding was not currently authorized, and that any future use would depend on the circumstances and would be subject to a Department of Justice opinion and on a presidential decision. Notice would also have to be provided to the Senate and House Intelligence Committee chairpersons and to the ranking members of the Judiciary Committees so that they might be informed that a change in "the program has taken place."[16]

A second press briefing took place on February 7. At that time it may have been possible for the Press Secretary to know of two secret legal memos prepared by the Department of Justice in 2005. They purported to authorize the CIA to engage in the waterboarding of terrorist detainees. He took the position that the use of interrogation techniques would have to take into account the Military Commission Act, the Detainee Treatment Act, "and the President's executive order on our compliance with Common Article III of the Geneva Conventions."

With respect to the then current policy regarding waterboarding Mr. Fratto added "it's not an authorized technique that is a part of this program."[17] When

pressed as to whether this policy would be continued in the future he responded that "it would be foolish to speculate on what the law would say
about the application of a particular technique in particular circumstances."[18]
He also observed that prospective changes would go through a process and
that the "process will include the notification of the Congress."[19]

Given the admission by the CIA that it had employed waterboarding in
three cases ending in 2003, and if this view cannot be proven to be untrue, the
likelihood of a detainee's success in seeking financial relief against the CIA
for alleged post-2003 conduct, based on being the victim of this torture technique after 2003 would seem to be highly problematical. On the other hand,
if it were proven that despite the government's disavowal waterboarding had
in fact occurred, it is likely that confessions based on this technique, properly
identified as torture, would not provide the basis for proving acts of terrorism
and the associated charge of conspiracy.

A. The Presidential Veto, March 8, 2008

On March 8, 2008, President Bush vetoed the measure. Reasons given included the view that "tough interrogation methods constituted one of the most
valuable tools in the war on terror . . . [and that forcing prisoners to talk was
critical saying] the best source of information about terrorist attacks is the terrorists themselves." Senator McCain had voted against the proposed statute
while both of his potential rivals for the office of the President, absented
themselves from the rollcall while campaigning for the nomination of their
political party. Senator McCain expressed the view that the bill would hamper CIA presidential authorized interrogations while repeating that he had
long since taken the position that waterboarding is "illegal." House democrats
immediately proposed an override of the veto, but failed to obtain the required number of votes. The Senate took no action to override the veto.

NOTES

1. The White House, Office of the Press Secretary. http://www.whitehouse.gov/
newsreleases/2007/07/print20070720-4.
2. S. Horton, Defending Enhanced Interrogation Techniques, Harpers Magazine,
June 15, 2007.
3. J. Mayer, The Black Sites, 83 The New Yorker, No. 23, p. 48, August 13, 2007.
A more detailed account is JANE MAYER, THE DARK SIDE: THE INSIDE STORY
OF HOW THE WAR ON TERROR TURNED INTO A WAR ON AMERICA (2008).
4. Los Angeles Times, A14, September 8, 2007.

5. Ibid. Compare, L.N. Sadat, Extraordinary Rendition, Torture and Other Nighmares from the War on Terror, 75 G. W. L. Rev 1200 (2007).

6. Los Angeles Times, A14, September 8, 2007.

7. Ibid.

8. New York Times, December 31, 2007.

9. The Group was co-chaired by James A. Baker, III and Lee H. Hamilton, U. S. Institute for Peace (December 6, 2006).

10. 437 F. Supp. 2d 530 (D. C., Eastern Dist Va. 2006). GEORGE TENET, AT THE CENTER OF THE STORM, MY YEARS AT THE CIA (2007).

11. No. 06-1661.

12. Los Angeles Times, A9, October 10, 2007.

13. 542 U. S. 692 (2004).

14. Reynolds v. United States, 345 U.S. 1 (1953); United States v. Nixon, 418 U.S. 683, 710 (1974).

15. Los Angeles Times, A33, December 9, 2007.

16. Press Release, Office of the Press Secretary, www.whitehouse.gov/news/releases/2008/02/20080206-12.html

17. Press Release, Office of the Press Secretary, www.whitehouse.gov/news/releases/2008/02/200807-12.html., p.3.

18. Ibid.

19. Id., at p. 1.

Chapter Fourteen

America and the Rule of Law

1. INTRODUCTION

Ask anyone in America if the United States believes in and conforms to the rule of law. The response of a clear majority will be an affirmative "Yes."

Support would be based on the fact the Constitution is the "supreme law of the land," that it contains a powerful Bill of Rights, that the American judicial process is highly respected and effective, and that the American political-legal process produces valued outcomes with all being buttressed by well-identified and operative principles of a vital democracy.

If a public opinion pollster were to ask American citizens if the United States were supportive of the world rule of law, responses probably would be more uncertain. Perhaps by introducing the word "world" only the most far-sighted would possess a background adequate to provide a meaningful response.

What, then, are the components which need to be present to justify the term "world rule of law?" It may be supposed that among its essential characteristics would be a body of principles, standards, and rules and processes governing their existence and use. For example, States would have to accept that they were bound by their international agreements (pacta sunt servanda) and that international law is also the product of customary practices (general principles) and that compliance contributes to a shared world order. They would also have to accept that claims of unrestricted national sovereignty are counterproductive and that in recent times creative new institutions, both global and regional, have come onto the international scene. Each may have wide-ranging rules relating to such subjects as an international criminal tribunal, governance of areas (oceans and outer space), protection of Human Rights,

232

including the rights of women and children, cultural matters, economic matters, educational subjects, as well as political, social, and security needs. The rapid emergence of dispute-resolving institutions and demands for the protection of Human Rights have been particularly remarkable. Laws and institutions are held together by an educated understanding that common interests are involved and that experience has demonstrated that common expectations constitute a powerful driving force.

This being the case how does one respond to the mid-2007 conversation between Secretary of State Condoleezza Rice and French President Nicolas Sarkozy when she reportedly said to him "What can I do for you" and he responded "Provide me with a better image of yourself." Like many observers President Sarkozy undoubtedly was influenced by U.S. policies highlighted in recent years and governed by unilateral outlooks including such subjects as global warming, the expenditure of huge sums for the development of new weapons, including plans for the militarization of outer space, the unilateral termination of arms agreements, and the fear, particularly in Muslim countries that the United States was not pursuing an even-handed approach to the resolution of the Middle Eastern conflict, the American opposition to the International Criminal Court, the fact that the United States occupied a hegemonic status with the attendant fears and frustrations flowing from this condition, and, above all, that in the "war on terror" the United States, through an overreach in the use of armed force in Afghanistan and Iraq, had created a "loss of faith in America itself, in the values and institutions that have historically defined this nation."[1]

2. U. S. PRONOUNCEMENTS SUPPORTIVE OF THE RULE OF LAW

Important public officials have not placed a high priority on support for the rule of law. When made the statements have been supportive. They have occurred in the context of advancing democratic principles and the protection of Human Rights. In their joint statement of November 13, 2001, Presidents Bush and Putin in referring to "New Russian-American Economic Relationships" stated it would be promoted through the strengthening of the rule of law. In a subsequent join statement on April 24, 2002, dealing with "Counterterrorism Cooperation," they stressed that "initiatives against terrorism must be conducted in an atmosphere of the rule of law with respect or universal Human Rights."

President Bush in his June 16, 2003 statement on United Nations International Day for Support of Victims of Torture stated that "Torture anywhere is an affront to human dignity everywhere. We are committed to building a world where Human Rights are respected and protected by the rule of law." In 2004 on the same occasion he stated: "America stands against torture and will not tolerate torture. We will investigate and prosecute all acts of torture and undertake to prevent other cruel and unusual punishment in all territory under our jurisdiction." These occasional statements emphasize he fact that President Bush has made no overarching statements attesting to America's high commitment to the principles of the rule of law. His application of the concept in domestic matters has been criticized in an American Bar Association Report of July 24, 2006, relating to the exercise of signing statements at the time of the adoption of legislation. In the report by a bipartisan task force of the Association it was concluded that such statements were subversive of basic principles contained in the U.S. Constitution.

General Colin Powell, as Secretary of State designate, on January 17, 2001 told the Senate Committee on Foreign Relations that he supported a presidential policy of cooperation with "any country that puts the rule of law in place and begins to live by that rule . . ." As Secretary of State his Memorandum to the President dated January 26, 2002, advising him of the vast importance of conforming to the 1949 Geneva Prisoner of War Convention was his most notable effort regarding the rule of law.

With a growing awareness in the White House that the United States was being perceived as having a luke-warm outlook respecting the rule of law Secretary of State Rice in November, 2005, addressed an American Bar Association symposium concerned with the promotion of the rule of law and the strengthening of legal institutions. In an historically oriented and detailed assessment of America's commitment to the rule of law in international relations, she noted that the United States was engaged in empowering "our partners in weak and poorly governed States to uphold the rule of law. We also expect them to meet their international obligations."[2] Among the considerations highlighted in her remarks were the need to support democracy and the protection of Human Rights within States, the obligation of the United States to empower weak States so that they might obtain the strength to enforce the rule of law, the need for the United States to support the rights of oppressed citizens, eliminating corruption in foreign governments through the offering of incentives for honest and transparent behavior, helping citizens in countries where immoral rulers and war criminals governed, to establish and operate international tribunals and special courts of justice, and, where peoples had been newly liberated, to assist them in adopting democratic principles. References were made to substantial monetary contributions to Afghanistan for new court houses, for the training of judges, and the reformation of the nation's regulatory system. She also called attention to grants to Iraq for the training and equipping of a new national police force, for the reform of the legislative system, for educational purposes all costing more than $1 billion and to help them "frame their new democratic constitution at a cost of $400 million."[3]

On December 6, 2005, following a conference with the German Chancellor, Angela Merkel, Secretary Rice stated that the two countries "share ideas and we do share a belief in the rule of law." She indicated that this meant the United States would live up to its "commitments under our own laws and to our international obligations." On April 26, 2006 Secretary Rice joined with the Brazilian Foreign Minister in a statement reaffirming a "commitment to our shared view that representative democracy and the rule of law are indispensable to building modern societies and political systems that provide growth, social development, accountability, transparency, and stability."

On May 1, 2006 she stated to the United States-Japan Security Consultative Committee that this partnership would promote "fundamental values shared by both nations including basic Human Rights, freedom, democracy, and the rule of law." On November 5, 2006, she referred to the conviction of Saddam Hussein. She applauded Iraqi officials who had advanced "the rule of law in Iraq."

By way of contrast neither Attorneys General Ashcroft nor Gonzales have made public pronouncements of any significance supportive of the rule of law. Vice President Cheney and Secretary of Defense Rumsfeld have been generally dismissive of the role of international law in foreign relations

The United States Institute for Peace, a federal agency, conducts a "Rule of Law Program." Its function is to "build upon and define principles of the rule of law as articulated by various international bodies." It seeks to provide "practical guidance for their implementation." To address these conditions to the extent possible the United States has embarked on initiatives conducted by Department of State officials and other agencies supportive of U.S. foreign policy such as the Voice of America and the U. S. Information Agency. Attention has been called to the government's commitment to care for the poor and the ill wherever such suffering takes place. Foreign aid has been an ongoing policy of the United States. Support has been given to the World Health Organization, the Food and Agriculture Organization, and UNESCO as well as other important specialized agencies of the United Nations dealing with the homeless and dispossessed.

As a result of their support for the rule of law, particularly its principles relating to the use of force in a time of armed conflict, as well as the detention and interrogation of combatants, the members of the American Society of International Law at the Annual Meeting on March 29, 2006, adopted a seven point resolution.[4] It was reported that it was approved by a "substantial majority" of the members present. Under its terms: 1. "Resort to armed force is governed by

the Charter of the United Nations and other international law (jus ad bellum).
" 2. "Resort to armed conflict and occupation is governed by the Geneva Conventions of August 12, 1949 and other international law (jus in bello)." 3.
"Torture and cruel, inhuman, or degrading treatment of any person in the custody or control of a state are prohibited by international law from which no
derogation is permitted." 4."Prolonged, secret, incommunicado detention of
any person in the custody or control of a state is prohibited by international
law." 5. "Standards of international law regarding treatment of persons extends to all branches of national governments, to their agents, and to all combatant forces."6. "In some circumstances, commanders (both military and
civilian) are personally responsible under international law for the acts of
their subordinates." 7."All states should maintain security and liberty in a
manner consistent with their international law obligations." The resolution,
adopted at a time when world-wide confidence in America's commitment to
the rule of law in international affairs was at a low ebb, was intended to re-
mind the American government of basic principles with an implied invitation
to meet their requirements. The terms of the resolution were not mere articles
of faith: they were obligatory requirements of law recognized in civilized societies. They are the very life blood of the rule of law.

High level military personnel, particularly those serving as Judge Advocates, have grave responsibilities regarding the rule of law. One response, allowing for conformity in the other branches of the Army, was the publication
in 2007 of "The Rule of Law Handbook: A Practitioner's Guide for Judge Advocates." With the need to engage in counterinsurgency operations in the conflicts in Afghanistan and Iraq the United States Army and the Marine Corp
have published a "Counterinsurgency Field Manual (U. S. Amy FM No 3-24
and the Marine Corps Warfighting Publication 3-33.5. They add to the "small
print" of the rule of law principle.

Another relevant position emerged on August 20, 2007, from the First
Chautauqua Declaration advanced by former Nuremberg prosecutors. The
group called attention to the statement by the Chief Prosecutor, Robert H.
Jackson, who said: "We are able to do away with domestic tyranny and violent aggression by those in power against the rights of their own people only
when we make all answerable to the law."

Several American universities support research on the rule of law. The
Georgetown University Law Center focuses on the advancement of the rule
of law in the Americas. Stanford University supports a Center on Democracy,
Development, and the Rule of Law. The American Center for the Rule of Law
emphasizes the importance of economic freedom and global progress. It pro-
motes the view that consistency, predictability, and transparency are essential
to an effective rule of law. The Center's approach is characterized by the view

that when legal rules are "variable, intrusive, and unclear . . . [they] stand in the way of economic freedom and global progress."

Citizen's organizations such as the UNA-USA call for governmental support for the rule of law. Its goal is to "encourage the US government to adhere to international treaties it has ratified and to join treaties that would advance US national interests." It noted that US non-conformity would serve as an invitation to others to disregard the law.

3. AMERICAN EFFORTS TO DEMONSTRATE ITS SUPPORT FOR THE RULE OF LAW

The United States turned to the Department of State's Legal Advisor to persuade foreign leaders of America's commitment to the rule of law. He addressed one group in San Remo, Italy, in September, 2005, and another at The Hague on June 6, 2007.

At San Remo he began by describing the role of international law in U. S. foreign policy observing that the United States had a vital interest in strengthening and promoting the development of international law.[5] He discussed the increasing use of the Security Council under Chapter VII to "create mechanisms that ensure accountability or to adapt and amplify" the law of war and Human Rights in particular situations. He referred to progress in the law of war being accorded to women and children as a result of Security Council resolutions. He referred to progress in the area of Human Rights that had resulted from the establishment of the international tribunals for Yugoslavia and Rwanda. He called attention to the Security Council's invocation of its Chapter VII powers "to create specific legal frameworks to address the threats to international peace and security" which the United States considered to be a "significant development."[6]

He then explained the American position on the ability of the Council "to modify or supplant existing norms when acting under Chapter VII."[7] Examples were selected from resolutions adopted during the early stages of the Iraq crisis. A second example was the "treatment of the political transformation of Iraq."[8] He added that caution was in order in taking such an approach, but he urged that "in order to address the most serious threats to international peace and security the UN Charter clearly contemplates that the Council may need to specifically address matters normally within the sovereign control of states, or to take action . . . altering the obligations of states under international conventions."[9] In his view The Hague Regulations of 1907 and the Geneva Conventions of 1949 dealt with a set of facts "that did not necessarily address political and economic realities of the 21st century."[10]

Although many of his observations may be deemed somewhat controversial, depending on special, nationally oriented, perceptions of the meaning and substance of international law, including its dynamic capacity to advance preferred goals and values, it must still be acknowledged that Mr.Bellinger's remarks clearly fit within the concept of the rule of law.

In a major presentation at The Hague on June 6, 2007, he introduced his remarks by acknowledging that "our critics sometimes paint the United States as a country willing to duck or shrug off international obligations when they prove constraining or inconvenient."[11] Relying on an earlier statement of Secretary Rice that the Department of State "along with the rest of the administration will be a strong voice for international legal norms, for living up to our treaty obligations, to recognizing that America's moral authority in international politics also rests on our ability to defend international laws and treaties," he urged that the foregoing perceptions were "wrong."[12]

In endeavoring to understand the reasons for hostile foreign outlooks he speculated that they might be the product of inadequate information, the fact that the United States has taken international law seriously has been construed as "obstructionism or worse,"[13] "that some of the most vehement attacks on our behavior—although they are couched as legal criticism—are in fact differences of policy."[14] that "our critics often assert the law as they wish it were, rather than it actually exists today,"[15] and that claims that the United States is in violation of international law has been the product of the failure of the United States to reach "the result or interpretation that these critics prefer."[16]

Mr. Bellinger offered three major conclusions. First, the treaty practice of the United States demonstrates a commitment to international law. Second, the treaty practice of the United Stats also demonstrates a belief in the important role of international law. Third, international law plays an important role in U. S. domestic law.

On his first point he asserted that America's treaty practice reflected "the seriousness with which we take international obligations, not our indifference to them. For example, whenever we consider taking on new obligations, we examine a number of factors—What problem is the treaty designed to address? Is it a problem susceptible to solution through a treaty? Will we be in a position to implement it, or will there be complications raised in domestic law?"[17] He pointed out the need to obtain the advice and consent of the Senate to a proposed international agreement, and the critical outlooks often reflected there. He noted that under such circumstances the Department of State was obliged to determine whether it should suggest or implement Senate promoted reservations, understandings, or declarations and also whether it had been understood in Congress that implementing legislation might be required, and, if so, whether a reasonably comprehensive blue print had been considered prior to a final commitment to treaty terms.

Mr. Bellinger then referred to several highly important international agreements to which the United States had declined to become party. Among them was the Kyoto Protocol. He took note of the fact that that the Bush administration had been vigorously opposed to it for identified reasons. While informed scientific opinion had almost universally rejected the Bush "reasons," as "unreal," such reasons, nonetheless, reflected the policy of the United States. Thus, policy considerations, rather than disrespect for the treaty process and international law, were considered to be the culprit. The principal fears of the United States were that the implementation of the agreement would create greater economic inequalities and general dangers than those that would be present in a polluted world.

Mr. Bellinger's second major contention was that United States practice demonstrated belief in the important role of international law. His focus was on how the United States had met its treaty obligations. He began his assessment by stating that the United States recognized that international law had a "critical role in world affairs and is vital to the resolution of conflicts and the coordination of cooperation."[18] Under this heading he addressed what he referred to as "probably the most divisive and difficult international legal issue that we have faced: our detention policies."[19] He continued: "Frankly, I don't expect that most of you will agree with the steps we took or the decisions we made . . . , but I hope you will understand the difficulty we faced after September 11, when we captured or took into custody suspected members of Al Qaida and the Taliban."[20] Noting that the United States was confronted by a dilemma, he asked: "What legal rules apply to them?" To be considered might be that "these suspected terrorists did not fit neatly within existing legal rules—whether domestic criminal law or the laws of war."[21] An important factor was that these terrorists could not be tried in American criminal courts since their jurisdiction did not extend to activities in Afghanistan. Further, in his view the "detainees did not qualify, as some critics claim, as POWs under the Geneva Conventions—which by their terms apply only to conflict between the High Contracting Parties and also extend special protections to persons who openly identify themselves as a part of a Party's armed forces."[22]

He also called attention to the fact that the United States Supreme Court had held that common Article 3 of the Convention was applicable, while "the Conventions as a whole do not."[23] Under these circumstances the United States endeavored to establish a more complete legal framework. This was accomplished through the adoption of federal legislation, notably the Military Commissions Act of December 17, 2006. He stated as a result of negotiations with European governments that a growing number of European officials and legal experts "have come to acknowledge that members of Al Qaida captured outside our own territories do not fit neatly into traditional criminal law rules or into the Geneva Conventions."[24] In his view the effort to resolve these problems through the application of international law "demonstrated the respect in which the United States holds international law."[25]

Mr. Bellinger's third theme was entitled "International Law Plays an Important Role in U. S. Domestic Law." In this section of his presentation he called attention to the constitutional provision that treaties are the supreme law of the land, that treaties share a legal equivalency with statutes, and that treaties can be self-executing or non-self-executing thereby requiring further action by the Congress. Selected as an example was CAT's Article 15 relating to the use in courts, including military commissions, of statements obtained via torture. To obtain the application of the treaty prohibition it was necessary for Congress to adopt a prohibitory statute.

He noted that countries, including the United States, do not allow unlimited private litigation of international law. Yet, the United States has adopted legislation allowing private persons to sue named individual defendants for specific violations of international law involving extrajudicial killings and torture, even though most countries reserve such matters for consideration only to their criminal courts. Congress has also enacted legislation allowing for private claims for compensation based on expropriations of property in violation of international law.

His remarks acknowledged that the United States and its critics had gone through a difficult period of reproach and incrimination regarding different outlooks on international law. Hoping that these conditions might be put behind he expressed belief that in the future members of the international community would "seek new ways to build international cooperation and the rule of law."[26]

4. THE CONCERNS AND RECOMMENDATIONS OF THE CAT TORTURE COMMITTEE, 2000–2006

Another way to measure America's commitment to the rule of law, with specific reference to its obligations under the 1984 CAT, is to examine U.S. reports to its Torture Committee, the Committee's concerns and recommendations, and American responses. The fact that these transactions have not attracted wide-spread publicity does not detract from the fact that understanding them provides another valuable basis upon which it is possible to identify and judge the extent to which the United States is supportive of the rule of law.

Article 17 of CAT made provision for a Committee against Torture. Consisting of 10 experts "of high moral standing and recognized as competent in the field of Human Rights" they are selected on the basis of their geographical status and legal experience.[27] The United States filed its Initial Report with the Committee in October, 1999,[28] and made oral presentations between May 15–20, 2000. On May 6, 2005 the United States submitted its Second Periodic Report updating relevant information arising since its first submission. The Report consisted of 148 pages.

Following a review of Committee conclusions and recommendations to the Initial Report the United States stated it was in compliance with the Convention. It explained the reasons for its RUDs, which it regarded as having continuing validity and necessity. Note was taken of Committee observations regarding prison abuses, detention of minors with adults, the use of electro-shock devices, and the presence of chain gangs. It was admitted that some of these may have taken place occasionally but they were not tolerated. It was pointed out that prisoners had the right to institute law suits in the event of abuse. It was concluded that "the United States legal system affords numerous opportunities for individuals to complain of abuse and to seek remedies for such alleged violations."[29]

The Second Periodic Report consisted of a point-to-point response to the Committee's previous recommendations. It addressed new measures and developments relating to the implementation of the Convention. It contained highly specific information regarding Articles 1 through 16. It provided additional information that had been requested by the Committee and concluded with observations and recommendations. It was supplemented by seven Annexes containing separate reports relating to individuals in the custody and control of American forces in Afghanistan and Iraq, a presidential statement, the December 30, 2004 Department of Justice Memorandum, a list of the American RUDs, relevant provisions of the U. S. Constitution, statutes and regulations, a sample of federal court decisions applying Article 3 of CAT, and to capital punishment cases. The Report was a full-fledged effort by the United States. It was intended to demonstrate[30] positive efforts to meet the terms and conditions of the CAT.

It was not until May 5, 2006, following a time-consuming review by the Committee of the Second Periodic Report, and prior to Mr. Bellinger's European presentations that the Committee convened to receive an oral statement from the United States. On that date he appeared before the Committee Against Torture where he highlighted the content of the Second Periodic Report. He told the members of the Committee that while cases of abuse and wrongdoing had occurred during the conflict with Al Qaida that these events had been relatively few and not systematic. Without acknowledging that waterboarding had occurred he stated that the technique was prohibited. He stated that the government of the United States was absolutely committed to "upholding our national and international obligations to irradicate torture and to prevent cruel, inhuman, or degrading treatment or punishment worldwide."[31]

Mr. Bellinger also told the Committee that federal legislation adopted after the ratification of CAT criminalizing the offense of extraterritorial torture was designed to implement the obligations undertaken in the Convention. He also noted that Federal laws were in force that prohibited acts constituting torture within the boundaries of the United States. He also indicated that the Committee did not possess jurisdiction to consider the extraterritorial transfer of persons since the CAT did not apply to such persons. In response to the Committee's concern relating to executive detention practices following 9/11, he "asserted that they are 'governed by the law of armed conflict' operating as lex specialis to the exclusion of the Convention."[32]

On May 18, 2006 the Committee issued a Report entitled "Consideration of Reports submitted by states parties under Article 19 of the Convention."[33] It contained the conclusions and recommendations of the Committee. The Report commended the United States for its exhaustive written responses and oral statements made during Committee hearings. Positive aspects of the Report included the assurance that the United States and its civilian contractors were prohibited from engaging in torture and the lesser included offences, the acceptance of the American statement that it was not engaged in the "transfer [of] persons to countries where it believes that it is 'more likely than not that they' will be tortured, and that this applies, as a matter of policy, to the transfer of any individual, in the State party's custody or control, regardless of where they are detained."[34]

The Committee also commented favorably on the assurance received from the United States that a Presidential Signing Statement "is not to be interpreted as a derogation by the President from the absolute prohibition of torture." The Committee expressed its satisfaction with the enactment of The Prison Rape Elimination Act of 2003 and that section of the DTA of 2005 which "prohibits cruel, inhuman, and degrading treatment and punishment of any person, regardless of nationality or physical location, in the custody or under the physical control of the State party."[35] Also favorably received by the Committee was the adoption in 2000 of National Detention Standards fixing minimum standards for facilities holding Homeland Department security detainees, the sustained and substantial contributions by the United States to the UN Voluntary Fund for the Victims of Torture, and the adoption by the Department of Defense of a new Army Field Manual for Intelligence Interrogation designed to insure that all military personnel comply with it when engaging in interrogations.

The Committee then turned to a criticism of the Report. It listed 24 concerns and made four recommendations. All were based on the view that the United States had failed to comply with the letter, spirit, and purpose of CAT.

The foremost of the Committee's concerns was based on the view that Sections 2340 and 2340A of the Criminal Torture Act of 2004[36] dealt only with extraterritorial instances of torture and did not deal with behavior within the United States with the result that the United States did not have "a federal crime of torture consistent with article 1 of the Convention."[37] To remedy the American approach to CAT the Committee urged that the United States "should enact a federal crime of torture [statute] consistent with Article 1 of the Convention. The Committee considered that the United States should include appropriate penalties, in order to fulfill its obligations under the Convention to prevent and eliminate all acts of torture causing severe pain or suffering, whether physical or mental, in all its forms."[38] The Committee also indicated that the United States "should ensue that acts of psychological torture, prohibited by the Convention, and not limited to 'prolonged mental harm' as set out in the State party's understandings lodged at the time of the ratification of the Convention, but constitute a wider category of acts, which cause severe mental suffering, irrespective if their prolongation or duration."[39] Moreover, it was urged that the United States should "investigate, prosecute, and punish perpetrators under the federal extraterritorial criminal torture statute."[40] This was occasioned by the finding that no prosecutions had been instituted under the statute.

Other expressions of concern dealt with the American position relating to application of the Convention in time of armed conflict. Concern was expressed regarding the definition of American territory in the 2004 Criminal Torture Act, which limited it to areas of de jure control. It was asserted that the statute should also apply to areas of de facto control. Additional concerns related to the failure of the United States to register all of the persons detained by it in any country, that the United States had established secret detention facilities, its role in dealing with "enforced disappearances," concern that the American statement respecting the nonderogation provisions contained in the agreement were inadequate thereby allowing for a justification or defense against acts of torture, that the "non-refoulement" guarantee did not apply to persons detained outside the territory of the United States, and the significance of "diplomatic assurances" given to the United states that a person was not to be subjected to torture in a host state once that person had been turned over to that state. Of critical importance was the concern that indefinite detentions of any person "without charge constituted per se a violation of the Convention . . . [particularly that detainees had been held for protracted periods at the Guantanamo Naval Station] without sufficient legal safeguards and without judicial assessment of the justification for their detention."[41]

Further concerns related to the inadequacy of training programs provided to all law enforcement and military personnel. It was feared that sufficient focus on the provisions of the Convention had been absent. Attention was drawn to deaths and serious abuses in 2002 in Afghanistan and Iraq, resulting from "confusing interrogation rules" that were overly vague and general thereby countenancing "stress positions." The terms of the DTA of December 30, 2005 withdrawing the issuance of writs of habeas corpus by Federal District Courts were heavily criticized. The difficulties confronting victims of abuse seeking redress and compensation in the courts were noted. Attention was drawn to the provision in the 1995 Prison Litigation Reform Act stating that "no federal civil action may be brought by a prisoner for mental or emotional injury suffered while in custody without a prior showing of physical injury." Taking note of the procedures employed by a valid Military Commission of not admitting statements resulting from torture into evidence, concern was expressed regarding the implementation of the rule and the opportunity of a detainee to complain regarding a Commission decision.

Concern was expressed that executions taking place in the United States "can be accompanied by severe pain and suffering."[42] Concern was expressed over reports that detainees were being subjected to sexual assaults and that these were not being promptly and independently investigated. Also raised were allegations that women detainees had been subjected to humiliation and that children were being held without segregation from adults, as well as that convicted children were being sentenced to life imprisonment. Separate concerns were voiced over the use by detaining personnel of "electro-shock devices." Concern was expressed over the use of "super-maximum prisons," where prolonged isolation was being practiced. It was believed that adequate investigations had not been conducted of brutality and ill-treatment of "members of vulnerable groups by its law enforcement personnel, and that such investigations be carried out in an independent, prompt, and thorough manner."[43] A special request was made for a report on the "investigations into the alleged illegal treatment by law enforcement personnel in the aftermath of Hurricane Katrina."

Additionally the Committee made recommendations on four subjects. First, it invited the United States to allow its special rapporteur on torture to visit the Guantanamo Naval Base and any other detention facility under "its effective de facto control."[44] Second, the United States was invited to consider its decision not to become a member of the International Criminal Court. Third, the Committee "reiterated its prior recommendation that the United States should consider withdrawing its reservations, declarations, and understanding lodged at the time of ratification of the Convention." Fourth, the United States was encouraged to "consider making the declaration under article 22, thereby recognizing the competence of the Committee to receive and consider individual communications, as well as ratifying the Optional Protocol to the convention."

Although, as pointed out, the Second United States Report was exceedingly detailed the Committee observed that it would benefit from the compilation by the United States of a data base which would allow for the compilation of statistics and information so that the Third Report would be more conclusive.

Within a few days after the issuance of the Report the White House stated that American conduct at Guantanamo was in compliance with CAT and that "everything that it does in terms of questioning detainees is fully within the bounds of American law."[45] Following the issuance of the Committee Report Mr. Bellinger stated that it contained a number of "factual inaccuracies and legal misstatements of the law applicable to the United States."[46] He indicated that it was "legally wrong" to say that existence of the detention facility at Guantanamo violated CAT, and that it was "factually wrong" to conclude that the detainees lacked access to judicial processes.[47] He characterized the Committee findings as being "skewed and reaching well beyond the scope and mandate of the Committee" and that the United States would comply with the Committee's request for the submission of further responses within the coming year.[48]

5. CONCLUSION

The concerns and recommendations of the Torture Committee were the product of a thorough analysis on torture and its associated crimes identified in CAT. It is possible that the Committee's report was the product of a "worst case" appraisal picturing numerous instances of law enforcement failures as representative of a national policy or policies thus overstating the significance of the reported delinquencies. It is probable that the Committee's view of the U. S. policy regarding its RUDs to CAT, namely that they should be eliminated, was unrealistic and weakened the report. In assessing the report it is necessary to ask whether an entire remedying of the committee's concerns and recommendations would have a substantial impact on America's image regarding its support for the world rule of law.

This would have to be weighed against America's adoption of wide-ranging and highly controversial policies having important ramifications. These have contributed very materially to the conclusion that the United States is not much concerned over its negative image regarding support for the world rule of law.

A major American effort would be required to respond to all of the Committee's concerns and recommendations including providing a factual basis for refutations. Even if further American reports were to respond in greater detail to Committee concerns the possibility might remain that frank and factual statements still would not be satisfactory to the Committee, and American efforts to advance the rule of law would not be advanced. It remains to be seen what the American Third Report will contain. It seems that concessions to unfounded charges by the United States would not serve to advance respect for the rule of law both nationally and internationally.

This is not to say that the Committee's concerns and recommendations were unreasonable. Many possessed merit. It is to say, however, that meritorious changes regarding CAT would not necessarily modify or alleviate entirely the existing perceptions of the government's tarnished image.

If it were possible for the United States to conform substantially to the Committee's concerns, what else might it take to establish that the United States was interested in improving its international image? To achieve such a goal the United States might (1) substantially restrain the use of armed force in response to foreign misconduct, (2) demonstrate a greater concern for the deterioration of the Earth's atmosphere, (3) engage in greater support for the world's judicial institutions, including ending the heavy diplomatic pressure on signatories to the Rome Treaty to exempt American citizens from the jurisdiction of the International Criminal Court, (4) reconsider its practice of taking unilateral decisions respecting new policies arrived at multilaterally resulting from globalization, (5) promote through education an understanding by an alert citizenry of the importance of political processes, (6) close the Guantanamo Naval Station, as has been suggested by former Secretary of State Colin Powell and the current Secretary of the Department of Defense, William Gates, and with it the termination of the detention policies that have been employed there, and (7) initiate on the part of all executive departments engaging in foreign policy activities a vigorous and cohesive program to eliminate foreign false impressions regarding America's basic values as applied to foreign relations. Many vehicles of communication are able to serve this task. In measuring the utility of these proposals account would have to be taken of the fact that any modification of foreign outlooks and attitudes will require serious and consistent work over a period of years. There have always been fears of international transgressions on the part of hegemonic countries. Thriving on uncertainties and the enormity of the risks now alive in the world the concept of hegemony has taken on a life of its own.

When one takes into account all of the aspects of American foreign policy stemming from basic security concerns, as well as the concerns and recommendations of the CAT Torture Committee, the United States at present will find it difficult to persuade other states of its commitment to the world rule of law. However, some changes in American policies relating to the need to address the pollution of the world's environment occurred in mid-2007. In 2009, with the advent of a new President in the White House, more pronounced changes may be in order, and there may be new opportunities for the development of a new and more favorable "image."

NOTES

1. Los Angeles Times editorial "What we've lost," A18, September 11, 2007. It continued: The Bush "war has not only undermined the liberties that make this nation worthy of emulation . . . [as well as] subvert[ing] U. S. military interests. That is the tragic and true cost of these past six years." Early in 2008 the Pew Global Attitudes Project released the results of an opinion survey comparing views held in foreign countries regarding America's image with 2002 and 2007 used as comparative dates. In 26 countries in 2007 the view was less favorable, in 5 counties more favorable, and in 2 countries about the same. With 2002–2007 the base period only in Russia was there an improvement in out look, but the jump was from about 10% to 20%. In the United States it fell from about 80% to 48%, in Italy from 43% to 30%, in Canada from 58% to 29%, in the United Kingdom from 50% to 23 %, in Germany from 31 % to 19%, in France from 19% to 14%, and in Spain from 26% to 9%.

2. 100 AJIL, No. 1, 216 (January 2006). President Bush in 2005 appointed Mrs. Karen Hughes, a close advisor, as his emissary to meet with world leaders, seeking a modified perception of the United States with respect to the world rule of law. She served until December, 2007.

3. Ibid. The State Department's International Law Enforcement Academy's mission is to buttress democratic governance through the advancement of the rule of law. Through international cooperation the particular goals are to combat drug trafficking, criminality, and terrorism.

4. Proceedings of the 100th Annual Meeting of the American Society of International Law 485, (2006).

5. His remarks were published in 99 AJIL, No. 4, 891–894 (October 2005).

6. Id. at 892.

7. Ibid.

8. Id. at 893.

9. Id. at 894.

10. Ibid.

11. http://state.gov/s/1/rls/86123. htm. p. 1.

12. Ibid. at 1.

13. Ibid.
14. Ibid.
15. Ibid.
16. Ibid.
17. Id. at 2.
18. Id. at 3.
19. Id. at 4.
20. Ibid.
21. Ibid.
22. Ibid.
23. Ibid.
24. Ibid.
25. Ibid. Mr. Bellinger expressed an opinion on "Unlawful Enemy Combatants" at http://www.opiniojuris.org/posts/11690000173.shtm.
26. Id. at 5.
27. The Committee was composed of representatives from Chile, China, Cyprus, Denmark, Ecuador, Egypt, The Russian Federation, Senegal, Spain, and the United States.
28. CAT/C/28/Add. 5.
29. Second Periodic Report, p. 63 (2005).
30. CAT/C/USA?CO/2.
31. D. M. Amann, The Committee Against Torture Urges an End to Guantanamo Detention, 10 ASIL Insights, No. 14, p. 1, June 8, 2006. The quotation is attributed to the author.
32. Ibid., p. 2.
33. CAT/C/USA?CO/2.
34. Ibid., p. 2.
35. Ibid.
36. Supra, Chapter Three, # 2.
37. CAT/C/USA/CO/2, p. 3.
38. Ibid., p. 3.
39. Ibid.
40. Ibid.
41. Id., at 6.
42. Id., at 8.
43. Id., at 10.
44. Ibid.
45 Christian Science Monitor, May 22, 2006, p. 2.
46. Ibid.
47. Ibid.
48. Washington Post, A1, May 20, 2006.

Chapter Fifteen

Conclusion

The time has come to draw together this recitation and analysis of the competing claims of American leaders as they pursue their legal and political goals, subject, as they are, to the constraints of the Constitution, applicable international agreements, and the constant influence of public opinion. Since 9/11 the United States has been confronted with two basic challenges: winning or prevailing in armed conflicts or wars against Afghanistan and Iraq and against terrorists and maintaining in this setting the constitutional principles essential in a free democracy. This drama has taken place on a stage where the presence of a militant and totalitarian Islamic terrorism, the claims of detainees, and the practice of torture have been powerful factors. It has become imperative to think about the high relevance of the rule of law to such situations while always being mindful of national security.

The institutions of government have been under pressure to provide acceptable answers to the on-going and seemingly never-ending crisis. It remains on going because of increases in terrorist activities and because the goals of Americans and the methods for achieving them remain unsettled and unanswered. In considering the methodologies of an effective national security system it is impossible not to give thought to the possibility of overreacting thus threatening America's historic respect for civil and political rights and liberties.

The wars produced a legal battlefield with its strategy and tactics no less well defined than those employed by commanders in the field of battle. The institutions of the legal battlefield were the Office of the Presidency, supported consistently, but not always uniformly by civilian "troops," composed of high administrative officials. The opposition consisted of many members of the Congress with its committee systems, and by the courts with their appurtenances. More often than not, bystanders, in the form of the media and academe provided substantial support to the parties, especially to the judiciary.

In positioning themselves on the legal and political battlefield the several branches of the government were obliged to perfect their understandings of the meaning to be attributed to the language appearing in the Constitution, statutes, international agreements, and the reasons advanced by the judicial system in the decision of cases. This was referred to as the process of the "moving sidewalk" in which facts and law are combined by courts in the event of disputes among litigants, certainly including the Executive and Legislative branches of the government, resulting in judicial decisions. In the process, for example with regard to treaty terms, it may be necessary to look to definitions employed in the agreement, as previously interpreted or construed by Congress or the President. In the case of CAT critical terms of the convention were subject to RUDs initially put forward by the U. S. Senate. The executive branch, speaking through the Department of Justice, put forward interpretive legal memos. They dealt with the elements of torture and the status of persons captured in armed conflict. They endeavored to differentiate what was legal in the matters addressed, and what was not permissible. An influential DOJ Memorandum dealing with the definition of torture was subsequently revoked. The change constituted a situation where the initial effort to "fine tune" a legal concept defined in an international agreement was counter productive. Substantial detriment resulted from that particular use of the interpretive process to provide guidance for anti-terrorist activities.

It is to the several branches of the government with their historic separation of powers functions that the public can look for protection. In a military battlefield there is a sense of command, founded on discipline, with identified goals and objectives. To be successful there is also a sense of personal loyalty and mutual protections against adversity. All of these may vary in intensity and duration, but they are the foundation stones upon which success depends. These same considerations became important factors in the Office of the Presidency during the wars. A major goal was the creation of a system of military law with supporting procedures applicable to terrorism and its consequences which would take precedence over traditional judicial procedures. Whether the Constitution could bear this challenge has become the burden and responsibility of the federal courts.

In time of crisis the United States must be attentive to constitutional principles, including unrivaled support for the Bill of Rights, and clear perceptions of the respective roles of the three branches of government as portrayed in the concept of separation of powers. Deviations from the tradition and practice which support the view that the Supreme Court has the final authority to say "what the law is," are not permissible or acceptable. With its declaration of the "war against terrorism" the Bush administration has emphasized the "war powers" of the President. Critics of the content of such "powers" have referred to a "unilateral" theory as descriptive of excessive claims. Congress has sought to preserve its prerogatives especially respecting the Senate's right to provide its advice and consent before a proposed treaty can be ratified. It has adopted relevant legislation, some of which, such as the Detainee Treatment Act of December 30, 2005, and the Military Commissions Act of October 17, 2006, have countenanced broad executive powers. At other times Congress has vigorously opposed presidential decisions. An overriding factor has been the defense by each branch, pursuant to its views, of the powers it believes that have been conferred on it emanating from the separation of powers principle. The Supreme Court has ruled on cases involving the respective rights of the government and detainees. It held that the President had exceeded his authority in creating military commissions by his Order of November 13, 2001, and the Order was voided.[1]

Nonetheless, the Bush administration made very substantial efforts to establish military processes and procedures to be employed against terrorists. President Bush has remained steadfast in his view that military procedures should generally prevail. Crimes were identified and procedures established both in statutes and in Executive Orders to deal with detainees. One goal was to acquire information on terrorism and the plans of terrorists. A second goal was to ensue that detainees not be tortured or harmed through identified forms of harsh treatment. To render this goal effective Administrative Review Boards, Combatant Status Review Tribunals, and a new Military Commission were established.[2] This approach resulted in opposing the initial reference of terrorism cases to the federal courts where trial procedures would adhere to constitutional mandates. Only through successful applications by detainees for writs of habeas corpus were they able to advance their rights. Rulings on habeas corpus petitions by trial courts provided opportunities for appeals to higher tribunals. The Supreme Court reversed a number of the decisions rendered by military authorities. The differences between the two branches produced responsible responses and while operating under judicially imposed limitations they endeavored to secure the implementation of their preferences. This opened the door to new executive orders and initiatives, legislative responses, and new cases for the courts. Mountains of supportive memorandums were published and reviewed.

One extremely important outcome was the enactment of the Military Commissions Act which contained a habeas corpus "stripping" provision which denied to Federal District Courts the power to issue the writ. This stirred up substantial debates whether there was a rebellion or invasion of the type allowing for a suspension. A number of influential Senators introduced legislation seeking to repeal the "stripping" provisions, but their efforts were not successful. Under the Act rulings relating to the writ were given to the United States Court of Appeals for the District of Columbia.

Following 9/11 the Bush administration was confronted with the question whether the Constitution applied to persons, who prior to capture, had engaged in acts of terrorism, including taking up arms against the United States. These persons fell into different categories: U. S. citizens, aliens, place where the person engaged in acts of terrorism, and place of capture, e. g., within the United States or abroad, with some aliens having been captured within the United States while in violation of their visa conditions. Depending on the variables some persons were prosecuted in Federal District Courts while others were held at Guantanamo pending administrative hearings before Administrative Review Boards or Combatant Status Review Tribunals or judicial proceedings before a 2006 Military Commission, with the latter not rendering opinions until June 2007 at which time the military judges held that their jurisdiction extended only to "alien unlawful enemy combatants" and dismissed the cases before them for failure to conform to the terms of the Military Commissions Act. This decision was soon overruled as having been too "technical" with advice to the Commission that it had the power to rule on its jurisdiction.

When the forum for detainees held in custody in the United States has been a Federal District Court a detainee defendant, even though an alien, is entitled to all of the constitutional guarantees of American citizens. But, where the person is believed, on the basis of a military determination rendered by a Board, Tribunal, or Commission, to be an alien detainee held outside the United States only the Sixth Amendment guarantees of a fair and speedy trial were available. This raised the question of whether this test, established in federal laws and Department of Defense rules and regulations, assured the protection of a fair and speedy trial particularly when there was the prospect of an indefinite detention either in a detention facility located in the United States or at Guantanano.

The problem can be viewed from the generally accepted principle that U. S. constitutional guarantees do not extend to aliens resident in foreign countries. Thus, a person suspected of being an alien unlawful enemy combatant and being held abroad, while being entitled to a fair and speedy trial, that person cannot complain of the unavailability of all constitutional guarantees. For such a person the inability to move through the military procedures identified above to a resolution of his classification by the military forces allowed for his detention based on security considerations. This is where petitions for writs of habeas corpus were lodged with federal trial courts. This is where the rulings and reasoning announced in the majority opinion in the 2008 cases of Boumediene v. Bush and Al Odah v. Rumsfeld, dealing with alleged alien enemy combatant detainees in U. S. custody at the Guantanamo Naval Station, have become of critical importance.

In these circumstances the executive branch asserted that military courts, because of security considerations, were better suited to deal with terrorists. Many challenges have been mounted to that outlook. Among them are fears that American civil and political liberties would be substantially and possibly permanently eroded, that civilian courts should in all circumstances be preferred over military courts, that such a dualism does not well serve the democratic needs of the country, that America's reputation as supportive of the rule of law would continue to be in disrepair, and that if the detention facilities at Guantanamo were to be closed that an early determination would have to be made which detainees were the most dangerous and who were the best sources of intelligence information and transferred to the United States and whether those who were of lesser value could be repatriated to the countries of their nationality or otherwise discharged.

Before 9/11 and new perceptions of terrorism the United States Supreme Court had ruled in cases involving the right of aliens outside the United States to invoke constitutional guarantees established principally in the 4th, 5th, and 6th amendments. In the Insular Cases (Bolzac v. Puerto Rico) in 1922 the Court held that the 6th amendment did not apply although the United States was exercising territorial sovereignty in the islands.[3] In the 1990 case of U. S. v. Verdugo-Urquidez it was decided that a citizen and resident of Mexico could not claim the benefits of the 4th Amendment relating to searches and seizures taking place in Mexico.[4] On the other hand in Player v. Doe an alien domiciled in a foreign country was held to be entitled of the protection of the due process clause of the 5th Amendment.[5]

In Johnson v. Eisentrager in 1950 the Supreme Court emphatically rejected the claims of overseas aliens to rights under the 5th Amendment.[6] Eisentrager, a German national, had been convicted in a United States military commission situated in China for violating the laws of war. He was transferred to a U. S. military prison in Germany. Extraterritorial claims calling for the use and protection of the writ of habeas corpus were denied. The meanings of these cases produced sharp disputes between the majority and minority justices in the Boumediene case.

The Supreme Court in Rasul v. Bush involving a Guantanamo detainee in 2004 expressed the view that a Federal District Court did possess jurisdiction respecting a claim advanced by an alien detainee held at Guantanamo even though the United States did not possess territorial sovereignty at the Naval Station and the litigants were not physically present in the United States.[7] In the Eisentrager case the prisoner was characterized as an "alien enemy" defined as the "subject of a foreign state at war with the United States." In Rasul v. Bush the majority distinguished the Eisentrager case on the facts, holding that an "alien enemy" was not entitled to a high degree of protection and that Supreme Court decisions in the years following the Eisentrager case had not followed that precedent. The majority in the Rasul case ruled that the then operative habeas corpus statute granted to district courts statutory jurisdiction over an enemy combatant, being held as a detainee, whenever and "as long as the custodian could be reached by the service of process."[8]

The Rasul decision also referred to the rights of an American citizen living in England who, when charged with criminal conduct, had claimed rights contained in the 5th and 6th Amendments. The court held that an American citizen enjoyed their full protection. But, as noted, an alien in custody outside the United States had access to the writ of habeas corpus when the custodian could be reached for service of the writ. The other two branches of the Federal government expressed dismay at the Court's holding and on October 17, 2006 enacted the Military Commissions Act containing jurisdictional provisions stripping trial courts of the power to issue writs of habeas corpus.[9] An interesting scenario awaited the challenging of this limitation. In the meantime the prospect that a detainee may face an indefinite detention has riveted attention on the need to address the situation. On June 29, 2007 the Supreme Court, in a rare reversal of an earlier ruling on granting writs of certiorari, agreed in the case of Boumediene v. Bush, to review in the October, 2007, term problems involving the jurisdiction-stripping provision relating to writs of habeas corpus and the military practice of holding a detainee for a seemingly indefinite time.[10] Chapter Nine dealt at some length with the impact made by the Boumediene case on legal rights of the Guantanamo detainees.

Several factors contributed to the events identified above. The Bush administration's decision to establish separate jurisdictional approaches—military and civilian—resulted from the asymmetrical nature of the war against persons who could not qualify as POWs under the Geneva Convention. The decision occurred under circumstances where American military forces were obliged to detain and to interrogate combatants captured in Afghanistan and in Iraq. American actions stemmed from inadequate prior military planning at the highest levels of authority. This resulted in the failure to establish clearly defined rules applicable to the armed forces in the field. These failures were compounded at Abu Ghraib where the laws and customs of war were not understood or implemented, where the basic requirements of military discipline were lacking, owing in part to unschooled troops, where a functioning registration process for detainees was not in place, where some captured persons were held as "ghost detainees," and where there was "rogue" behavior on the part of both military personnel and civilian employees at the prisons. Concurrently extraterritorial (extraordinary) rendition had been initiated by CIA personnel.

Not all of the blame should be attributed to the forces in the field. Uncertainties flowing, from opposing outlooks in the Departments of Justice, Defense, and State relating to the meaning to be given to the Torture Convention and its implementing statutes and to the POW Convention undoubtedly contributed to the indefensible misconduct.

Seeking to avoid a repetition of this debacle the Department of Defense called for the preparation of formal policies and procedures. One important step was taken in 2004 with the issuance of a directive to the Joint Chiefs of Staff to prepare applicable rules and regulations. A document entitled "Joint Doctrine for Detainee Operations" was issued on March 23, 2005.[11] It was based on the premise that the war against terrorism is a continuing struggle. This culminated with the issuance of Army Field Manual 2-22.3 on September 6, 2006. For the history of the efforts of the Department of Defense and the Army to rectify such matters the reader is referred to Chapter Eleven. With the publication of the Manual and the accompanying trial instructions it became evident that unrivaled efforts had been made to insure that persons who were to be prosecuted would receive the very highest procedural guarantees.

Several other topics deserve at least brief mention. With terrorism continuing to be with us international efforts should be made to clarify the status of unlawful enemy combatants. This is a matter confronting almost all countries, especially those that have embarked on higher levels of globalization. The extent to which humane considerations should be accorded to such persons requires universal consideration. Since terrorism is expanding the immediate need for international efforts is evident. This initiative is a function of the Executive branch of the government.

A fair appraisal of the situation requires an international perspective. At the world level vital attention must be given to important international agreements such as the Universal Declaration of Human Rights, the U. N. Charter, and relevant international agreements such as the 1949 Geneva Conventions dealing with Prisoners of War and Civilian Populations, and the 1984 Convention Against Torture. It is also necessary to take into account the laws and customs of war. An overarching consideration is to prove to world leaders that the United Stats is deeply committed to the world rule of law and has taken and is taking effective means to make this a matter of reality. This will require consistent action over a long time. Words and affirmative commitments must be proven through observable acts.

In the United States searching questions will have to be asked and answered whether the "military" approach to the disposition of Guantanamo

Bay detainees was or was not effective. There have been vast delays in bringing such persons before the Administrative Review Boards, the Combatant
Status Review Tribunals, and the Military Commissions. This has allowed for
intensive interrogations, and was, perhaps, preconceived. On the other hand,
observers can agree that the military forces have engaged in very serious efforts to establish fair inquiry processes. The future record may be better than
the past. This is also a function of the Executive branch.

The Congress also has major responsibilities. Following 9/11 it created the
Privacy and Oversight Board charging it with ensuring that "concerns with
respect to privacy and civil liberties are appropriately considered in the implementation of laws, regulations, and executive branch policies related to efforts to protect the Nation against terrorism." To make this body more effective the former chair and vice chair of the 9/11 commission, Thomas H. Kean
and Lee H. Hamilton, have suggested reforms including political balance in
the composition of the board, granting it subpoena powers, periodic reports to
Congress consisting of findings, conclusions, and recommendations, and giving it greater freedom as an independent agency of the executive branch. Implicit in the proposal is the heightened presence of international terrorism.
The Legislative branch would be responsible for this action. As has been
noted there is substantial interest in Congress for the repeal of the jurisdiction-stripping legislation relating to writs of habeas corpus. Congressional in-
activity in this matter may be alleviated through the growth in confidence in
the functioning of Military Commissions and the supervision exercised over
their decisions by the Court of Appeals of the District of Columbia.

Committees of the Congress can conduct hearings seeking a clearer understanding of fitness of nominees to high office. The members of the Senate Judiciary Committee have demonstrated an ongoing concern as to what constitutes torture. From a legal point of view this entails the meaning of the
definitional terms contained in CAT and the American RUDs. This concern
found expression in the October-November, 2007, hearings conducted by the
Senate Committee on the Judiciary to determine the qualifications of Judge
Michael B. Mukasey, designated by President Bush as the replacement to suc-
ceed Alberto Gonzales as Attorney General. Members of the Committee endeavored to learn during the hearings whether the nominee considered the
practice of "waterboarding" to be torture. His answer, apparently aware that
such a practice had been employed by government officials, but premised on
the basis of his unawareness of the precise aspects of waterboarding procedures, was that as it had been portrayed by Senators as inducing the sensation
of drowning, it was "over the line" and "repugnant." But, he declined to say
that the described practice was a form of torture, as then described or defined
in federal statutes and DOD Orders, and would be illegal in all cases.[12] This

response occurred following an earlier request on the part of ten Democratic Senators asking him to declare it to be illegal and to express his opposition.

He wrote "As described in your letter, these techniques seem over the line or, on a personal basis, repugnant to me, and would probably seem the same to many Americans. But hypotheticals are different from real life, and in any legal opinion the actual facts and circumstances are critical. Any discussion of coercive interrogation techniques necessarily involves a discussion of and a choice among bad alternatives. I was and remain loath to discuss and opine on any of those alternatives at this stage."[13]

This resulted in charges of equivocation and dissembling and became the litmus test for determining if it were possible to obtain a sufficient number of Committee votes to refer his nomination to the Senate. He found himself in the predicament of having to provide a "yes" or "no" answer in the absence of federal legislation specifically designating "waterboarding" as a crime, taking into account judicial rulings on the subject, and on the conflicting opinions of the Department of Justice during 2002–2004. This would mean that the response would be his personal opinion, which nonetheless would contribute to the belief that this specific practice was either legal or illegal. He could have referred to Army Manuals prohibiting such conduct or to the involvement of the CIA in such practices. But any legal finality would be lacking. Further, it could be expected that an affirmative response would also open the door to requests as to the legality of other ill- or non-defined acts claimed to be torture, with the result being that an affirmative response would contribute to the belief that such act constituted torture. To avoid such uncertainties the Congress should in the ordinary course of its procedures arrive at acceptable definitions containing prohibitions, which while providing the required legitimacy would undoubtedly, depending on the times and places, in the course of application still produce valid critics. In the meantime there are a number of Federal statutes identifying the crime of assault which are available for the prosecution of the actions resulting in the particulars of "waterboarding."

With such prescriptions for the White House and Congress, what might the judicial system contribute? One answer might be: Why should the courts be asked to "contribute" anything? Or, is it not enough to go about their future work with the trained perspectives that have always been characteristic of the judiciary? At the very least federal judges must understand the sources and relevance of international law and take international law into account in arriving at their decisions. The justices of the U. S. Supreme Court have often been divided, on one ground or another, in the light of opposing litigants with opposing legal theories and arguments. The absence of unanimous opinions is not surprising. Still, it is not the role of the Supreme Court to be unhelpful. For example, in Justice Kennedy's opinion in the Boumediene case, in referring to the granting of a writ of habeas corpus, reference was made to outlooks and procedures that would assist trial courts in performing their functions. Still, the print in the Boumediene case was hardly dry before questions arose as to whom the term "alien enemy unlawful combatant" applied or what evidence would be controlling in deciding if a detainee continued to be a security threat. The question arose as to the burden of proof, i.e., whether the government had to prove that a detainee fit into the above category and was dangerous to the United States or whether the detainee had to prove he is innocent of the government's claims. The Executive branch has taken the position that these are matters for the Congress to decide; members of Congress have placed this burden on the courts. In either case the final disposition of the detainee cases will be delayed despite the goal of expediting matters identified by the majority in the Boumediene case.

In the future detainees at Guantanamo will have the option of having their cases processed through a Military Commission or by seeking and obtaining a writ of habeas corpus. The question is presented whether their legal rights will best be achieved through one or the other of the procedures. Counsel for habeas corpus petitioners in the past by the use of that option have expressed a preference. With the emergence of holdings favorable to a detainee in the Court of Appeals, counsel may deem that process to be preferred. In making a decision in such a matter counsel will have to weigh the length of time involved in coming to closure. That may not be an easy decision, but should undoubtedly be a controlling factor. Also, the detainee population is diminishing. Releases will occur as a result of decisions made by Combatant Status Review Tribunals. The pools of detainees are not being replenished as fast as they are being reduced in size. Many leading Americans have called for the close of the Guantanamo detention facility, although the legal ramifications of such a move have not been explored fully.

In conclusion it can be stated that the challenges to America resulting from terrorism, detainees, torture, and treaty interpretation, as well as many unpopular foreign policy decisions, have quite properly raised questions as to America's commitment to the rule of law. More recently another critical issue has been raised, namely, whether the American legal process is equipped to deal with terrorism and the prospect of indeterminate detentions. However, the fact of dissatisfaction with policies and procedures should not result in conclusions that where detrimental policies and procedures have been implemented this must necessarily be considered to be a disavowal of the rule of law. It is the function of the rule of law to correct such mistakes.

Pains have been taken to identify the concerns and recommendations of the CAT Committee on Torture and the detailed responses. Major attention was also given to the very substantial efforts made by military authorities following misconduct at Abu Ghraib and at Guantanamo to provide detainees with basic legal protections although such protections fall short of those belonging to United States citizens. Critics will have to determine if such efforts meet America's continuing acceptance of the rule of law, and if not then what is required to cross the threshold. That this will not be easy is suggested by the highly divergent views on the subjects dealt with in this book.

Another approach is to examine America's domestic political-legal processes gathered in our separation of powers principle. The fact that the legislative, executive, and judicial branches of the government with their intense rivalries and periods of considerable friction are nonetheless committed to the well-being of constitutional traditions suggests ultimate respect for the rule of law by those who have been called upon to serve. Very little discernment is required to know that when public policies fail to meet with public approval that such policies are changed, some with considerable speed, others in a longer time frame.[14] This is true whether the issue is identified as domestic or international. Images will change. An abiding faith in the rule of law will serve as the cornerstone underlying an ongoing American tradition. When all of these verities are not fully understood and actively pursued by a president and his close advisors confidence in him and their leadership is diminished. Demands for change become the order of the day.[15]

NOTES

1. Hamdan v. Rumsfeld, 126 S. Ct. 2749 (June 26, 2006). Were it not for the heavy involvement of the American judicial system in this scenario a striking parallel would exist to the contest between the executive branch and Congress formalized in the 1973 War Powers Act or Resolution, Public Law 93–148. The Resolution identified the tension between the two branches and focused on the importance of collective judgments while fixing time periods within which the President could embark on military measures while obliged to make reports of such measures to the Congress. The causes of concern were different. In the more recent situation acts of terrorism challenged American security; earlier it was national conduct seeking territorial expansion.

2. The Department of State Legal Advisor, John B. Bellinger, told an audience at the London School of Economics on October 31, 2006 that "every detainee in Guantanamo has his case reviewed by a formal Combatant Status Review Tribunal, which determines whether a detainee is properly classified as an enemy combatant. The detainee has the assistance of a military officer, may present evidence, and may appeal the determination of the Combatant Status Review Tribunal or to our federal courts." www.state.gov/s/rls/76039.htm. He also noted that at the end of October, 2006, that some 75 detainees, whose cases had not been referred to a Tribunal or to a Commission, had been released or transferred.

3. 258 U.S.298 (1922).

4. 494 U.S. 259 (1990).

5. 247 U. S. 202 (1982).

6. 339 U.S. 763 (1950).

7. Rasul v. Bush, 124 S. Ct. 2686 (2004).

8. Id. at 2695, citing Braden v. 30th Judicial Court of Kentucky, 410 U. S. 495 (1973).

9. In the debate several Senators argued that the availability of Combat Status Review Tribunals constituted a sufficient substitute for writs of habeas corpus.

10. The case is discussed in Chapter 8 at 5.

11. Joint   Publication   3–63,   Final   Coordination, http://hrw.org/campaigns/torture/jointdoctrine00705.pdf.

12. For a more detailed assessment of the situation see Chapter 11 at 2.

13. Los Angeles Times, A10, October 31, 2007.

14. That Congress can act in a hurry is evidenced by the passage on September 18, 2001 of the Authorization for Use of Military Force, on October 8, 2001 of the Patriot Act, on December 30, 2005 of the DTA, and on October 17, 2006 of the MCA.

15. SCOTT McCLELLAN, WHAT HAPPENED INSIDE THE BUSH WHITE HOUSE (2008).

Index

5468607